STARTING
OUT

STARTING OUT

The Guide I Wish I'd Had When I Left Home

LILI KRAKOWSKI

STEIN AND DAY/*Publishers*/New York

First published in 1973
Copyright © 1973 by Lili Krakowski
Library of Congress Catalog Card No. 73–79339
All rights reserved
Designed by David Miller
Printed in the United States of America
Stein and Day/*Publishers*/Scarborough House, Briarcliff Manor, New York 10510
ISBN 0–8128–1634–X

For the T.

CONTENTS

INTRODUCTION

Starting Out intends to help you live well and happily on the minimal budget, and in the circumscribed surroundings, of a student, artist, or novice worker.

The book makes certain assumptions, which you should keep in mind throughout:

1. That you are one of the thousands of young people from well-off homes who are facing antique urban housing, poverty, and being-on-your-very-own simultaneously and for the first time. If you have experience with poverty, or old houses, or have been without parents as a backstop for a while, some of this book will seem silly. I *know* that. Skip those parts.

2. That your poverty is temporary, but also real. If you make only fifty dollars a week, but your mother sends you constant, huge CARE packages of delicacies or clothes, you are only playing poor. God bless, and I envy you, but as the French say, "You are not serious." Some of *Starting Out* is specifically for people who will be poor only a year or two—five at the most. I would not recommend foil baking dishes, for instance, to the forever poor.

3. That you intend to enjoy a good, rich, and beautiful life despite financial limitations. That you want to eat as well, dress as well, live as well as possible. If you are out to prove some philosophical point with your diet (and I don't mean vegetarianism), or overthrow our economy by the disarray of your dress, you will find this a disappointing guide.

Starting Out has a viewpoint: that skill is freedom, and freedom happiness. After you've read and used this book, you will know how to get on with little, how to cope with some problems you never tackled before, how to live pleasurably without enslaving

9

luxuries, costly gadgets, "conveniences" as addictive as any drug. You will know you can be poor without having to deny those values of order, calm, and beauty essential to creative serenity. Most important, you will have lost that fear of penury that devastates so many lives.

NOTE: The U. S. Department of Agriculture and its Extension Services will deluge you with fantastic, mostly free, information at the drop of a postcard. What's not free is extremely low in price. Subjects range from clothing to roof repair, canning to building storage refrigerators.

NOTE: It has been our experience that manufacturers and their associations will supply one with free, informative material, explaining products and their use. If the material is not free, the charge is minimal. I send away for, and keep on file, every booklet possible—whether it explains welding, the uses of manmade fibers, or offers canning recipes.

PART ONE

1 / A Room of One's Own: Finding a Home

One promises oneself, when writing a book such as this, that one won't be one's usual preachy, opinionated self, but will be easygoing, cool, and please everybody.

In this chapter, however, resolution yields to conviction. And it must, if I am to write it at all.

When you look for a room of your own—one you can afford, one that gives you enough space—you are destined, in most of today's American cities and towns, to land in an integrated, working-class neighborhood.

So before you start to look, examine your innermost feelings about your prospective neighbors. I am not talking about political small talk or religious good intention. I am talking about the nitty-gritty gut reaction you *personally* have to people as unlike those you know as any you will ever meet abroad.

One *cannot* lead a happy and productive life among people who make one uncomfortable. If it is any help, these feelings of antipathy or malaise are *not* a sign of prejudice or contempt. They can be quite as sharp when one is cast in with one's social "betters" as when one is with "inferiors"—a fact long recognized by novelists and playwrights, and only more recently by social scientists.

The reason you must confront your innermost feelings *before* you start house-hunting, is that, as soon as you go into the "slums"—as integrated working-class communities are fashionably dubbed—you will be bombarded from all sides by Horror Tales and Ghastly Stories. All are meant to make you quit. And they will succeed unless you have come to grips with your actual feelings calmly, rationally, and beforehand.

Your family may well feel that their friends, or Daddy's boss, will be appalled should they learn The Truth about Where Betsy

Lives. Real-estate agents have a practical reason for wanting you in a "better" neighborhood. They are normally paid a month's rent on each flat they let—so they try to move the costly ones first. If they think panic will make you or your parents shell out more. . . . Politicians and media are making much hay out of exaggerating the differences between the rich and the poor.* It has sold lots of papers and won lots of votes, particularly among that large segment of the upper-middle class that rose from poverty. Nothing makes the newly rich as smug as to disparage the still-poor. (It is much the same psychology as that of the Saved Sinner who never can hear enough of the Unsaved Ones' transgressions.)

Social workers, city planners, and other bureaucrats all have selfish reasons to preach the evil of neighborhoods like ours. *Be prepared.*

Preparatory Facts

1. Integrated, working-class neighborhoods are exactly like others. They have individual characteristics, their own *train de vie*, their own values. Some you will find charming; others may repel you. I love it when the streets are full of people at 6 A.M.; I loathe the music the record shops blare into the street.

2. Although we have a large number of welfare mothers and their children among us, remember how recently divorce, contraception, and abortion have become available to the poor. Welfare is their alimony and child support. (And the upper-middle class made it so!) I hope Women's Lib will soon achieve meaningful reforms. But as long as we live in a male-oriented, male-dominated society, any man who does not need a résumé and references to get a job can "disappear" overnight, leaving Society-at-Large to support his family. The statistics tell only the facts. They ignore the deep cultural differences in values and priorities.

3. While we have a rather steep number of social failures,

---

*The charming line attributed to Fanny Brice—"I have been both rich and poor. Rich is better"—is as close to the truth of the matter as one can get.

who inevitably drift to where rents are low, we also have a great many highly individualistic, gifted, imaginative, personally successful people. Low rents, without doubt, attract a greater variety of people than high rents. That is why neighborhoods such as ours are so lively and challenging.

4. Some of our housekeeping standards are, of necessity, lower. We live in older houses, have older plumbing, and so on. Many architectural features we have to live with have long been abandoned in new construction. You cannot compare the way we live to the way people live in brand-new houses. You can only compare us to how people lived fifty or seventy-five years ago, when even the rich heated with coal, shared hall toilets, and took the garbage out.

As with everything else, you get what you pay for. Old houses don't have the features of new ones, any more than old phonographs have those of stereo. Old design plus the consequences of aging account for the low rents.

We are, however, thoroughly clean. We spend as much time as anyone on housework. If the results are not as spectacular as they ought to be, it is not from want of trying.

5. *There is no more crime in "slums" than in other parts of the same city.* Startling, but true. Many poor sectons rate lower on the burglary/mugging scale than the high-rent districts or the tourist-attracting central areas. Burglars and muggers know exactly where the money is; they get about town as easily as anyone and have the advantage that they can travel at nonrush hours. We do seem to have a slightly higher murder rate. This is due to ethnic differences in settling personal grievances and affects only the people directly involved.

That more people in prison give poor neighborhoods as their home address reflects on the system and not the areas.

All one can say honestly is that different types of criminals come from different neighborhoods. According to the newspapers, gigolos, call girls, embezzlers, tax evaders, stock waterers, jury tamperers, toxic food processors, corrupt politicians congregate in high-rent districts. It all boils down to what kind of thief you prefer as neighbor.

And as far as drugs go, your generation knows infinitely more than mine about the universality of the problem.

6. One of the stories that *is* true is that municipal services are less adequate in slums than elsewhere. The cities and towns don't care. They pretend that a garbage collection schedule designed for low-density areas with crushers and incinerators is equally good for a high-density neighborhood with only garbage cans. So our streets are in worse repair, our lights and traffic lights take forever to fix, and so on. If you live among us, you will spend a couple of dollars a month on phone calls to prod public officials to earn their keep. Or you may get a big broom and sweep your own street!

Now you are ready to plunge in.

How to Look for a Home

I was well into my thirties before I discovered that some people have neither need nor desire for a workshop. Up to then, I knew only people who, in every new town, got a studio first. With money left from *that* rent, they found a place to live. Otherwise they doubled up, or camped in their studios.

Consider:

What kind of space do you need?

What are your priorities?

What will you sacrifice for what?

Will you climb five long flights to get an extra room for the same money? Is an extra room worth the sacrifice of a separate bathroom? Are two more rooms worth sharing a hall toilet for? Is the extra light on a top floor worth the added burglary risk?

Make your mind up before you house-hunt. Have a clear idea of what you want.

Investigate the neighborhoods that come in question. Check them out as thoroughly as possible. Evaluate possible locations on the basis of distance from school, job, where your friends live. In a big city, try to locate yourself conveniently to where you go at night. It is better to travel your longest routes by day—not only for safety, but because buses and subways run less frequently at night. If the traffic patterns are unbalanced, try to find a place that lets you travel against the mainstream.

From window signs, phone book, or ads in the paper, choose a few rental agents. In most larger towns, agents specialize in specific neighborhoods. See a few agents. Tell them exactly what you need. Don't let anyone rush you. If anyone tries, be doubly suspicious. There is likely to be some catch. Visit as many apartments as possible. There *are* differences in value.

Remember, a lease is a binding contract. No wiggling out. Check everything before you sign.

NOTE: An agent may ask how many are in your family, how many of you plan to live in a place. Many communities have fire and health laws that prescribe the size or the number of windows of rooms let as bedrooms. In old houses, a formerly legitimate three-bedroom flat, may, under current law, have only one room that can be rented as a bedroom. It also happens that a landlord wants a bit of extra rent if two or more unrelated people share a place.

Check these points:

1. Is there a hidden handicap? Noise, bad smells from shops or restaurants?

2. Who collects garbage, makes repairs, cleans communal parts of the building? Is there a janitor? Where does he live? If the landlord himself does the maintenance, where does *he* live?

A live-in landlord or janitor may be a big plus. But if they are crabby, they are frightful neighbors. Try to meet the janitor. Find out, if you can, how much time he spends on the job. (Many janitors get nothing but free rent from the landlord and hold outside jobs to earn cash.)

The state of public halls is a fair guide to maintenance.

3. Who pays for repairs? Are they made promptly? Again, the hallways tell a lot.

4. How is transportation to where you work or study? Essential fares are part of your rent. It may be cheaper to pay more rent in a one-fare zone than less in a two-fare or three-fare zone. Transportation *time* must be counted if it interferes with your wage-earn-

ing hours. (If you only can work three hours as a waiter because of travel time, and could work four if you were closer, the loss of income is part of the rent.)

5. Check shopping facilities. Yours may be a low-income block, but the nearest supermarket may be in an expensive area. Chain-owned supermarkets do not charge differently from store to store on specific items, but they frequently stock only costlier lines in richer areas. Services—dry cleaners, barbers, shoemakers —definitely cost more in high- than in low-rent districts.

6. *Check the building by day and night and on weekends.* Try to check during those hours you need quiet. If you sleep by day, a printing shop downstairs may keep you up; a bar won't. It may be fun to live in the old "owner's flat" above a store; but if the store is closed weekends, and there are only warehouses on both sides, it may be un-fun to live there alone.

Try to meet your neighbors. Ring bells, and say frankly that you are thinking of moving into the house. Ask what you want to know about the building. *All people everywhere are interested in having good neighbors.* The people next door are as keen to look you over as you are to chat with them.

Once You Have Found a Home

1. Go over the flat with the agent, janitor, or landlord, and check for existing damage. (Take along a friend as witness.) Point out *all* existing damage. *Be hawk-eyed about minor things.* The big ones are obvious and will *have* to be fixed prior to your moving in—a missing window pane, a dangling light fixture. But the little things—a cracked toilet tank, a chip out of the formica, a badly painted scratch on the fridge—may well be the defects for which the management has withheld the security of the last half-dozen tenants.

After you have moved in, send your landlord, or the management,* a friendly letter listing these "small" and often irreparable

*Many buildings are operated by management companies that act for the landlord but do not necessarily own the building. Some act as rental agents as well for the properties they manage.

defects. Keep a copy of the letter. Make it clear you don't necessarily want repairs. You just don't want to be held responsible for pre-existing damage. *Include in this letter a list of repairs that were promised to you and not yet completed.*

2. Read your lease, carefully. Every syllable of that tiny type affects you. Most leases are preprinted forms incorporating local custom. Read the lease anyway. If you can, get a lawyer friend to explain it. Only what is written in the lease is binding. Promises mean nothing. If the dog-loving landlord promised you could keep Fido, but the lease bars dogs, Fido may be chased out if the landlord sells to another. (You might, under such circumstances, have a legal claim, but it won't be worth your time.)

3. Try to get a sublease clause. Sublease means you can rent your place to someone for a time—during the summer, for instance. The subtenant generally pays the tenant, who pays the landlord. The landlord is under no obligation to give you a sublease clause. If he does, he may ask for extra rent while the subtenant is there. He will, quite certainly, ask for approval of the subtenant.

Never sublet your place without a sublease clause in your lease. A major violation of your lease can mean eviction. (The "Just tell them you are my cousin" routine has a grand chance of backfiring. Besides, it's not honest.) *Never* become a subtenant until you have seen the tenant's sublease clause and spoken to the landlord or management. We've all heard of someone who sublet on the hush-hush, and remains happily ensconced after fifteen years. We have heard far more stories of evictions! We've also heard of people who sublet to unwary strangers, got a good chunk of key money,* and then vamoosed—leaving the subtenant twice cheated when the landlord lowered the boom!

4. See how much the landlord will do before you move in. Ideally he will paint, exterminate, and make all repairs needed before you move in. The extermination is much to be desired. (See page 00.)

5. Make sure the refrigerator, stove, and any other appliances

---

Key money may be a cash payment to a superintendent to give one preference over those who've waited in line for a particularly desirable place. It may also be, as in this case, the "purchase price" for fixtures, bookshelves, etc. which the tenant leaves behind for the subtenant. It boils down to a payment to let one have the place.

now in the flat will remain. In some communities the tenant provides his own, even on rented premises. It also is possible that once the flat is rented, the lovely stove and fridge will be replaced by less desirable ones. *Make triply sure of this if you are the first tenant in a building.* Agents may partly furnish a place and give it appliances far better than those the tenants ultimately get. The agents then claim the "model" flat was only decorated to "give you an idea" of what the place could look like. See the apartment you actually are contracting for. Don't take anyone's word it's just like the model.

6. See what the landlord will let you do before you move in. In many cases the landlord will give you access to the place before your actual moving-in day. This is very desirable, because it is much easier to work in an empty place.

7. Get permission *in writing* for all changes you plan to make. (Written permission is called for in many leases.) As mangy as the carpet is, you may not remove it without permission. The landlord has every reason to want to keep your security money at the end of the lease; "damage" is the best excuse. On the other hand, he legitimately may feel that your improvements—exposing lovely brick behind tacky plaster—damaged his real estate.

NOTE: Neither landlords nor agents are monsters. They are hard-working people to whom every calamity has happened, from willful damage to Acts of God, from bouncing checks to smoldering fires. If they are cynical, it's tenants who have made them so. Play fair as a tenant, but be a little skeptical too.

NOTE: You are fully responsible for all "improvements" you make. *Do not,* for instance, open a sealed-up fireplace without consulting experts. *You must not* start a fire in a fireplace unless you know it has been safely used, or inspected. If you cause structural damage, or start a fire that smokes out your upstairs neighbors you will not only be in trouble with the landlord, but the neighbors may sue you for ruining their curtains.

Getting Ready to Move In

Most old apartments need what all historic buildings need: *restoration.* The order is: scrub, patch, paint.

1. Scrubbing comes first. Walls covered with flat (nonshiny) paint are extremely hard to wash. It often is easier to give them an extra coat of paint. Shiny walls (enameled) are easier to wash, and the scrub will, most likely, save you that second coat.

Use heavy-duty cleaner according to directions. Or get trisodium phosphate—often sold as "wood bleach"—and use just enough in warm water to do the job. Wear heavy-duty rubber gloves bought at a work-clothes store.

When you wash walls, start from the bottom, work up. For some reason, soapy drips onto a dry area leave marks that may show through the paint (particularly when you give only one coat, which is what the scrubbing is all about). Rinse well. Residual soap may hurt the paint.

2. Scrape floors now. The temptation is to use the old floor surface as a drop cloth; but then, when you do scrape the wood or rip up old linoleum, the dirt will ruin your paint job. Exception: if you will paint your floors, you can strip, sand, etc. them *now*, then paint them *after* the walls. Ditto for installation of carpet and new linoleum.

Consult the linoleum store *before* you rip out old lino. Linoleum or vinyl flooring sold by the roll covers a multitude of lumps and bumps that tile will not. But it may be wiser to leave one layer of the old linoleum as a subflooring under the new. If you go down to the wood, and it is very uneven, you may have to put down hardboard before the new linoleum can go on. Try to get the store to come have a look. (They most likely will if you have bought their linoleum and certainly if they are to install it.)

3. Spackle and plaster. *Spackle* is a plaster mix intended for small holes. It comes in a powder (cheaper) and in a vinyl-based paste (better). Spackle is for small holes (no bigger than 4 by 4 inches or so) and cracks. For bigger holes *patching plaster* must be used. Plastering any big area—more than a foot in any direction—or a corner is very difficult. Plastering a ceiling is next to impossible. Don't try it. Anyway, a job that size is the landlord's responsibility.

You should use spackle to level chipped paint or dented wood. The vinyl paste is best here too.

4. Paint. Water-soluble paints—latex or vinyl latex—are the best to use. No special solvents are needed for cleaning up, and

they are almost odor-free. Flat paint is used for all rooms except kitchen and bath. Enamels—satin, low gloss, semigloss, or high gloss—are best for all rooms whose walls get splashed or washed. (The high-gloss enamels with latex base are quite new on the market. But beautiful.) Reserve oil-base paint for those surfaces that really get scrubbed a lot—kitchen cabinets, window sills. Walls so greasy that you are not sure all the grease has been washed off may *have* to be done in oil. Water-soluble paints will not adhere to greasy films. The best for a greasy wall is a double coat of paint with a twenty-four-hour (or more) drying period in between. The first coat will lift and hold remaining grease. The second coat will finish the job.

NOTE: Water-base paints dry very quickly. And once dry, they are as tough as oil paint. Wipe up spills and splashes, rinse tools as promptly as possible.

NOTE: *Never* use plastic drop cloths on the floor. Since these are nonabsorbent, paint spots remain wet a long, long time. Paint spots are as slippery as banana peels. Use plastic to cover furniture, mirrors, and such. Use cloth or newspapers on the floor.

Buy the best rollers you can afford. Cheap ones are fragile, rarely can be washed and reused. The smoother the wall, the shorter the nap on the roller can be. Medium-nap is best for older, not-so-even walls.

Get the very best paint. Price difference in paint is based principally on amount and quality of pigment. Better paint covers better, may save you from a second coat in an iffy situation. The price difference between the cheap and the best can't be more than fifteen to twenty dollars for a whole apartment. Since you are investing a lot of time and effort, use only the best materials.

Buy ready-mixed colors. If you shop around among different brands, you will come up with something almost exactly like what you had in mind. If you really can't find what you need, get a color sample of a custom blend and get an artist friend to mix. My own system is to examine the swatch, read the directions (2 A 1 B in a gallon of white), examine the dispenser, and take note of what color is A and what B. I then buy tubes of chrome yellow and ivory black, let us say, measure with a measuring spoon, and not only have my custom blend, but the possibility of repeating it.

Best buys in paint are private labels or house brands. The higher-priced lines of national brands are excellent, but too expensive. A local department store or hardware chain will have a house brand, and the best of that is the best for you. There also are local brands, mainly sold to professional house painters, and these often are superb. I have heard good things about the house brands of mail-order houses but have never used them.

NOTE: *Filled paint, textured paint, sand paint:* it's all the same thing. A sandy filler of some kind is added to the paint to give a rough finish. Sometimes the filler is in the paint, sometimes it is added by you. Worthwhile to cosmeticize a lumpy, bumpy wall, not worth it for purely decorative effect—and quite a dust-catcher.

NOTE: Stir oil paint to mix. But water-base paints should be poured back and forth between buckets to mix well. And unless a paint is mixed thoroughly, it won't cover properly.

NOTE: Avoid wallpaper if at all possible. Not only is it a bitch to put up, and hell to take down or paint, but it quickly becomes a rodent and roach haven. Self-adhering vinyl may, however, be the best and only solution for a really ugly wall area.

Problems You May Run Into

1. *Soft, broken, gray or green looking plaster, generally around sink or tubs, occasionally in a wall adjacent to bathroom or kitchen.* Plaster can develop mildew from moisture. If kept wet long enough, or rewetted often enough, it will begin to effloresce, soften, and look leprous.

If the plaster in this condition feels no cooler than the plaster of adjacent areas, there may be a number of causes, *all past:* a previous tenant splashed a lot; there was a leak or flood but all was fixed. In this case, your worry is to make the thing look good. A chlorine bleach and water solution should wash off the mildew. Spackle and sandpaper (sand in overlapping circles) should make the surface presentable. You then paint.

If the plaster *is* cooler, either a splasher was there recently, of there is an active leak in the wall. The splasher may be the ten-year-old upstairs—a sopping wet bathroom floor will let water seep through the tile, and it *will* find its way down. A leak, likewise, may be way upstairs or even in the roof.

Wet plaster near windows—*on wall or ceiling*—can mean a leak around the window frame or missing mortar outside. In either case, water gets into the outside wall and "wanders" inward.

If the plaster is actively wet, call your landlord, the management, or the janitor. Unless action is taken within a reasonable time—three or five workdays, depending on the complexity of the problem—write the landlord or management a letter. Specify what is wrong, and point out what it is endangering; that is, the wet spot in the living room is smack above the built-in (immovable) bookcase; the wet bathroom wall is the one the medicine cabinet is on (your pills and perfumes are in danger!). If this letter does not bring action, repeat the letter, mentioning calls and previous letters, and send it registered, return receipt requested.*

Plaster that once was wet can be repainted. Wet plaster can, theoretically, be painted with water-base paint, but it won't hold properly. In case your bathtub is so close to the wall that splashes are inevitable, hang a shower curtain along the wall (with the bottom draining into the tub) or affix a panel of outdoor (waterproof) hardboard or vinyl tile wallboard. (Be sure the plaster is dry before you try to attach anything to it.) You may have to put up lath first and attach your wallboard to that. If you use a waterproof "splashboard," be sure to keep a rug or some other absorbent cloth under the tub to catch the drips.

2. *Poor wiring.* Inadequate wiring is wiring insufficient to the needs of our day. If you have no appliances, this will not create a problem. *Poor wiring,* however, is sparks coming out of

---

*This procedure should be followed for all complaints: If there is a janitor, mention the problem to him first. Follow up with a call to landlord or the management (whomever you send the rent to). If *that* call breeds no results, a plain letter (keep a copy), then a registered letter, return receipt requested (so you know he got it), is the order of business. *Do not take it upon yourself to withold rent* or part of the rent as "punishment." You may get evicted before you get plastered!

outlets, droopy wires leading to permanent light fixtures, and so on. Also wires that get hot, or smell burnt, when the lights are on.

Remove any extension cords left by the previous tenants and check them very, very carefully. In old buildings, where there are few wall outlets, people become extension-happy. The cords generally are cheap, puppies nibble them, children try their scissors on them; they are a screaming fire hazard. Junk any cord that looks imperfect, or that has become stiff and brittle.

Do not install more extension cords than you absolutely need. Get heavy-duty ones at an electric supply house. Attach them to the wall so they don't trip you or permit *your* puppy to test his teeth. Plug appliances into different outlets, preferably different circuits, and don't run two from the same outlet at the same time.

If a fixture splutters and sparks, it generally indicates moisture. If it happens once to your bathroom light, it may be only a puddle in the bathroom upstairs. More than once may indicate a leak.

Do not play electrician. Old wiring is brittle and unpredictable. It is often laid in crazy ways. A fixing job you might safely have done in a new house, like back home, could spell disaster here.

3. *Holes, cracks, etc.* Wooden floors shrink. When they shrink a lot, there are gaps between the boards. These are dust catchers, but unless you see little creatures going in and out, do not bother with them. You can stuff the cracks with wood putty, but it will only work its way out again, since the boards have a great deal of "play." Even nautical caulking works loose. Big gaps can be fixed with molding strips or lath. Genuine holes can be done with floorboard or plywood or hardboard. Talk to the man at the lumberyard.

Likeliest problem is gaps where the floor meets the wall. This matters little in living areas, but in kitchens and pantries it is a haven for rodents and roaches. Stuff the cracks with steel wool— from the hardware store, not the supermarket. Get 0 or 00 (fine, in both senses of the term). Borax is said to discourage roaches, so you can stuff some of that in too. If the crack is small, a tightly packed wad of steel wool should do the trick. If a visible gap remains, cover it with molding strip. (Molding strips come in a great variety of shapes, adapted to many purposes, and the lumber-yard will help you choose the best.)

4. *Badly damaged doors, window frames, etc.* As we've dis-cussed above, the landlord should repair and replace really bad things before you move in. But let us say he gives you the place for a song and does not feel like replacing something that is on its last legs but will last a while. Discuss the problem with him. Offer to pay part of the cost. If pleading fails, ask his permission to have the saggy window or the splintered and patched door re-placed. (I very much doubt he'll refuse!) A new window costs about $25; a door about $20. A fire-retardant front door (such as is required in New York City, for instance) is about $50. Even if you must hire someone to install it (the janitor may do it), it is well worth the price. Remember this is your home, you will live here, and you too are human!

5. *Bathtub and sink have lost their enamel.* A common problem with no real solution. Years of being scrubbed with abrasives will make any enamel-on-metal quit. In case of a sink the only complica-tions are that the sink is pitted, hence hard to clean (solved by a scrub brush and strong detergent, plus an occasional soak with chlorine bleach) and a snagger of undies (get a plastic dishpan to soak undies in). In case of a tub the thing looks unhygienic and is unpleasant to the skin. You can paint the tub with an epoxy paint, the only worthwhile ones being those that come in two con-tainers that have to be mixed together for the reaction to start (these paints dry by chemical reaction, not purely by evaporation). Epoxy paints emit dangerous fumes and cost a fortune. A good double coat on a much-used tub lasts, I'd say, two years. My feeling is—if you take baths, it's worth the effort on the tub. If you take showers, don't bother.

NOTE: I've discovered that if I keep the brush I used on the first coat in the refrigerator overnight (wrapped in plastic), it is soft enough to do the second coat. I use a cheap brush and throw it out—as the epoxy solvent also costs a lot.

6. *Door locks.* In many cases the lock is fine. In others there will be signs of damage—that is, burglars having tried to pry the lock open. If you live where burglary is a problem, invest in a

double cylinder lock or a police lock. A *double cylinder lock* requires a key to open or close it from either side of the door. (A burglar who has come in through the window cannot get out through the door.) Such locks are hard to pick. *Police locks* come in different styles. All work on the principle that a metal rod becomes wedged in tight if the door is opened without the lock being unlocked. They are a fancy version of the chair-under-doorknob technique dear to westerns.

Just about any lock can be picked, and the door opened. All you can hope is to delay intruders so long as to discourage them. Even a padlock on your front door will help—if the hasp is solidly bolted in, and if the padlock is high enough so that one cannot saw it off without standing on a box or ladder.

Use tamper-proof screws, or file down screw heads and bolt ends. Burglars are not above opening doors by removing the locks. A special type of tamper-proof screw exists (a good locksmith will stock them) that can only be screwed in, *not* out. If you can't buy those, use a file to "ruin" the groove in the screw heads, so they will not hold a screwdriver. If you are using hasps and padlocks, bolt them through the door and strip the thread off the bolt below the nut (once it is tightly in place). These rather primitive methods make removing the screws or bolts next to impossible. (If you ever wish to remove them, you'll need an electric drill.) The law or your lease may require you to give the landlord a set of keys. Do not ignore this rule—it's for your safety.

7. *Bugs and beasties.* As much as I dislike these creatures, they do very little actual harm. One hears stories of small children being attacked by rats, but that is *so* much less likely than their being attacked by malevolent and/or drunken adults as to be trivial. Far, far more children die from human malice than from animal assault.

Nevertheless, a room of one's own should be just that.

We've agreed on the desirability of having the landlord fumigate and exterminate while the flat is empty. If the landlord cannot or will not do it, hire your own man. Ask him if it is better to have the job done before or after you paint. A thorough, professional job costs about twenty-five dollars. It's worth every penny. Where there were children (notoriously messy eaters), or old people who could not maintain much hygiene, I'd call the services of an exterminator essential.

If you cannot get an exterminator, buy bug killer in a can. *Don't buy spray.* Read the directions on the can. Then, with a soft brush apply the insecticide to all cracks and fissures, particularly in areas that are likely to be constantly damp, dark, or greasy (around the stove, sink, under closets and refrigerator). Do this after you paint. (Pesticides have a slightly oily base, which would prevent water-base paint from sticking.) Give your paint as much time as possible to dry before *you* exterminate.

If there are places you simply cannot reach with a brush, you will have to resort to a spray can. I cannot begin to tell you my abhorrence of these things. When one uses sprays, one should have an industrial respirator with goggles—the kind that protects against fumes, not dust. Perhaps you can borrow one from school (either a lab or the maintenance department) or from a body shop. Buy one if you can swing it. (Cost: about fifteen dollars.) If there's no way, goggles plus a thick pad of cloth held over nose and mouth will have to do. *Spray thoroughly.* Then rush out into the fresh air. The extremely fine droplets ejected by spray cans hang as a mist in the air for a long time. If there is enough to harm the bugs, there's enough to harm you. *Cover as much of your body as possible during this process. Wear rubber gloves throughout. Whether you use the paintbrush-and-liquid technique, or the spray can, wash any splashes off your skin immediately. Rush home after you have finished and shower and shampoo with extra care. Change all your clothes. Wash the clothes you wore thoroughly before wearing them again.* (If you already live here, have fresh clothes at a friend's, go there to wash, change and, ideally, spend the night.)

After you've massacred with insecticide, the best roach preventive is the *roach trap.* (There also are very effective ant traps.) These are small tins, the size of a shoe-polish can, into which the animal is lured to its death. Although we have no roaches, we keep the traps around in case some wander in. In apartment buildings, particularly, they *will* wander in.

NOTE: An outstanding "source" of roaches is the supermarket bag. Roaches are passionate about the glues used in making bags, cartons, etc. Do not stockpile bags; and transfer all groceries out of cardboard boxes into tin or plastic containers.

Use a cat or traps against *mice*. Depending on how squeamish you are, get the traps that kill or those that catch 'em alive. The ones that kill can be used only once, because the smell of mouse blood warns other mice to keep out. In any case, "defuse" traps before you go away for weekends or longer, or you may come home to a very unappetizing spectacle.

If you followed the how-to-look instructions above, it is unlikely you will end up in a place that has rats. Yet even good places can be troubled by them, if below street level or near the waterfront.

The first step in rat prevention is keep 'em out. And rats can gnaw through almost anything. You may have to use long strips of L-shaped tin along the crack where floor meets wall. You may have to replace plaster with cement. (Use ready-mixed, powdered *mortar-mix concrete*.) Make sure all doors and windows are really tight in their frames, and their frames set in tightly too. Check that all pipes leading into the street have no space *whatsoever* around them where they enter the wall.

Even so—if you are in a basement or cellar, if there is a basement or cellar below you, or a grocery next door, you may occasionally be troubled by a rat. Set out poison. The best of these contain an anticoagulant that turns the rat into a "hemophiliac." (You can identify such a poison because the antidote listed under the "warnings" is a coagulant.) This is *very* dangerous stuff, but also the safest. It is adjusted to the body weight of rats, and so if, God forbid, your dog or cat should get at it, he would have to eat a really huge amount before it would hurt him. A snack of the stuff won't be fatal, but be sure to call the vet, pronto! Keep the poison under some kind of "shelter" so that your pets can't get at it, and you can't step into it accidentally and get it on your shoes. (A coffee can with both ends removed, and cut with tin shears into a little quonset hut, works well.) *Never* use *any* poison where young children might come.

After all these dire warnings, take comfort. It is unlikely you will have any of these problems except roaches. And as a recent article in a posh magazine reassured its even posher readers, roaches are endemic to cities and call on the cream-of-the-cream as well as on the dry-skim-milk peasantry!

In all likelihood the previous tenant was as spic and span as your mom. After all, the previous tenant may have been the woman who kept your mother's house spic and span! So it goes.

2 / Cleaning

If you live in a city, particularly in an old building in an old street, *dirt* will be your constant enemy, particularly in the kitchen.

This is not good, clean dirt like sand and grass, or even clay and ink. This is grubby, greasy soot and grime—man's principal urban products.

There's no escape. Even if you seal all doors and windows, and use only air-conditioners and filtered fans for ventilation (as our friends, the G's did), the city dirt will find its way in.*

But dirt can be fought. The nose can be kept above water.

1. *Avoid the unnecessary.* The less you own, the less there is to clean. Streamline your house. Do not stockpile canned food. Keep clothes and objects not in *constant* use in trunks or big plastic bags. Get rid of everything that requires great care. Time for that later in life.

2. *Avoid frills.* No shelf paper, no venetian blinds. No curtains, even. Use cheap roll-up shades from the dime store, and replace as they get dirty.

---

*If your flat has a dumbwaiter used for garbage collection, you are well advised to seal off that roach promenade with masking tape (the plastic kind, but wide adhesive tape will do) and take out the garbage yourself.

3. *Keep food in sealed, washable containers.* Old coffee cans are fine. Wipe all canisters with a damp cloth after use. Wash all drips and sticky fingerprints off bottles immediately. If you don't have tin, plastic, or glass containers to keep flour and sugar in, place the bags inside plastic bags, close tightly with rubber bands or wire. But remember: cardboard or paper food packages are first-rate roach lures.

4. *Have a good garbage can, with a good lid.* Buy garbage-can liners and use them. Plastic bags are all right, but fragile. Metal cuts them. Plastic-coated paper bags are better. Or place a plastic bag inside a big shopping bag, inside the garbage pail. Wash the pail inside *and* out at least once a week. Wash the lid (which gets messy from sticky fingers) more often. Empty the garbage at least once a day. Be sure you get rid of all garbage if you go away weekends.

Be generous with wastepaper baskets. Avoid fancy ones such as wicker baskets that catch dirt on their own. Have baskets at frequent intervals. It's easier to keep a place tidy if it's easy to dispose of trash.

How to Clean and What One Needs (Besides Patience)

My husband feels that not to make a mess, ever, is the road to cleanness. He cleans and tidies and puts things away as he works. I prefer to get the job done, *then* clean up when I am through. Different temperaments, different styles. Regardless: clean up thoroughly after each activity. Put everything away and tidy up before starting the next task.

1. *Organize.* When you have an idea of the rhythm of your life, what your hectic, what your easy days are, plan your cleaning around your schedule. Allow *plenty* of time. (Cleaning actually can be relaxing if one is not pressed for time.) Clean all at once on a slack day; or space your cleaning an hour at a time, over the week.

Schedule those chores that aren't weekly. I do them in rotation:

window cleaning one time, refrigerator washing the following, and so on.

Priorities

1. *Daily.* All dishes, all ashtrays. Counters and stove top as used or necessary. Sweep kitchen. Dispose of all garbage.

2. *Weekly.* Change beds, towels, dishcloths. (In summer in a damp climate you may have to do this twice a week.) Scrub bathroom and kitchen fixtures and floors. Sweep and dust throughout.

3. *As necessary.* Laundry, refrigerator, windows, bookshelves, closets, etc.

If for some reason you cannot do a task as planned, avoid making it worse. If you cannot do the dishes after the meal, soak the dishes. If you cannot scrub the stove or oven after a very messy cooking spree, spray with cleanser or set a small glass or china dish of ammonia in the oven to prevent the grease cooking or drying on. If you cannot clear your desk before leaving for the weekend, and soot is likely to pile up on papers and books, cover the desk with a newspaper or sheet of plastic.

Prevent (or localize) messes. Keep a "fire ditch" space between work and living areas. When I come in from garden or studio, I take off my clothes before entering the living area. We keep a shallow cat-pan-like plastic pan for wet or muddy boots. All greasy, muddy, clayey, manury clothes are removed at the door and *stored* there. (Our farmer friends always remove their coveralls at the doors to their houses.)

The Nitty-Gritty of Cleaning

Assuming you do all cleaning at once, I would recommend this order:

1. *Tidy.* About half one's cleaning time is spent tidying. Pick

up clothes, gather up dirty laundry, empty ashtrays, change and make the bed. (If you do not have a bedspread, use one of the removed sheets as a temporary spread while you sweep and dust.)

2. *Do floors.* After some experience—including as a professional chambermaid—I find floors first, then dusting best. Sweep and vacuum.* If you have no vacuum, use a small stiff corn broom on rugs. What about wax? I have asked a number of dealers. All agree wax on linoleum, tile, vinyl floors makes them look good but does not affect wear. Real parquet floors (which you're unlikely to have) should be dewaxed and rewaxed periodically with a machine (rentable). But if you want to use liquid wax on the lino, clean floor first, wax, come back when the wax is dry to do your dusting.

3. *Dust and wax.* I do windowsills with water and ammonia or borax. For dusting I use a silicon-treated cloth, or a spray on an untreated cloth (either makes the dust adhere instead of fly). I never use furniture polish, which makes things greasy and catches dust. Good furniture deserves a twice-yearly treatment with a first-rate paste wax or, if oiled, with an oil mix—both available from a cabinetmakers' supply house.

For oiled surfaces, or those finished in shellac or natural varnish (not plastic varnish), Leigh's polish is excellent. Mix one-third each boiled linseed oil, real (gum) turpentine, and white vinegar. Apply generously, allow to sit about five minutes, rub off *thoroughly*. The stuff smells a bit, but it is the very best.

4. *Bathroom and kitchen.* Although the kitchen sink should be washed after use, it deserves a good scrub—drainboard, splashboard, and all—once a week. Do all fixtures with detergent, borax, or baking soda. Remove bad stains by applying chlorine bleach and letting it sit a while. Do only *ceramic* fixtures with scouring powder.

Scrub the bathtub, sink, adjacent tiles. Wash the outside as well as the inside of fixtures. If there is mold in the cracks between

---

*As much as I dislike and shun appliances, a vacuum cleaner is close to essential to people with dust allergies or dusty trades like potting, woodworking. The best vacuum is the five-gallon shop type with domestic attachments. It's cheap, strong, picks up lots of stuff the home vacuums ignore—and lasts forever.

tiles, or at the edge of the tub, scrub with a brush and water plus ammonia. It will keep the mold down, though I have never been able to get rid of it completely.

Wash bathroom shelves, and give tooth mugs* a thorough wash. This is the time to do brushes and combs in water and ammonia. (Hang real-bristle brushes with wooden backs to dry them.)

If you have a rubber bath mat, scrub it well.

While we all know how unlikely one is to pick up germs from toilets and tubs, it does no harm to use disinfectant. Particularly in the hot, damp summer days, fungi, such as athlete's foot, can be a problem, and prevention is the safest approach.

About the john. *Scrub it.* Inside and out. Wash the toilet seat top and bottom. Use a disinfectant solution on a paper towel. Keep a separate sponge or brush or cloth for the inside of the bowl. Wear rubber gloves if you are squeamish. Or do it bare-handed and disinfect your hands afterward.

Scrub the kitchen and bathroom floors with soap and water. Rinse with clear water. Again, there is no need for great floods—just enough water to do the job.

I do not use sponge mops, because those miserable cellulose sponges cost a lot and are quickly destroyed by chlorine bleach, strong detergents, and disinfectants. I use a string mop or a heavy floor cloth. These can't be obtained here anymore—my mother sends them to me as presents from Belgium!—but several layers of Turkish toweling (quilted on a sewing machine is best) do a good job. Use disinfectant when washing the bathroom floor, or spray the disinfectant on afterward—particularly if people walk about barefoot.

Rinse, dry all mops and floor cloths well before storing.

About Cleaning Products

1. *A nylon broom is best.* Corn brooms are too stiff for most

---

*Tooth mugs really can be a source of germs and should be kept as clean as drinking glasses.

floors; hair too costly and fragile, and hard to clean. A soft nylon (or other synthetic) broom is best for wood, linoleum, tile.

2. *A dustpan and small broom.* The small dustpan-broom is not essential, but the dustpan is. Get one of metal or heavy flexible plastic. The thin, rigid plastic ones break very easily.

3. *Cloths.* Old cotton or cotton-rayon underwear is ideal. Old sweat socks make perfect dust mitts.

4. *Sponges.* As for sponge mops, so for sponges. Have a few around for odd jobs that don't involve the strong detergents: wiping the kitchen table, washing dishes.

5. *Scouring powders.* Get the cheapest. Some have virtues others lack, but not worth the price difference. Use only on ceramic tile, or all-ceramic fixtures (like the toilet bowl). Do not use on enameled metal—as your sink and tub are likely to be. Wash those with detergent; or borax, washing soda, or baking soda, plus detergent, worked into a paste. Reserve abrasives for dirty pots and pans and really desperate jobs.

6. *Cleaning* products.* First there is soap. Reinforced with a dash of ammonia, borax, or chlorine bleach, it works extremely well. Then there are heavy-duty detergents, *which must always be used with rubber gloves, if you will get them on your hands at all.* The detergents fall into two categories: the alkalines, which contain ammonia, washing soda, or trisodium phosphate, and the petroleum-based detergents. The heavy-duty detergents in powder form are—as far as I see on my grocer's shelves—all alkalines. If your nose cannot tell you which is which in their liquid form, note that the alkalines generally warn you not to soak aluminum in them (it would discolor), while the petroleum derivatives proclaim they are phosphate-free and noninflammable (I suppose once they burned?) and that, in their pure form, they remove tar and paint from tools and brushes. (Don't use on hands; great for brushes.)

Interestingly, *waterless hand cleaners*—sold in hardware, paint, and garage supply shops—are cousins of the petroleum-based detergents and great to use on those jobs you must somehow do bare-handed.

I cannot warn you strongly enough: *If soap and detergent solu-*

*Look up *cleaning* and *cleansing* in the dictionary. Most amusing.

tions are strong enough to do a serious cleaning job, they are strong enough to hurt your skin. What you think is simply a case of chapped hands may be the first sign of some kind of dermatitis. Dermatitis is a son-of-a-bitch to cure, sometimes requiring cortisone (which is *not* good for one) and often leaving a lifelong sensitivity. *It is better to leave a job undone than to do it without rubber gloves.* In a pinch a plastic bag, worn as a mitten and secured at the wrist with tape or a rubber band, will replace a rubber glove.

Cleaning Ovens and Refrigerators

Both these jobs are A-1 hateful. Use a commercial cleaner for the oven, and use it with *extreme* care. If your oven is very old, it may not be cleanable. If the inside looks rusty and the enamel is off (a condition called fire scale and caused by repeated heating and cooling and so on), cleaning is impossible. Line the oven with heavy-duty aluminum foil (keeping the foil away from burners and vent holes and pilots), and change the foil whenever it is dirty. *Oven cleaners are supremely caustic. Wear safety goggles, if possible, while using the spray ones. Follow directions to the letter.*

Cleaning the refrigerator is a bore, not a risk. It's best done when the icebox is at its emptiest—just before the week's shopping trip. If the fridge needs defreezing, do it now. Newer refrigerators have a defreeze setting that keeps food safely cold while allowing excess ice to melt. Old iceboxes may have to be turned off, and the process hastened by keeping the door open. In summer the defreezing of such an older fridge is a great big bore, as food that must be kept cold must be stashed with plenty of ice in a picnic cooler, or wrapped in lots of newspaper, with lots of ice, in a heavy cardboard box, for the duration of the defreezing.

Wash the icebox out with water and baking soda or borax. Remove the shelves and wash them in the sink.

NOTE: Take advantage of icebox-cleaning time to get rid of leftovers, consolidate bits of jam (all except marmalade can be mixed together) or ketchup bottles (dilute with a bit of boiled-hot water to make pouring easier), and tidy up.

An Ecological Note

You may hate me for not shunning all phosphates, but their guilt in the ruin of lakes is far from proven. Latest studies make their guilt doubtful. Anyway, biodegradable phosphates are *not* a considerable worry in our oil-and-industrial-waste-laden, raw-sewerage-fed waterways. And while I mostly use cloths, I use paper towels wherever they make my work easier. I make up for this use of wood pulp by not buying newspapers, writing on both sides of stationery, refusing paper bags in stores, and using cloth table napkins.

3 / Furniture and Such

In New York State, and I suppose elsewhere, secondhand mattresses may not be sold. They are "given away" free with a bedstead you buy. *Do not accept a secondhand mattress, even if free*. Uphol-stered furniture must be sterilized before being resold and wears a tag saying so. *Do not* buy secondhand upholstered furniture without a tag.

When one buys privately, one is well advised to buy only brand-new upholstered furniture, or to insist everything be dry-cleaned—preferably at the seller's expense—*before* delivery.

Secondhand furniture is one of the biggest sources of fleas, roaches, and even mice around. Get your pets at the Humane Society!

Where to Buy

1. *Department stores* are hard as heck to deal with. They seem to have open-ended delivery dates. Friend after friend tells of furniture promised within six weeks and not delivered after twelve. If you are in a hurry, get something you can take home with you

that very day. There is no point in sitting at home weeks waiting for the truck and then getting your money back!

2. *Specialty stores* are my favorites. Chairs at a chair store, beds where only beds are sold. Specials are very good here, delivery immediate, and the complaints are handled knowledgeably.

3. *Unpainted furniture* shops vary in price-worthiness and quality. *Do not* order by mail unless you have a friend who has bought and can show you a sample. No matter how it comes to you—truck, U.P., parcel post—it is a monstrous nuisance to repack and reship anything big. (And if it is too big for parcel post, you're just about stuck.)

A cabinetmaker friend tells me staples are preferable to nails, the construction of this type of furniture and staples and glue fantastic. I prefer hardboard to plywood for drawer bottoms and cabinet backs; plywood splinters.

Unpainted furniture, if of good quality, offers modest savings, pleasant, simple designs, and of course lets you have your way with the finish. It is not, however, an earthshaking bargain (particularly because the finishing costs extra money).

4. *Secondhand or antique stores.* If you proceed with the thought that you probably will be rooked, and haggle on price accordingly, you'll be okay.

The mahogany dresser probably is stained something else—a cheap, pretty wood used during the Great Mahogany Era to make cheap furniture. That hand-caned chair is not *hand-caned* (each individual strand is fitted into an individual, little round hole) but *machine-caned* (a previously woven cane "cloth" glued into a groove, and held in place with a thick fiber called *spline*). Hand-caning is worth at least four times what machine-caning is. What the woman *thinks* is oak or cherry is or ain't. (Even antiquarians don't know it all. We bought an oak desk which, upon stripping, turned out to be walnut. It was a bargain as oak, but a windfall as walnut!) The man says: "All it needs is a dab of glue"? The whole thing may have to be reassembled with $200 worth of clamps by a specialist who will charge accordingly. The chair that can be recaned for a few bucks? It's no bargain if you can't do it yourself. (The handicraft magazines and some antique magazines list suppliers of caning material, if the Yellow Pages are no help.)

5. *Ads in the paper.* Genuinely risky, often rewarding. They really may be moving into a trailer and no longer have room for the four-poster bed. But that antique actually may be a 1923 imitation of an earlier piece, and never worth more than fifty dollars. By the time the old folk are in their trailer, you are well stuck. Sellers' hard-luck stories are as often fiction as fact; none is a guarantee.

Never pay more for anything because it is touted as an antique. If the desk is worth forty-five dollars *regardless* of provenance, buy it. If you are being asked twice the reasonable price because it is an antique, insist on a receipt that spells out the facts—one table, cherry and hickory, built 1820. A receipt not only proves the seller means it, but can be produced in court should it turn out you were had.

Remember thousands of people get stuck each year with old copies of older antiques. (They are not alone! Many masterpieces in which museums took infinite pride were revealed by X-rays and Carbon-14 tests to be seventeenth-century copies of fifteenth-century works.)

6. *Secondhand office furniture stores.* My flat-out favorites. I'm crazy about these stores. Not only do they sell sturdy, turn-of-the-century oak furniture at tiny prices, but assortments of vermin-free almost-new stuff, some of it exciting and challenging. (They outdo themselves in bargains after political campaigns, when campaign headquarters furniture floods the market.) For some reason an armchair sold secondhand at an office furniture store costs palpably less than the same chair from a regular store. The only explanation I find for this miracle is that office decorating is handled by professionals who don't care *what* happens to the old stuff, as long as they get rid of it.

These stores often have doctors', architects', or other specialized furniture—all of which can be used imaginatively.

A receptionist's desk is a great kitchen table. Use drawers for cutlery.

Desks are good bedroom tables. The drawers act as bureau.

With "modern" furniture, drawers and rails can be removed easily, the drawers plus hardboard becoming a separate chest.

A man we know uses an old library-card file for socks and handkerchiefs. Blueprint drawers are heaven for shirts. A small drafting table, plus some L-shaped molding, is a superb reference-book stand. An expansible showroom "pipe" rack (plus a curtain if you wish) makes a fine clothes closet. (Clothes do not remain cleaner in a closet than out—under normal circumstances—but you might get plastic garment bags for rarely worn things.)

And no one should be without a regular file cabinet for booklets, papers, correspondence, magazines, notebooks, recipes, and the like.

Stripping vs. Painting

One generation strips, the next paints. So it goes. Painting is in fashion right now, and the horrors of stripping have been minimized by the appearance of stripping (or, more accurately, *dipping*) services that dump the whole piece of furniture into a chemical bath that removes all stains and paint. (I am told it also kills all bugs.) But, as an antiquarian warned me, the dipper must know his stuff. Different woods need different baths, and the wrong bath can ruin a good piece.

Even the best dipper has no control over the glue. Older pieces may come apart, inset pieces may come out. Much antique painted furniture was *built* to be painted—the plank seat may have knotholes that were filled by an inset of wood (which can easily get lost). Much furniture that is stripped and comes out ugly should never have been stripped at all—neither the quality of the wood nor the original construction being meant for exposure.

Discuss possible gluing problems with the stripper beforehand. See if he will handle them, and at what price.

There is nothing shameful about painted furniture, and I'm glad to see its revival. Stained pieces may need a first coat of shellac, or white alcohol-base paint (sold specifically to keep stain from bleeding through paint). The new high-gloss latex paints are good for all furniture that will not need frequent washing. If scrubbing will be the furniture's lot, use a high-gloss oil-base enamel. (If you don't like the shine, it can be removed by automobile rubbing compound—once the coat is really truly dry.) For painting and other finishes, consult the Popular Science book *How to Do Your Own Wood Finishing*.

If you want to oil, or stain and oil, dipped furniture or new unpainted furniture, you have three choices. The easiest (and simplest) is to buy one of the highly reliable trademarked products the paint stores carry. As good, cheaper, but more complicated to use, is the house brand of a cabinetmakers' supply house. But if you are planning to do a good many pieces, the cheapest procedure is to get a book such as *The Furniture Doctor* from the library and use one of its recipes. Cheapest, most instructive, but also most cumbersome.

NOTE: *Please do not use spray-can paints unless you have a fume-proof respirator, preferably with goggles.* I recently made a test, using such a can in a "well-ventilated" place: all available windows and doors wide open. I used the spray *as directed*—and found that it ricocheted three feet in all directions. Which means (as my arms are *not* three feet long) I was getting a lot of spray on and into me. Spray lacquer is even *more* dangerous to inhale than spray enamel. The "well-ventilated" on the can is an understatement if there ever was one. If you must use spray, do it outdoors—and even then wear a proper mask.

4 / Safety in the Kitchen and Health in the Home

Most accidents happen at home because we feel so *safe* there. That handy chair is convenient to stand on: *Crash!* Breakfast in bed is so cozy, one forgets about one's floppy housecoat sleeves: *Flash!* "Why disturb her by turning on the light, when I know my way downstairs?": *Oops!* And saddest of all: "I know what pills are in the cloisonné box."

All these accidents do happen—sometimes to those one loves, sometimes to oneself. Most of the scars I have are from accidents at home, not from any in my far-more-dangerous studio.

Safety in the Kitchen

1. *Keep the kitchen organized.* What you use frequently should be within reach. You should not have to climb to get it. What you use rarely should be kept out of the way. (A neighbor with a tiny kitchen suspends rarely used pots from the ceiling, using an old sausage rack.) Have a good stepladder and use it. Keep knives in a knife box (easily made) or on a magnet board. Keep other sharp objects in boxes or containers. (One of those heavy leather tool-holders such as electricians wear on their belts is good.) *Never* strew sharp or pointed tools in a drawer.

2. *All electrical appliances must be kept in good repair.* Never poke at them with a metal tool while they are connected. At the slightest sign something is amiss, *disconnect and unplug* the appliance. Do not trust thermostats or switches.

Keep appliance cords out of the way. More than one person has gotten a bad jolt by accidentally slicing or chopping through an electrical cord.

3. Always turn on the kitchen light if you cannot see clearly. As you reach for a tumbler, you might grab a raggedy-edged can.

4. *Concentrate on your work, and insist others keep away.* Particularly true when you make last-minute preparations while the guests are already there. It's one of the entertainment industry's biggest idiocies to show the 'over sneaking up to kiss the neck of some poor girl who's chopping parsley or frying eggs. I've gotten many a cut or burn by becoming distracted from my task by a sudden noise.

5. *Burns are the worst kitchen hazard. Always wear clothes.*

A splash of sizzling fat is bad enough on arms or hands. It's excruciating on breasts or genitals. *Wear good, well-fitted shoes.* Simone Weil, you've read, put herself out of the Spanish Civil War when she spilled boiling oil on her feet. Not only should your feet be safe from what might *fall* on them—a knife, or something hot—but from what you might *step* on. Shoes should be solid enough to give you good footing when you carry heavy or hot dishes.

Avoid loose sleeves, long skirts, baggy pants. Remove beads and bracelets. Tie up your hair. Anything that can trip you or catch or get in your way is to be avoided. My favorite serious-cooking clothes are jeans, a long-sleeved cotton turtleneck shirt, boating sneakers. My hair is short, but long-haired friends wear kerchiefs.

Have good, thick potholders and use them.

Keep fire extinguishers accessible and in working order.

Warn others or leave a note about hot appliances, including electric stove tops that take a long time to cool. Beth comes home, finds the iron out, grabs it carelessly to put it away. Josie has this minute finished ironing, dashed out on a date. Result: burns. A freak accident? Sure. But also avoidable.

6. *Nonfood items do not belong in a kitchen.* A sound basic rule. But we all break it with cleaning products under the sink or in the broom closet. If nonedibles must be stashed in the kitchen, give them their own separate closet. *Never* transfer a nonedible into a food can without clear and ultra-visible labeling. Paint thinner in an old gin bottle can be disastrous.

7. *Keep pills out of the kitchen.* We all laughed when we visited a friend and opened the jar with the pretty candies, only to be driven back by the awful smell of fish oil and yeast. The jar was full of vitamin pills! But not all pills smell.

8. *Have all medication labeled clearly as to content by the pharmacy.* Most pharmacies think ''one a day as needed'' is enough to keep the patient happy. It isn't, particularly if the patient has a bad reaction to the medication and neither prescribing doctor nor dispensing pharmacy is on duty.

9. *If you live with others, have a separate canister for each person's medications, and be sure labels are loud and clear.* You

could grab a roommate's allergy pills when you think you have your own vitamins. Not funny if you're starting on a long drive.

NOTE: All of the above must be emphasized in spades if children will come visit. Before the little guests arrive, tour your apartment, check that there are no razors abandoned on the sink, appliances in the way, medication left about.

Safety in the Bathroom

Bathrooms—with their hard, sharp fixtures, hard tile floors, and generally crowded layouts—are hazardous. Keep glass out of the bathroom. Buy shampoo and such in plastic jars, or transfer into plastic. Get antiskid tape for the tub. If you live with others, color-code towels, tooth mugs, toothbrushes. Not only should this guarantee against the transfer of fungi and some germs, but people *do* vary in their hygienic criteria, and to each his own is best.

If there is any illness in the household, ask the doctor to be specific about household hygiene. Most doctors do not issue warnings unless specifically, insistently asked.

Personal Safety

(*Not* about locks, dogs, and gas bombs!)

Now that you are on your own, you are responsible for yourself. No one in the area knows your folks, or that you are old Doc Prins's patient. If anything happens to you, *you are the only source of information about yourself.*

Carry identification with you at all times. Bursar's or social security cards or driver's license is *not* enough. Even a Blue Cross card is no help. The identification should list blood type, any medication you are taking, any known allergies—particularly to medication a first-aider might give you. It also should tell your parents' phone number and another number to call if something happens to you. (Be sure that other number knows how to reach your parents.)

If you have any permanent medical condition—including antibiotic or anesthetic allergies—join some group such as Medic Alert and wear their identification tag at all times.

Tell a close friend about any such condition. (Let that be the friend whose phone number you carry.) If you have something like epilepsy or diabetes that just might make you suddenly very ill, tell someone at your office about it.

If you share a flat, share medical information. Even spouses rarely know each other's blood type, or exactly what medication is being taken. Know where your roommate's family are. Know how to reach them night and day. Know who his doctor is. A friend saved me from disaster once by calling my doctor while I was reacting to a new medication. The scariest scene I ever witnessed was a sudden asthma attack a girl at the dorm had! None of us had ever encountered asthma, we had no clue what was wrong.

Post emergency numbers near the phone. Identify them clearly.

Keep the first-aid kit stocked. Keep medication you need—even if rarely—on hand. Fewer and fewer drugstores are open nights—and I do hope you buy at a discounter who might be miles away. Know where your nearest hospital emergency room is. Know how to call an ambulance.

A last, related, warning.

Don't disappear.

Two sad stories I remember from my twenties go something like this: A girl took off for a long weekend and was in a serious accident. Her companion, thank God, knew mutual friends, and some nimble-footed detective work located the girl's parents. She was okay, and her parents were there when needed. But they arrived hours after they could have been there, had the girl carried sufficient identification. In the second case, a family desperately tried to locate their daughter because of an emergency at home. By the time the girl returned to her school—no one had been able to find her—it was too late. Great sorrow was made more terribly by simple thoughtlessness.

Even today, when we are as adult as we will ever be, we tell close friends where we are going. (TV news spreads terror quickly. If your parents hear there was a gas explosion in Rochester, and can't locate you at home, it's only fair they should have another number to call, to find out your whereabouts or welfare.) When my husband travels, we use two friends as contacts. If he does not reach me at home, M. or C. knows just where I am. They, in turn, have copies of his schedule and could call him should I need help.

Cherish your privacy, by all means. But don't run risks or cause others needless worry. If you are taken ill, call a friend and tell him. An older friend was taken ill during a blizzard. He called no one so as not to be a bother. By the time he was sick enough to accept help, his phone had been knocked out by the storm. Lucky for him, the woman who lives down the hall is both motherly and observant. Not seeing him about for a few days, she went to investigate. Since he had pneumonia, she probably saved his life.

5 / Clothing

Clothes tie up a considerable amount of money, particularly in cold climates, where one needs at least two complete wardrobes (the winter one being the costlier).

I don't propose to tell you how to buy clothes, as Americans seem to select their own from the time they can point. But here are a few thoughts to consider, now that you pay all bills.

1. *Staples vs. fashion.* Those blue jeans that have not changed style since Mr. Levi invented them are *staples*. Bell-bottom jeans (even of *blue* denim) or printed ones are *fashion*. Blouses and panties are *staples;* melded into a body suit, they are not.

Staples are items that are the same, year in, year out. *Fashion* is ephemeral.

Some fashion items quickly become staples—*vide* pantyhose, turtleneck shirts, boots. Once a fashion becomes so established the manufacturers are assured of a long-range market, and do not face the threat of complete retooling every few months, the prices drop.

Given the above, you see that the identical fabric and identical construction will make a cheaper *staple* shirt (regular collar, barrel cuffs) than a fashion one (wide collar, frilled cuffs). Conversely, given two shirts at the same price, you can be reasonably sure that the staple one has a better fabric or sounder construction.

Staples are your best buy, particularly in clothes that have to last a long time.

NOTE: At end-of-season sales, however, fashion will be reduced more sharply in price than staples. When buying, make allowance for the original overpricing. A classic sweater cut from $26 to $13 probably still is a better buy than the mohair argyle extravaganza reduced from $55 to $13.

2. *Washing vs. dry-cleaning.* Ten-dollar pants that must be dry-cleaned will cost you over $30 before you are through. A $20 pair of pants you can wash will cost perhaps $21 and is bound to last longer.

Clothing maintenance is a heavy budget burden, and maintenance should be a prime consideration when buying.

Some years ago I accompanied my most elegant friend to a boutique. While she shopped, a very expensive young lady in an ankle-length white melton coat zoomed in.

"Oh," she cried, "I made *such* a mistake when I bought this coat."

("You bet," I thought. "White? Melton? Ankle length? In New York? In winter?")

"Oh, this coat spends so much time at the cleaners," she went on. "I should have bought *two*."

Dry-clean only is no longer a sign of good quality. Today it frequently masks poor construction. Some of the worst goods on the market are marked *dry-clean only* because the manufacturer knows they cannot survive a wash.

Woven woolens and worsteds, cottons, most linens and silks can be washed. So can a good number of synthetic fibers and blends. We always have washed my husband's lighter suits, my skirts, our slacks. The only reason heavy suits or winter coats can't be washed is that they are interfaced. The interfacing may shrink, but the bigger problem is that the thickness of the fabric layers makes it impossible to rinse the garment properly and dry it quickly enough to prevent "souring."

Knits and heavily textured linens and silks are iffy. A normally knit garment, such as a sweater, can, of course, be hand-washed. Double knits and other knit *fabrics* may or may not withstand a water bath. Heavily textured fabrics are apt to lose their looks. I would not experiment in violation of a label directive unless the garment were on its last legs anyway.

Cold-water soaps are great but not essential. You can dissolve granulated soap or hand-dishwashing detergent thoroughly in hot water, allow to cool, and then add it to your cold water (which need not be glacial, just cool).

NOTE: *The most important factor in washing is drying!* When you hang up a wet cloth, the water gathers at the lower edge. The thicker that edge—a hem or cuff—the more it will hold the water. This exerts a great pull on the upper part of the garment, creating little "cherub wings" where the fabric is clipped to the line, or distended pockets, uneven hems, and so on. All woolens and linens, all knits (except those whose hang tags permit machine drying), *all fabrics you hand-wash are best dried flat.*

A sweater-drying rack can be bought for little at a housewares store, or built for less out of dowels and nylon netting. The rack can be made like a screen, or like a hammock. The idea is to suspend the washed garment so that air reaches it from the bottom as well as top. No matter how good you are at stomping out excess water into a turkish towel, there will be drips of water. Build or set your rack above the tub, or on a very thick layer of newspaper on the bathroom or kitchen floor.

NOTE: The hidden key to clothing longevity is *construction:* how the garment is assembled, how the seams are finished, whether good or chintzy interfacing and lining were used. Even if you never hope to sew, read a book on home tailoring. Try to get an experienced friend to show you the difference in construction at a department store that carries several differently priced lines.

Buying Clothes

Sales. Clearance or end-of-season sales are a fine source of clothes, but worthwhile only at better (more expensive) shops. For serious clothes such as business suits or for winter coats, the clearance sale at a well-known specialty shop is worth the wait.

If yours is an offbeat size, however, the store is unlikely to have anything left for you at end of season.

NOTE: A detestable habit of many stores is to supplement their own leftovers with manufacturers'. The latter goods, nine chances out of ten, were rejected by the same store at the beginning of the season. Or they will be of a poorer quality than the store normally carries. These supplemental goods will be identified (on signs as invisible as local law allows) "Special Purchase," "Manufacturer's Overstock," or some such. Until you know construction, avoid these racks—and shun as you would any con artist the table marked "Bathing suits—were $6 to $35" *unless the original price tags are still on each item.*

Discounters. The big discount houses are quick and easy for sneakers, pantyhose, and other clothes that represent a small investment. Quality on serious clothes, however, runs from fantastic (a couturier needed quick cash) to crummy (A Hong Kong bankruptcy). Do not buy something that needs to last unless you have a savvy friend as guide (or know construction).

Thrift shops and secondhand stores. A thrift shop retails donated new and old clothes for the benefit of some charity. The Salvation Army and Goodwill Industries stores are best known, but in a sizable town there will be schools, old age homes, and so on that operate or share their own thrift shops. New merchandise was donated by a store or manufacturer, and rarely is there an exceptional buy. Much of the secondhand clothing has survived its original owner and will be of excellent quality and outdated style. *The buys in thrift shops are in women's clothes,* which will be first-rate castoffs from ladies of high fashion and higher income. Again, those in the extremes of the size scale won't be lucky here.

Secondhand stores used to be found only in poor neighborhoods, where they specialized in out-of-pawn overcoats, lost-and-found galoshes, the clothes of the dead, and shirts confiscated by unpaid laundrymen. Today secondhand stores (veiled by cute names) are springing up in expensive neighborhoods. They buy and resell the wardrobes of men and women of high fashion but insubstantial income. They are outstanding sources of good business suits, I am told. Again, the closer your size is to the median, the luckier you will be.

Army-Navy or work-clothes stores. These used to be about the same thing, with the A-N stores specializing in uniform items the military man must buy for himself, or simply extra socks and underwear. Government standards are good, and clothes made to their specs reliable buys. After World War II, A-N stores also carried lots of government surplus—again, good buys. Of recent years, however, flagged on by the youthful cult for paramilitary dress, the A-N stores have stocked secondhand clothes from every army, navy, and police force in the world. The prices are fanciful, and the buyer must be wary. *Work-clothes stores,* which used to be Outfitters by Appointment to the Working Class, also have succumbed to fashion. The fad that has turned blue-collar outfits into high fashion has encouraged these stores to diversify, and they've added pseudo-work clothes, such as bell-bottom overalls, that are not necessarily hard-wearing.

NOTE: Denim clothes often are labeled by weight—this weight, as with other cottons, representing a square yard. For real work, 13- or 14-ounce denim is the only kind. For summer casual wear, lighter weights serve. (They are a lot cooler.)

Wholesalers. Excellent, particularly for staples. Every big town has some wholesalers who supply the small neighborhood stores, In New York City the wholesalers concentrate around Orchard Street. As staples come price-tagged from the factory, you instantly see exactly how much you are saving. Some wholesalers also handle seconds or irregulars, which are clearly stamped as such—sometimes on the label, sometimes inside the garment, generally both. These items have minor defects, and while I would not buy something as fragile as a nylon tricot as a second, I would buy coveralls and sweat socks.

Mail-order houses. If you are very busy, or an unusual size, and have a safe mailing address (your office or school, for instance), by all means buy by mail. The savings are negligible. What is knocked off from the retail-store price is added back on under shipping and handling. *But* you do save carfare. More important, catalogues give you far more description than you ever get from a salesclerk (compare *full* description of *all* items in *each* price range before deciding which to buy); very large or very small sizes are always available; orders and complaints are handled swiftly and politely. The biggest advantage of mail-order houses is that you can compare values of different price lines without having to trot from department to department, and can buy a diversity of objects without leaving your house.

Factory outlets, cancellation, surplus stores. As with other goods, so with clothes. *Outlets* carry both regular stock and seconds. We have found them remarkably honest, and quick to point out what and where the defect that makes the item a second is. (They have, of course, every reason to want to keep your confidence in their label.) *Cancellation and surplus stores* seem to buy canceled orders, bankruptcy stock, merchandise other retailers have left *after* end-of-season sales. I have only bought shoes at such stores, picking according to the manufacturer's or retailer's label (which is generally kept on), and have been very satisfied.

Sewing: Your Best Source of Fashion

You cannot buy better fashion than you can sew. Twenty years ago, when I was broke and shabby, R. urged me to start sewing: "Don't worry," she said. "It can't possibly be worse than ready-to-wear." She was right. Even my beginner's efforts were of better quality than what I then could have bought. Today I sew a lot better and could buy costlier ready-to-wear. But what I make still is better than what I could buy. A home-sewn item costs about one-third of the retail price. And it lasts longer because of better construction and finishing.

An acceptable sewing machine costs about thirty dollars. It

is likely to be an ancient treadle machine, converted to electric portable, but it will sew a straight seam and that is all you need. The major pattern companies have patterns specifically for beginners, and very reasonably priced how-to books.

The above is addressed to men as well as women. If you've ever lived abroad, you know there is nothing sissy about tailors and nothing exotic about custom tailoring for men.

If you still are anxious about plunging in, take an adult-education course in sewing. But it is not necessary.

The only problem is time. While one can dash to the stores during lunch hour (investing perhaps a week's worth into a skirt), one must sew in one's leisure time. (The skirt will take only three hours.) Since I am not a standard size and have always had to add time spent on alterations to time spent shopping, I quickly learned to set aside two or three whole weekends a year for sewing. A professional seamstress taught me to work assembly-line style. I cut out *all* garments, baste, fit, stitch, etc. *all* garments, thereby saving hours over doing one item from beginning to end while the others wait.

Remember we are talking fashion, not staples. You cannot buy the fabric for 13-ounce blue jeans as cheaply as you can buy the jeans. Shirts and blouses are worth the effort only when you move into really costly fabrics. The same goes for pajamas, robes, and the like.

6 / Miscellaneous Counsel and Hints

If you live with others—as contrasted to living as a couple— problems about money arise quickly. Psychiatrists will tell you most people are more troubled by money than by sex, and have stranger financial than sexual hangups. Money wrecks friendships as well as marriages. Care should be taken.

A budget of some kind is a good idea. Several perfectly good methods exist, and one will work for your household.

1. Plan all purchases together, share all expenses alike. Buy nothing that is not approved by the others, shared by all.

2. Plan and share certain expenses, leave others *ad lib.* to each individual. This could mean basic food, toiletries, cleaning supplies are bought by the group, while optionals such as soda, beer, magazines are bought by those who want them, and remain theirs.

3. Share costs after reviewing expenses at the end of the month. When I had a roommate, our schedules were so different we rarely saw each other. We kept lists of needs, and each did what shopping she could and noted what was spent. At the end of the month, we'd straighten things out, agreeing on what should be half-and-half, what personal. I consume tons of coffee, she ate tons of cookies. But sometimes she served "my" coffee to her guests, or I fed "her" cookies to mine. It worked out extremely well because we are dear friends, and equally frugal.

You can't be tied to a method. So much depends on temperament that no method is *best*. I like the third method because I hate restraints, and this system is free, fair, and treats people as adults. The first method, however, might be best for a household of several people, some of whom are rich, others broke.

Keep your money at a savings bank. Forget checking accounts. The ideal bank account is at a bank that compounds interest on a daily basis. (In New York these are called *day-of-deposit/day-of-withdrawal* accounts.) These exist only at savings banks (as contrasted to savings accounts at commercial banks).

Big-city commercial banks (the ones with checking accounts) have, of recent years, developed the practice of charging for checking *accounts*, as well as per check written. (The exception they make is to give a few free checks to those who keep enormous balances.) This means that $300 in your checking account costs you something like $0.50 a month *just for nothing*. And if you write a check, you are charged at least $0.10 per check. The same $300 will earn you about $1.25 a month in a savings bank, and should you need a check, the bank will write you one for a tiny fee. If you have a job you will, in all likelihood, cash your paychecks for pocket money and "transform" some of your paychecks into other checks to pay bills. That part of your finances won't be affected;

but the bits and pieces you accumulate will benefit greatly by being in a savings bank.

Get a tax accountant if you have more than one source of income, or unusual expenses. If you do any money-earning work at home, some of your rent may be tax-deductible. In certain work situations carfare is deductible. Having an accountant requires record-keeping and exactitude, but the more complex your financial and work setup, the likelier it is to be a good investment, even with a small income.

Insurance

This is so complex a subject that I can only alert you to *think about it and consult a good reliable agent.*

Your college may have a medical plan covering students. Your employer may have a medical plan for employees. You should, however, read the policies and see, in the case of your college, what happens during vacations, what happens if you take a leave of absence, become an exchange or graduate student. How soon after graduation are you "cut off"? Are nonmatriculated spouses covered? (In the past, wives of students frequently were, while husbands of students were not. I do not know if and how far this has changed.) Is the plan *convertible?* (Which means that after you are separated from the group plan you can, within a reasonable period, buy the same plan on your own, without losing any of the waiting-period benefits.)*

Just because your employer's plan is free or partly paid for does not make it good. You may find that your coverage is based on your salary and is not enough to meet realistic needs. So you may need a supplementary plan.

If you pay for any of the insurance, check all details with the agent or representative. Even if the plan is *all* free, check it out carefully before accepting that it's *all* you need.

Consider a plan that pays you a salary while you are ill.

*Many plans require you to be a member for more than nine months before they'll pay for a baby. Many plans disqualify you if, within a certain time of joining, you come down with some chronic diseases. That is why convertible plans are attractive.

I am quite devoted to such plans and carried one in my penniless youth. Had I been unable to work because of illness, the plan would have paid my then-salary for life, if necessary. I bought the plan because my family could not have supported me without hopeless sacrifice, or without leaving me a ward of the Welfare State. The plan called for $50 a week, twenty years ago. That $50 still would meet my basic needs. Which shows such plans are not worthless, despite inflation.

Now you have a home, protect it. Dog nips super. Guest breaks leg. Overflowing bathtub drenches bookshelves of downstairs neighbor. All the *tzores** that once were your Dad's are now yours. You need some liability insurance on your home. (The guest with the broken leg may *have* to sue to meet medical bills. She's not being mean.)

Granny gave you a typewriter when you graduated from high school. How will you replace it if it gets stolen?

The New York City joke "If I can get burglary insurance at such-and-such an address, I can't afford to live there" is probably as true in other cities. Burglary insurance is almost impossible to buy in New York City, and, I suppose, elsewhere.

A form of insurance called a *floater* might, however, be available to you. A *floater* is insurance on a specific object and on it alone.

It covers it against damage or loss wherever you are. (Photographers carry it on their cameras, reporters on their typewriters, and so on.) Floaters are hard to get, but try.

If the article you want to insure earns you money, you may have to get a commercial policy, which costs more, but also is easier (I'm told) to get.

My guess is, you would be better off paying yourself "premiums" by placing a sum of money in a savings account for the replacement of stolen property.

Nevertheless this is a subject to be discussed with an accountant or insurance man—or with your Dad.

Tzores (Yiddish, plural, never used in singular form; how could it be?), an umbrella word that combines worries, anxieties, frets, and nibblings of paranoia.

Discuss insurance problems with your parents, even if they don't live in the same city or state. Get together with your parents' insurance agent. In some perfectly legitimate way your parents may be able to combine some of your insurance needs with their own and save you money.

Some of the more common types of insurance needed by homeowners or apartment dwellers are combined into *homeowners' policies.* For a given premium they allow x for a fire, y for liability, and so on. These policies commonly are cheaper than the same coverage bought separately.

Professional societies sometimes have group policies that are very advantageous. If there is a professional society in your field, it may have group insurance available to its members. If it does, you are likely to save money by joining and getting their plan. As a rule of thumb, it is cheaper to pay dues and group insurance than to have individual (nongroup) coverage.

Don't kid yourself about the generosity of public assistance. What charities tell one at fund-raising time is not necessarily so. When it gets down to cases, you might really have to *make* yourself penniless before they will help, and you might regret not having carried plenty of insurance.

A Checklist of Expenses

The following checklist should see you through your first months in a home of your own. If you have a job, and feel secure in it, you can reduce my three-month quotas to two. If you are new at your job, insecure in it, or not eligible for unemployment insurance, stick with the "this month *plus* two" model.

Call the utilities and ask about deposit requirements and monthly rates. Look at the paper and estimate what an apartment will cost. And so on. Then you will be able to fill in this checklist and see if you need to borrow some cash from your folks, or hustle a little harder to get it together yourself, before embarking on a room of your own.

DEPOSITS (returnable, or applicable against bills after a time)
1. Apartment security $_____

2. Telephone company (generally must be paid in full before they install.) _____
3. Electric company _____
4. Gas company (if separate from electric) _____

MONTHLY EXPENSES
1. Three months rent _____
2. Three months phone bill _____
3. Three months electric and gas (This would include purchase of a bottle of gas where needed.) _____

INSTALLATION
1. Trucking or car rental to move you $_____
2. Hardware and paint (make list, check suppliers) _____
3. Furniture and linens _____
4. Kitchen equipment see page 41 _____
5. Rental agent's fee _____

INSURANCE
1. Health _____
2. Homeowners (fire, liability) _____
3. Car _____

NOTE: If you have just moved from one state to another, find out what the requirements are for getting your driver's license in your new state. Some states give one a very small grace period, and a big fine if one forgets. The fee for the new license should go under *installation*!

PART TWO: Cooking

7 / About Cooking and Cookbooks

You don't really need cookbooks. But they are as irresistible as mysteries, so we had better discuss them.

There are two books I think should be in every kitchen. The first is Adelle Davis's *Let's Eat Right to Keep Fit,* which is a life-giving book on nutrition. And while Miss Davis takes her cause a bit more seriously than I think necessary, she goes a long way toward debunking much of what Big Food and Big Pharmaceuticals have dinned into our brains. Second is the U.S. Department of Agriculture's Home and Gardens Bulletin #72, called *Nutritive Value of Foods.* Write the Department in Washington, D.C., and the booklet is yours free. If you can spare $2.35,* get *Composition of Foods,* Agriculture Handbook #8, instead of, or along with, H & G #72. This is an amazingly complete book on exactly-what-you-are-eating and includes information on soybeans, Jerusalem artichokes, carob flour, as well as on regional foods such as mangoes and ground cherries.

The U.S. Department of Agriculture and the Extension Services are the most generous and informative sources for every-which kind of home and garden information. A postcard inquiry generally brings a flood of material, all of it terrific.

With these two books you will be able to discover what you ought to be eating, and exactly what nutrition your food dollar buys. You will learn, for instance, why fresh peanuts may be a breakfast food far superior to any commercial cereal, and how to plan food spending around nutrients.

If you still want a "real" cookbook, get *The Joy of Cooking*

*Prices are correct at time of writing. This includes prices of foods referred to in shopping advice, where the information is presented to indicate the merits of price comparison, and not as a recommendation of one product over another.

(my by-far preference), *The Settlement Cookbook*, or *The Fanny Farmer Cookbook*—which is the only one of the three currently in paperback.

These are standard references and best owned in hardcover. You do not need the current edition (in fact, a young woman told me the other day she preferred a very early edition of one of these, because it included recipes calling for "real" ingredients rather than their "instant" or "convenience" form). Look about the secondhand bookstores.

You should have one of these references before you buy any other cookbook, because they explain fundamental techniques and procedures of cooking. They are an essential introduction to any other cookbooks.

Most sophisticated cookbooks, including specialized regional ones, and most of the excellent paperbacks on the market assume you know all the basics—the difference between poaching and steaming, for instance. Even the paperback "originals"—that is, those not reprinted from a hardcover book—require one to be a good-to-excellent cook.

Good Sources of Recipes

1. *The women's magazines.* Unliberated men love to sneer at these magazines from behind their *Sports Illustrateds* or *Playboys*. But the women's magazines remain the housewife's trade journals and deserve as much respect as *Business Week*. They are excellent sources of recipes and full of general household advice *most of which is as useful to men as to women.*

If you keep in mind that magazines survive by juggling the interests of their advertisers and those of their readers, and frequently exaggerate the satisfaction the latter will get from the former's products, you will find women's mags invaluable helpers.

Family Circle and *Woman's Day* are the cheapest and the best for us, as they address an audience that has five kids and a median-or-lower income. They frequently have big food supplements—like "A Thousand Ways to Prepare Hamburger"—and if the basic food, that is, hamburger, appeals to you, get the issue. (Checkout counter, supermarket.)

The glossier ladies' mags—*McCall's, Redbook, Ladies Home Journal, Good Housekeeping*—all come up with fine recipes but geared to a plusher audience which means costlier ingredients, more time-consuming preparation. Anyway, they cost too much. Two of these slicks cost as much as a good paperback. Their recipes are sound, however, and good for copying.

2. *The farm magazines.* If you can get hold of them, they are great for good, healthy recipes for busy people, and far removed from the gourmet-circuit nibblies of the slicks.

3. *The public library.* Now that most public libraries feature copying machines, the world's your oyster. Check out the old W.P.A. regional cookbooks—a treasure trove of pre-gussied-up, uncommercial food. There are of course any number of cookbooks to browse in, and you can glean and photocopy twenty recipes you really will use, for the price of a paperback.

4. *Daily papers.* I like *The Christian Science Monitor*, whose weekend edition often carries fine recipes, frequently exotic. The *Monitor* can be read free at C.S. reading rooms, and they will give you back issues. *The New York Times* recipes are generally complicated, costly, and lean heavily on gourmet-shop gewgaws. Local, small-town papers are written for low-income families, and their recipes are sensible and practical in an unromantic sort of way.

Choosing a Cookbook If You Must

1. *Do you like the foods or cuisine involved?* Don't buy an Indian cookbook unless you are sure you like Indian food. Why buy a seafood cookbook when the only fish you can eat (because of allergies) is represented by a lone recipe? *Divide the price of the book by the number of recipes you truly will use. Is it worth it?*

2. *Do you have time for the techniques involved?* As dearly as you may love casseroles, they are beyond your means if you never have more than an hour to fix dinner.

3. *Can you afford the ingredients?* In the section "What Cooking Is All About," page 70, there is a discussion of how basic recipes, such tried and true stalwarts as stew and clam chowder, can vary greatly in cost, depending on which cookbook you follow. A cookbook that relies on heavy cream, butter, brandy, mushrooms for its "effects" is not for you. When buying regional cookbooks, compare several for availability and cost of ingredients for the same recipe. (Some "foreign" cookbooks list American suppliers by state and city.)

4. *Does the book offer something new?* Or only variations of recipes you already have?

5. *Are the directions easy and clear enough for you at this stage?*

6. *Do you have the kitchen equipment and the space needed?* No sense getting a *hibachi* cookbook if you have no *hibachi*, nor the well-ventilated space it requires.

How to Use a Cookbook

As with most things, the two basic methods can be labeled "inductive" and "deductive."

1. *Inductive* (frequently cheaper). You have a number of ingredients—leftovers, this week's supermarket specials—you want to use. You look up the ingredients in your cookbook and pick a recipe that uses the available ingredient. (That's why you should never get a cookbook without an index.)

2. *Deductive*. You don't know what to make for dinner, or you yearn for a particular dish. You check the index for inspiration and guidance, and do your shopping accordingly.

3. *When you have decided on your recipe, read it from beginning to end.* American cookbooks generally list all ingredients in their proper quantity before describing preparation. But they often surprise with time required, techniques or utensils involved. British

cookbooks* often combine technique and ingredients in a pleasant narrative and surprise one by calling for a key ingredient at the very end. (This ingredient always seems to be violently expensive, or out of season.)

4. *Figure total cost.* That pound of mushrooms that turns chuck into a king's delight may cost more than the chuck, or even steak.

5. *Figure total time involved.* If complicated shopping is called for, or a great number of pots and pans, or hours of preparation, do you *have* the time, is it best spent that way?

6. *Will you be able to use leftovers before they spoil?*

NOTE: *Cookbooks give quantities for four to six servings within the context of a full meal:* something to start with, a main course replete with vegetables and potatoes, a salad, and a dessert. This means that a four-serving stew is just enough for two hungry people who are *not* having anything else. Bread-and-butter and a piece of fruit and some cheese do not count. So before you divide a recipe or, for that matter, double it, take into account what other food will be served at the meal you are planning.

NOTE: *Some recipes cannot be subdivided.* Many soups, or vegetable dishes such as *ratatouille* (see index) which want one each of a great number of vegetables, cannot be made in small quantities. Will you be able to use leftovers before they spoil? The quickest way of wasting your food dollar is to waste food.

How to Use This Part of STARTING OUT

1. At the beginning of each recipe you will find *have* and *buy*.

Listed after *have* are basics such as salt, sugar, tiny quantities of flour—what one can safely assume you have in the house. If, before starting on the recipe, you discover you are out of one of

---

*British cookbooks use the Imperial gallon as liquid measure, and give dry ingredients in pounds and ounces instead of cups. This is unlikely to cause a crisis except in baked goods, custards, some sauces, where proportions have to be exact for good results.

these staples, you can muddle through without. And it will serve as a reminder to get whatever it is, on your next shopping trip.

After *buy* you will find the basic ingredients for that recipe—things that (unless you have a freezer) you won't have around. The *buy* list doubles as shopping list, and it is its ingredients you add up when figuring costs.

In some cases the haves *become* buys. While flour and sugar are mostly *haves*—where only a tablespoon or so is called for—they are listed as *buys* in baking recipes (among others) because so large a quantity is needed and the ingredient is essential to the dish.

2. *Directions are given in approximate sequence.* You can interrupt whatever it is unless warned not to, and with two permanent notable exceptions: any dish involving baking powder must be completed once the baking powder has been moistened; any recipe involving beaten egg whites must be cooked to the end after the whites have been beaten.

3. *Cooking times are approximate.* There are so many variables in cooking—the toughness of meat, the size and shape of pots, how strong a flame you use—that, with this, as with any cookbook, time can only be estimated. Give yourself twenty minutes leeway if you have a deadline (such as dinner guests).

4. *Variations.* Most cookbooks list variations as separate recipes—because tiny variations mean big changes in name. A *boeuf bourguignon*, for instance, is a *carbonnade flamande* made with wine instead of dark beer. A *hollandaise* sauce gets a dollop of whipped cream to become a *mousseline*, and a few herbs plus some vinegar to become a *béarnaise*.

As a result, many cookbooks are big, fat, impressive, and terrify or confuse the novice.

I have simplified everything as much as makes sense. Variations, regardless of name, are listed after the basic recipe. As a rule of thumb, the first recipe is easier to make, and like, than its variations. The variations are never—as you will see—earthshaking. They are meant to show you the fantastic range of possibility, and the extraordinary simplicity, of cooking.

A Note on How Food Is Flavored

There are a number of ways in which a single food can be flavored—and these should be understood before one sets foot in the kitchen.

The most primitive way of flavoring food is to vary the method of cooking. A chicken, with nothing added, can be "flavored" by boiling, roasting, frying, or charcoal-broiling it. Method of cooking alters taste.

The next method—in simplicity, and probably in antiquity—is to combine other foods with the basic one. Our chicken can be cooked with tomatoes, beans, or bananas.

While the vegetables add bulk, and stretch the chicken to feed more people, we can add only lemon juice or wine or coconut milk to the plain chicken. This addition of highly flavored liquids soon leads to the addition of herbs (stems and leaves of aromatic plants) or spices (flavorful fruit, bark, flowers, or seed).

One can skip entirely the addition of other flavors during the cooking process, and season the dish once it is done. Mild sauces such as *hollandaise,** sharp sauces such as mustard or chili, can be poured on the dish just before it is served. Or the sauce can be served separately *à la* ketchup. With Indian food, a variety of sauces is served separately with a blandly cooked main dish—the guests choose exactly how they prefer to season the main course. This method of flavoring food has the charm that the basic food remains intact; it can be used in something with a totally different flavor later (as cold boiled rice can become rice pudding), reheated without danger of curdling or scorching (as might happen with a yogurt or flour sauce), and refrigerated without the extra danger of spoilage (which would occur with an already-mixed mayonnaise dish).

Each of the above ways of seasoning is quite enough in itself. Beginners tend to overdo a good thing in their search for greatness

---

*Although I make hollandaise, it's a big nuisance. If you must have it *now*, buy one of the ready-made brands at a gourmet shop.

—to marinate a chicken, charcoal-broil it, add more herbs, and serve it doused with relishes—thereby totally overpowering the essentially delicate flavor of the chicken.

Herbs and spices, sauces and relishes never are, and never should be, more than an accent—like a bright tie with a dull suit, or a flower in one's hair.

Throughout these recipes the use of herbs and spices is optional. Except, of course, in self-evident cases where the spicing is the point of the recipe—as with *aïoli* or lemon chicken. But don't discard a whole recipe because you don't care for that ¼ teaspoon of oregano.

Five Notes of Caution

1. Salt is not a harmless food additive; and salt must be eliminated from the diet in a number of severe illnesses. I am wary of the stuff, use it with a very light hand, and often skip it altogether. Salt is a flavor enhancer, but never a substitute for careful and clever cooking. If you season wisely with other things, you will be able to keep your salting to a minimum.

2. The same danger flag goes up for sugar. Thousands of Americans are sugar addicts, and the many books and articles that warn them sugar is a health hazard, and a contributing villain in many illnesses, go unheeded. But parents and schools nevertheless allow children to guzzle sweets and soda pop—often as part of their publicly funded school lunch. Refined sugar is not good for one. Period. Cut back as much as you can on it. Use honey or maple syrup (the pure kind) instead of sugar whenever possible. Use dried fruit instead of candy bars for pick-me-up snacks.

3. In most cases (see below) I suggest you add salt and sugar *at the end of the cooking time*. Do this at least till you have more experience as a cook, although, after all these years, I still do it that way.

I have never found the slightest difference in taste between foods salted or sugared at the beginning or in the middle or at the close of their cooking time. And as my mother says, it is much, much easier to add salt and sugar than to remove them. Now if the food becomes condensed in cooking, or you use a number of prepared foods such as bouillon cubes or dried soup in the preparation of the dish, you will be adding salt above and beyond what the recipe calls for. (If the recipe suggests wine or bouillon, and you use bouillon, the proper amount of salt for the wine will make the dish with bouillon too salty.)

The same applies to sugar. Sugar is a born troublemaker. It tends to caramelize, it tends to stick, and so on. So one's best bet is always to add it at the end of cooking while the stuff is still hot enough to dissolve the sugar.

Exception to above: All dishes like meatloaf which cannot be stirred and mixed after cooking; all dishes like cake, jellies, conserves which need sugar in them from the start for the chemical reaction in cooking.

4. This section is written with healthy, nonpregnant adults in mind. I am not a nutritionist, and my views on nutrition, strongly influenced as they are by the "organics" and "health food" buffs, are the amateur views of a longtime housewife. If you have any disorder, or are feeling more poorly than you think you ought to, a complete medical checkup that includes a discussion of your diet is in order. If you are planning to become pregnant, or are pregnant, discuss diet with a good obstetrician. The lackadaisical attitude I have toward the balanced diet may not be the best way for you.

5. I am an organic gardener and, to the extent we grow our own, an organic cook. But I buy commercially grown and canned foods when I need to. I buy only things like bulgur and buckwheat flour at health food stores—because I can't get them elsewhere. I have become extremely mistrustful of the health food stores, some of which charge more for the self-same products the supermarket carries. Also, many of the health food stores carry imported processed foods that, from what one learns from the label, do not contain additives, but which nowhere claim to be made from organically grown ingredients. I mention this here because canned and processed foods appear throughout the book. My suggestion is: Read all labels with care, buy as much as you can at the supermarket, be wary of exaggerated health food store claims. (One of my pet peeves

is *organic honey*. DDT and some other poisons are fatal to bees; *ergo* no bee can bring contaminated pollen into the hive. But other bad things may not be fatal to bees and might get into the honey. Who, except God, can tell where the bee sucks? Or what contaminates that flower?)

What Cooking Is All About

In Anthropology 101, you learned man has survived so well (as has the rat) because he can, and will, adjust his diet to what the environment provides.

Seaweed, lizard, honey, dates, mushrooms, woodchuck, walrus, eel, octopus, breadfruit—all are part of the almost endless list of what man has eaten and learned to enjoy. Everywhere, in every age, people have made the most of available food. So evolved the delicious, astonishing complexity of regional cuisine. French cookery is nothing more than a combination of foods readily available in France, and easily prepared in the kind of kitchen the French home provided. Chinese cooking is what China cultivated, prepared as was easiest for the Chinese. (The reason stew is so prevalent in Nordic cuisines is that it is made from odds and ends, and cooks forever on the slow fire used to heat a house.)

Today—with refrigeration, canning, freezing, dehydration, plus our excellent transportation facilities—purism in national cuisine is obsolete and anachronistic. People who yowl with anguish when you put sour cream in your Irish stew forget that the American potato changed Irish history more than St. Patrick, or Cromwell, or Parnell.

I mention this to make you feel the enormous freedom of the kitchen. Cookery is simple, exciting, and it can be joyful. You can throw together just about anything. Cook it in any way possible. All cooking only has one aim—to make the inedible edible, and the edible delicious.

Which is why I am so appalled to discover cookbooks written, apparently, for such as you, and full of ghastly ways of combining canned foods of dubious merit into what my stepfather called "concoctions." Some of the food is repulsive. More is beneath the dignity of a five-year-old. All of it presumes bad food is easier to prepare than good. Which is totally untrue. There is no need to eat poorly, even while poor. Cooking is perfectly simple, and good food surprisingly cheap.

What frightens people about cooking is that restaurant food (particularly the expensive variety) is *not* simple. When restaurants serve simple food, they gussy it up in some (frequently lamentable) way to justify an outrageous price tag.

Remember that restaurants try to practice *haute cuisine*—the deliberately complicated, status-symbol, and costly cookery of eighteenth- and nineteenth-century upper-class establishments. *Haute cuisine*, to which far too many cookbooks are devoted, is the realm of the competitive professional cook. What *you* will be doing is household cooking—the kind every tired mother-of-eight, every weary peasant, illiterate sailor, or exhausted hunter has coped with admirably since the dawn of history.

This book is full of regional recipes because one of the secrets of eating well cheaply is to make—and stick to—peasant fare from all over the world. As my beautiful friend Judy says, Calabria, Greece, Spain, northern France are among the poorest regions in the world—and when you are broke, their cuisines will keep you going well and cheaply till plusher days. (This is not 100 percent true, since some ingredients that grow wild and abundant in the Mediterranean are delicacies here. But it is basically true.)

Learning to Cook

Preparing most recipes in this book requires no experience. But following recipes isn't cooking. You must develop your palate so you can imagine combinations of food and understand why certain methods of preparation are advisable in certain cases.

This requires practice. And the first step is to *learn to taste*. If you limit yourself to "Boy, this was great!", you are an eater. If you say, "This chicken was better than last week's," you're on your way to being a taster. There's nothing difficult about identifying the factors that make a dish good or bad. It is merely training a pattern of thought—something you began doing as a child when you loved one brand of peanut butter and despised another. Analyze your food preferences. Think about what you are eating as you eat it.

One way of educating your palate is to try as great a variety of food as possible prepared by experienced cooks. Which mostly means eating out, and is easier said than done on a budget. Still, you can turn necessary dining out into a tasting tour. Try the same basic dish—chicken for instance—in as many inexpensive restaurants as your town affords. Southern-fried, in fricassee, in Brunswick stew, roasted, barbecued, as *cacciatore* (Italian) or *coq au vin* (French). You will discover that while the fowl is constant, the method of preparation and the additional ingredients vary almost to infinity. From there you can proceed to your own inventions—and most likely will invent some classic dish anew.

By this method you will learn that ground beef can become hamburger, *moussaka*, Swedish meatballs, lasagna, meatloaf, *pâté maison*, stuffed cabbage (to name but a few). An egg "contains" an omelet, a soufflé, a custard, and so on, as well as plain fried egg.

Your expeditions will be more rewarding if you take a friend or two and order a variety of dishes to share. People do this in Chinese restaurants, as a rule, but hesitate, for no good reason, to do it elsewhere. Nevertheless you probably would not try squid (like rubbery shrimp and delicious) unless you could hedge your bet by sharing the dish.

Don't be afraid to ask questions. Most small restaurants are owner-operated, and the waiters (sometimes literally) are part of a happy family. Don't ply them with questions during rush hours, or on weekend nights, but on a calm day they will answer questions like "What's in this?" and "How is this made?" Such chitchat should be reflected in your tip, unless the questions are essential to your ordering.

If wine is appropriate to the cuisine, order it. It is pretentious to go on about wines and vintages, and I, for one, have taken savage glee at watching a date, or host, get his comeuppance at the hands of a savvy wine steward. (The most common mistake people make is to assume the oldest wine is the best. Only a minority of wines improve with more than a year's aging, and then only for a very few more years.) However. In the restaurants we can afford there will be one wine in each category, and that's that. They will have vermouth (which, sweet *or* dry, is only an aperitif), dry or sweet sherry, sauterne, port, Madeira, Tokay—none of which go with main-course food, but are heaven with nuts, nonacid fruit, and pastries. (Sweet wines with cheese can be exciting, but the combination is very, very iffy. Experiment with a nutty sherry in the privacy of your home.)

What you want at the restaurant is a dry wine—red or white—that goes with salty, acidy things (which is what most entrées are). Dry wines can be "identified" by alcohol content, which ranges from the rarely seen 9 percent (most are around 11 percent) to 13 percent. The lower, the drier. The making of a dry wine depends on more than just alcohol content—the actual flavor of the grape used plays a big part.

Ask the waiter what he would suggest with what you ordered. Ask for a glass or, if there are several of you, a bottle. Remember what you got: Chablis, Graves, Rhine, Moselle, Rioja. Characterize the wine in your mind. Soon you will know why you like Rhine with your fish, and a white Bordeaux with turkey.

Rosé wines—which, contrary to what their enemies say, are not made from leftovers of white and red mixed—are chancy; except for that astonishingly virile Greek wine Roditi, which is adaptable and reasonable.

Never sneer at American wines. California wines, bought by the gallon, or half-gallon, are delightful, and your best buy. New York State wines, handicapped by the New York State grape which gives a peculiar, so-called foxy, taste, are recommendable only in sweet or blended wines—sherry, Tokay, Madeira, port.

One more word.

If you have a choice, eat in restaurants at lunch time, and make lunch your main meal. The price difference can be as much as 50 percent. So, if you plan to eat out on a weekend, consider having your dinner at 1:00 P.M. and a light supper. Where I've lived, the saving will pay for a movie.

●

8 / Getting Your Kitchen Together

Well and good. Into the kitchen then.

To start to cook you need the following:

Two frying pans. One should be 8 or 9 inches in diameter, with sloping sides. This will be your *small frying pan.* The other should be at least 12 inches across. Bigger is better, and its size should be determined by how easily you can lift it with one hand while it contains something weighing two or three pounds. (It can have straight sides; there's enough room to maneuver a spatula anyway.) This is the *big frying pan.* Ideally the big one has a fireproof handle (some have easily detached handles) and can be put in the oven.

Two saucepans. Again one big, one little. The small should hold 1½ pints, the big 2 or more quarts. Lids are nice, but not essential, and need not match. Fireproof handles are best.

One big gigantic pot. An old-fashioned blue enamel canner does fine, and a seamless stainless steel pail will do. You want a pot that easily holds a gallon, is perhaps 12 inches across, and low enough so you can safely stir the contents easily. (If you're short, a pail won't do; if you're tall, it's fine.)

One kettle or coffeepot—depends on what you drink. A saucepan can replace a kettle, but kettles are designed to utilize and retain heat best—they save on fuel and are safer to pour from.

One or two 1-pound fire extinguishers.

You also will need:

One each: Can opener or combination can and bottle opener. Measuring cup (preferably the pint size). Cooking fork. Large cooking spoon. Slotted spoon (a spoon with holes in it for draining).

Knife with a 9-inch blade or longer. Paring knife—one or more, of which at least one should be of stainless steel, to cut acid fruits and fish without affecting flavor. Long-handled wooden spoon, and as many small ones as you can afford (buy seconds if you can). Pancake turner or spatula. Set of measuring spoons, metal preferred. Six-inch (or larger) strainer.

Two large, thick potholders and one potholder mitt.

I do not list bowls here, because a saucepan can double as a bowl. But a few bowls are handy, particularly big ones.

If you are clever with chopsticks, you can skip the wooden spoons and the kitchen fork and buy a package of the long cooking chopsticks at an Oriental store. I use them for scrambling eggs, tossing salad, stirring sauces, turning bacon, and so on.

You are free to skip any of this list on your first shopping trip except the fire extinguishers and the potholders. We discussed kitchen hazards on page 42, but remember old stoves are in and of themselves fire hazards, and burns are your greatest kitchen risk. Locate your fire extinguishers so that you *do not* have to reach across the stove or even walk past it to get the extinguisher.

Later on you might add an egg beater, additional spoons and knives, a few more saucepans to your *batterie de cuisine*. But so far, this is all you need.

Sources of Supply

The best idea is to ask your mother, and other longtime house-holders, to make contributions. Most of us who've kept house a while have odds and ends of kitchenware we do not really need. Couples whose children have grown up, and whose cooking volume has been reduced accordingly, are particularly good sources for *big* pots and *big* frying pans.

1. *Junk stores, rummage sales, thrift shops.* These often have good used kitchen stuff. Here is where you may find the pots with nonmatching lids! Thrift shops are also good on appliances such as toasters, electric irons, pressure cookers. Before buying any of these, *make sure* the manufacturer still is around and still

provides spare or replacement parts. (I received two pressure cookers as wedding gifts. For one I have no trouble finding gaskets and safety plugs, which are the wear-outable parts of a pressure cooker and last from six months to six years. For the other I have had to send away to Cleveland or some place to get gaskets!) If you buy any electric appliances at a thrift shop, have the store plug them in to see if they work. If that cannot be done, *make sure* the store will let you bring it back and get a refund if the thing cannot be repaired at a pre-agreed-on price.

2. *Five-and-tens and discount stores.* These carry nice, reasonably priced ware, which certainly will last through your bohemian period. From my observation, however, *discount stores* are not cheap enough to make up for the inconvenience of shopping there, and the greater inconvenience of getting things exchanged, repaired, and so on.

3. *Department stores.* I hesitate to put them in at all, because what they carry varies so much, and you need experience to choose wisely. Some department stores, appealing to the lower-middle class, carry *just* what you really want. Others carry elegant wedding-present-ware in the main section of the store and hide the stuff you, me, and yonder peasant want in the recesses of the basement. Others, still, carry only elaborate, overpriced gourmet-shop items. So find out what the store carries *first* (ask an old-time resident of the city you're in), and then set out to buy. Department stores are, however, good about replacing defective goods.

4. *Restaurant supply houses.* Believe me, these are mentioned only to obviate people saying I forgot. Because of the rough life pots and pans lead in restaurants, the supply houses carry only the roughest, toughest—hence *costliest*—ware. In some restaurant supply houses (because of the high bankruptcy rate of restaurants) you can get secondhand ware—which is likely, however, still to be more expensive than what you could get at the five-and-ten. For the dedicated householder/chef/gourmet these stores have great professional charm. For you, I doubt it. Except for dishes. (See page 00.)

Outlet or "seconds" stores. I do not recommend them for cooking ware. (See page 81.)

Kinds of Cookware

1. *Aluminum* pots and pans come in several weights, that is, thicknesses of metal. The heavier the gauge, the sturdier the pot, and the better its heat distribution (a key factor in the prevention of scorching). The lightweight stuff, which is what you are most likely to find in poor-neighborhood stores, is no good. Except perhaps for a tiny extra saucepan for boiling eggs. The medium weight is not cheap but worthwhile. The extra-heavy ware (which is what you see advertised in the magazines) is almost as expensive as stainless—and, for my money, not as good. Reason: aluminum is harder to clean (if really dirty, or scorched) than any other cooking ware, because you cannot use washing soda or ammonia without turning it a putrid color. Also aluminum imparts a tinge of flavor to highly acid foods. For frying pans, however, and one saucepan, medium-weight aluminum is fine.

2. *Stainless steel* pots and pans are my clear favorites. I have bought these secondhand at restaurant supply houses and thrift shops and been happy with them for years. The copper-bottomed kind is more expensive, a nuisance to keep clean, but like all stainless steel ware, lasts forever. (We've had some "in the family" for over thirty years.) It is easy to clean, does not discolor, cooks beautifully, and so on. If you can, get some as a present, or when you have some extra cash, or are really making a lifetime investment. It is worth it.

3. *Enamelware* can be tricky (like patent leather, which the Germans cite as the prototype of unreliable). But it is your best bet. Enamelware used to be so flimsy it was a gyp. You may still find this paper-thin kind at rummage sales, but if you buy new enamelware you are relatively safe. There are *two* varieties, of which the cheaper is your best buy.

As with other cookpots, the price and weight (or thickness) of the ware are directly related. This is expressed by gauge, but you will soon learn to evaluate and compare by heft. The cheaper kind, the one you want, is quite likely imported from Japan, Yugoslavia, or Poland, though some is Made in U.S.A. It is sold in houseware/hardware stores, five-and-tens, and the less expensive section of the department stores. It is bright in color, mediocre in design, and (see below) not eternal. It lasts a sufficient number of years, however, is cheap enough so as to be no disaster to replace, looks nice on the wall, or used for serving, and is easy to clean. (If scorched, soak overnight with straight chlorine bleach or a strong washing soda solution.)

There is also a very costly and often beautiful lead-heavy enamelware, sold under some very well-known brand names. It is mostly imported, though I see, from mail-order catalogues, that it too is now made here. This good enamelware, as far as I know, is all enameled cast iron. Nothing gives as good heat diffusion as cast iron, but nothing is as fragile either. This is one of those absurd, but little-known, paradoxes. A fall that would not hurt any other kind of pot can crack cast iron like the Liberty Bell. A thermal shock can do the same thing. This crack can come after a week of use or twenty years, and in my experience the stores and makers are unresponsive about complaints.

NOTE: All enamelware is made by heat-bonding a glaze to metal. This union is not eternal. A thorough overheating, a too-quick heating of a cold pot, or too-rapid chilling of a hot one, a fall, a bang, even old age—all can cause chipping or crazing (the development of a spiderweb-like pattern of fine cracks in the enamel). Both can lead to rusting and make cleaning more difficult. So, whatever kind of enamelware you use, handle it with some care and try to have it at room temperature before heating or chilling.

4. *Glass cookware*. There is a whole range of this stuff, sold under various trademarks. I am very down on it. It did its thing during the metal-short years of World War II, but it is ridiculously fragile, cannot be used over a direct flame, is extremely susceptible to thermal shock, and hard to clean. That it can be used for serving hardly compensates for hatefulness.

The *good* kind of glass cookware is made, as far as I know, only by Corning under the name of "Corningware." It is white, opaque, can be heated straight from the freezer, is durable and easy to clean. The lids (which some pots have) are, however, made of regular "ovenware" glass. I have asked the Corning people about lids and thermal shock, and they say they have never had any trouble there.

5. *Cast iron.* What applies to enameled cast iron applies to the regular. The old stuff has become an antiquarian's delight and is priced accordingly. The new stuff is, I feel, risky, and your money is better off elsewhere.

Still, at a rummage sale you may find a rusty and/or grease-encrusted Dutch oven (antiquarians get $35 ⅜ for these) or cornbread griddle or whatnot. So since for $1 or $2 you won't resist . . .

To clean: use Naval jelly, or washing soda and water, taking care to protect your eyes and hands. Soak and scrub (being sure the vessel you do it in is not aluminum if you are using washing soda). Finish scrubbing with steel wool of a fine grade. When the pan is clean, wash it, rinse, dry, and oil it thoroughly with edible oil. Let sit an hour or so, wipe off all oil you can with a paper towel, and set the pan in a warm place (atop the radiator, near the pilot light, inside a turned-off oven). Repeat this process once or twice, letting the oil "bake on" for eight hours or more. *Do not use too much heat* or the oil will burn instead of drying. If and whenever you scrape through this oil finish, you must renew it. But a well-seasoned pan will come clean in plain soap and water, and never require finish-killing steel wool or scouring powder.

NOTE: There are diverse kinds of cookware on the market which feature a bonded-on inner coating that allows one to fry without fat. Even if you use fat for flavor, these coatings prevent sticking and are easy to clean. They are great on pots, in which the residue left at the top by evaporating liquids usually becomes hard as enamel and murder to remove. These antistick coatings are new on the market, and I cannot tell you how long or well they wear. But they probably are worth their higher-than-other-pots-of-the-same-quality price.

NOTE: These coatings are dark brown or black. But not all pans enameled black or brown on the inside have this coating. Check labels and hangtags carefully.

Odds and Ends

1. Get wooden-handled, *never* plastic, spoons, knives, etc. Plastic breaks easily, discolors, and if it catches fire, goes up literally

in a flash. Wood wears well, and should it catch fire, burns slowly enough to let you save the piece.

2. Stainless knives do not hold their edges as well as regular or carbon steel. The latter must be washed and dried immediately and benefit from an occasional rubdown with #400 wet-and-dry sandpaper. They also impart a slight flavor to highly acid food (like lemons). Quality in knives can be determined not only by the kind of blade but by its length—the best knives are a full-length piece of steel with wooden handles sandwiching the noncutting end. Cheap knives are merely blades stuck in a handle.

3. *Avoid specialized dishes and tools.* For once-a-year occasions like roast turkey, use foil pans. Specialized tools and pans tie up money, waste space, and are a bloody nuisance.

Plates, Glasses, and Cutlery

Here I reverse my frugality-first dictum, because elegance is a great spice. Better scrambled eggs off a nice plate, than steak off a newspaper. My husband tells of calling on some people once to find them eating a supper of smoked salmon, herring, pastrami, and other delicacies out of the plastic bags from the store! On a picnic, in a pinch, this may have to do. In a house, *no.* I write this not to impose my aesthetics on you, but to point out that eating together is quite as much of a civilized ritual as sleeping together—and possibly *more* of a ritual—and attention should be paid. Having delivered myself of this opinion:

1. *Plates.* If you live alone, or as a couple, six big plates, six dessert or salad plates, as many cups and saucers or mugs, as many bowls or soup plates, should see you through. Japan produces some lovely ware, some of which is ovenproof. A local craft school may have sales on pretty odds and ends. Even the five-and-tens carry simple, handsome ware. And there are two further sources worth investigation: restaurant supply houses and "seconds" outlets.

At least in New York City, the *restaurant suppliers* who sell dishes are different and separate from those who sell pots and pans.

(Both are found in the Bowery, however.) They have very nice heavy-duty restaurant ware, and some carry the more elegant and delicate hotel ware. They will have stuff that was made for (or sold to them by) clubs, fraternities, railroads, and schools and—if that sort of thing amuses you—you can buy dishes with the insignia and mottoes of exotic organizations. The ware is quite cheap, attractive, and takes hard use.

Outlet stores, or places that sell seconds, often are connected with a local factory. But in cities like New York, you will find stores that carry only, or mostly, seconds from a great many sources. The untrained eye rarely finds the defect. It may be a speck of glaze where it does not belong, a warp in a cup, and so on. Only the most expensive goods are worth selling as seconds. So you are buying luxury ware at medium (not cheap) prices. Understand that these are seconds: items that did not meet the eagle-eyed production standards of the manufacturer. *They are not supposed to be functionally defective, unless you have been forewarned.* The store may have a corner in which chipped or damaged stuff is sold "as is" at dirt-cheap prices. If you have not been forewarned, and find a chip, crack, or other real defect, get your money back.

Outlet or seconds stores that belong to a manufacturer logically carry only what his factory makes. They are particularly good about telling you what is, and what is not, a second, as they have their name to protect. Independent outlet stores carry all sorts of table ware.

NOTE: While you are buying plates at a seconds store, you might be tempted by their pots and pans. Be very careful—an off-center handle does not matter on a cup, but it might cause a saucepan to tilt in your hand. A badly fitting lid (which allows too much evaporation) might be no good at all.

Stay clear of plastic. For camping it has to do, though stainless steel is better. Plastic is hard to clean, stains easily, and cutlery makes a sound on it like chalk on blackboards. *Wood is nice.* I have some 12-inch wooden plates we dearly love. But wood must be dried after washing, aired before storing, and oiled with salad oil from time to time.

If you have room for some extra plates, a few big enamel

ones are fun. They are about 12 inches and have a rim, which makes them practical for tableless dining. They can be cleaned easily, are easy to keep warm over a saucepan of hot water, and very pretty as serving dishes. They are, however, as fragile as other enamel, and cutting on them makes a fierce noise. They are not cheap.

2. *Cutlery.* Have enough knives, forks, spoons, and teaspoons for six—then buy three more spoons, three more teaspoons, and two more forks. These extras are for serving and need in no way match the first set—which need not match either. All the above suppliers have what you need. Bamboo, wood, and metal handles are fine. Nylon handles are the only acceptable plastic ones; okay for table use, but not for cooking.

Pawn shops and secondhand stores sell single forks and spoons —often quite lovely antiques that may cost as little as $1 for plate, and as much as $5 for a sterling teaspoon. These luxuries are decorative and, bought singly, can be worked into the budget.

We have bought utterly denuded silver plate for pennies and, when we had gathered a few pounds of it, taken it to a silver plater to replate. It is not expensive, and the final result is extremely attractive.

3. *Glasses.* Get half-a-dozen 8-ounce or 10-ounce glasses. These will serve for beer, wine, water, milk. You may want smaller glasses as well, but there is no need. Using a measuring cup, pour 3 ounces (the usual wine serving) and 4 ounces (the usual juice serving) of liquid into your big glass and train your eye to judge the proper serving level. That way you can use your big glasses for everything. (And by not filling your wine glasses very much, you will be doing the connoisseur thing, as the "extra" glass catches and enhances the bouquet! How about *that!*)

If you decide on footed glasses, you must get a few glasses without feet as well, for worktable and bedside use. Footed glasses tip very easily when full; tumblers do not, despite their name.

Appliances

The word is *no*. Electric frying pans, rotisseries, even toasters are costly, and costly to operate. They spend a lot of time breaking

down, and it costs a lot to fix them. If there is a shipshape toaster
at a rummage sale for only two dollars, get it. But don't *invest*
in any of these things. Toast can be made on an open flame with
the use of a long-handled fork. Or on a cheap (about a dollar)
rack that sits atop the stove burner. Or by baking it into a kind
of zwieback in a slow oven.

If You Have a Generous Godmother

If someone offers you a housewarming gift, and you can't
think of something better, consider these:

1. *A pressure cooker.* After World War II these were extremely
popular. Now no one but me seems to use them. I suppose so-called
convenience foods and TV dinners have, for most people, replaced
the pressure cooker as a great time saver. Convenience foods cost
too much and taste too little for us. I still use my pressure cooker,
a lot. Pressure cookers cut cooking time down by two-thirds on
most foods. Besides saving a lot on fuel costs in these times of
rising energy prices, this means stew and pot roast in one hour,
spaghetti sauce in minutes! They are an enormous convenience
and a three- to four-quart nonelectric one is what you might request.

*If you have heard horror stories about pressure cookers, believe
them.* What no one told you is that the victim ignored the actually
simple and sensible safety rules the manufacturer's directions outlined.

2. *A meat grinder.* Sizes #5 and #6 are small, #10 is the
largest. The number indicates the size of the hopper into which
the food is fed. I had a #5 for years, got a #10 recently for
convenience. With any size you can grind meat, dried fruit, liver
for pâté, nuts for breakfast food.

Even without a godmother these tools are a boon. Each can
be found at rummage sales or thrift shops. For the pressure cooker
be sure the manufacturer's directions are with it, or that the manufacturer is around to send you some (also spare parts that might be
needed). Do not use the thing till you know how. (An experienced
housewife might show you.)

When buying a secondhand meat grinder, be sure all the parts are there. With a new one there should be no problems, since there generally is a diagram in the box. But with a secondhand one—again, unless you are familiar with the thing—get them to put it together for you at the store. The problem is that some grinders have a separate knife—a cross-shaped piece that looks a bit like a fan—and some *only* have cutters, which are metal disks with holes that control the size of the grind. Most grinders come with a couple of cutter blades.

3. *A freezer.* This really is godmother territory. But even if you buy it yourself—a freezer that holds about 4 cubic feet of stuff costs "only" $120. They are not easy to find, but large department stores and mail-order houses do have them. Particularly if you work very intensely, with whole days off in between, a freezer is a tremendous time and money saver. It allows you, for instance, to spend one day a month cooking and freezing; it allows you to buy and stock favorites when they are "specials"; it allows you to take advantage (assuming your oven is big enough) of the periodic turkey sales shops have (the turkey can either be roasted, carved, and stored or, if bought unfrozen, carved raw and stored). If that freezer saves you one dining-out a week it will earn its keep within a year.

A final word: Don't overbuy. It's a tremendous temptation to buy an extra little pot here, a gadget there. *Don't.* As your household becomes established there will be plenty of lacunae to fill. But avoid extras. They require storage space and cleaning and maintenance just as much as the things you really need. If you move, they must be packed and shipped. Later on you really may want a timer, a thermos, an oven thermometer. But please wait till you need them to buy them.

9 / Shopping: The Fine Art of Getting What You Pay For

You now have the basics and are ready to go to the supermarket to stock your pantry.

Here is a basic moving-in-day list. Buy, of course, only those items you use. An asterisk means I'm assuming a one-or-two-people-only household.

Cereal
Coffee—instant, freeze-dried, or regular, to suit your coffeepot
Tea—in bags or loose (cheaper, but you must have some sort of pot)
Sugar
Salt
Pepper (black)
Bread, muffins, or crackers
½ pound butter*
1 dozen eggs*
1 pound bacon or breakfast sausage*
Fresh or dried milk (a fresh half-gallon should last a few days)
An assortment of the following: fruit juice, cheese, peanut butter, jam, sardines, tuna, canned soups, canned fruit, cookies or cake (the noncream variety). Take advantage of the "2 for——" bargains here.

Also buy enough precooked or delicatessen food—canned ham, barbecued chicken, cold cuts, etc.—to feed yourself and moving crew. Beverages for same.

Also:

1 roll 12-inch aluminum foil (lightweight)
1 roll 24-inch aluminum foil (heavy)
1 package plastic garbage bags
Bath soap
Toilet paper
Plain soap in cakes for dishes
Scouring powder
Facial tissues
Strong detergent (it says on bottle for whitewalls, floors, etc.)
1 bottle chlorine bleach
1 package washing soda
Paper towels
1 string mop
Sponges

Heavy-duty rubber gloves
1 large plastic pail

You will find you will need more cleaning supplies later. Things like soap for the laundromat and so on. You also might have some of these items already if you persuaded your landlord to let you into the apartment to scrub it before moving-in day (see page 20). Get these things now. The rest can wait.

Get a shopping cart. The price is outrageous, but carts are a necessity of city life—unless you do your shopping by car. Otherwise you are reduced to doing your marketing in easy stages, since you cannot possibly carry that much at once. If you own a backpack or an Indian basket, these will do instead. But buying them for this purpose is also a waste, as they cost more than the carts.

If possible, do all of the nonperishable part of this shopping ahead of time. Move the items along with your other goods. Or get a friend to do the actual shopping on moving day.

Daily Shopping

The above lists the basics. But day-to-day shopping, wisely and well, is a constant art and demands as much craft and thought as anything else in housekeeping. Upon one's ability to shop wisely depends much of one's standard of living. You will soon discover that it isn't prejudice that makes many social critics observe that the essential difference between the educated poor and the ignorant poor is their ability to analyze expenditures and control or plan the way they spend money—with the result that the ignorant poor get much less in goods and pleasure for their money than the educated poor.

Shopping wisely takes patience, judgment, stamina, and time. Also quick wits and flexibility. Our shopping is done by my husband, who has all these virtues in which I am sadly deficient. (I am, however, strong on theory.)

1. *Allow yourself plenty of time to shop,* especially at the

beginning of your career as a householder. Hurrying precludes careful analysis of value, comparison shopping between different items, changing one's mind when necessary.

2. *Keep a complete record of what you buy and how much you spend,* so as to have as quickly as possible a clear picture of your consumption (and shopping) cycle. A knowledge that you use one quart of milk every two days, one dozen eggs and one pound of coffee per week, two rolls of paper towels per month, and so on not only allows you to budget your money, but your shopping time. (We make one special trip to the store each month for paper products and cleaning supplies "only.") Record-keeping also tells you when *x* dollars have to be available for the repurchase of slow-moving items (laundry soap) or when in-between shopping forays are needed (milk, bread).

3. *Comparison-shop on staples.* You may find that the house brand of tissues in one supermarket is better than in another, and of equal quality to a nationally advertised, more expensive brand. Always buy the cheapest *first;* work your way up if dissatisfied. *Read all labels carefully.* Remember you are interested in something working for you, not in sales talk.

a. *Don't be misled by "truth in labeling" tags and blurbs.* That's right, misled. Price per ounce is meaningless. What you need to know is *price per satisfactory portion, or job done.* Brand X instant coffee calls for 1 teaspoon per cup on the label. So does Brand Y. But in practice you need 2 teaspoons of Brand X and only 1 of Brand Y to get a good cup of coffee. Obviously the fact that the 8-ounce jars of X and Y cost the same is meaningless in practice. Try several makes of each product in the cheapest price range before moving up.

b. *Beware of superconcentrates.* The mouthwash claims that three drops in a glass of water are all that's needed. True. But you cannot tap less than half-a-dozen drops out of the bottle. The solution (!) is to transfer the mouthwash into a bigger bottle, and add enough water so that a *capful* of the diluted mouthwash in a glass of water is just right. This is a big bore, however. When a cleaning product with a bottle mouth ¾-inch wide tells you on the label that a drop in a bucket is all you need, remember the manufacturer is betting on your impatience; he knows you are going to splash the stuff into the bucket—and on that splash he makes a killing. (Worse than that, you will get too strong a solution that will hurt your skin and may damage whatever you are cleaning.) A less concentrated soap product (bound to be cheaper) will probably save you money, every which way.

c. *Beware the meaningless additive*. A number of food products boast herbs and spices which add disproportionately to the cost. You are better off (as a rule) buying the untampered-with food, adding the spices yourself. This is true *only* if you use enough of that food to warrant stocking up on spices. If you make saffron rice once a year, the prefabricated mix is worth the extra cost. If saffron rice is a weekly feature on your table, by all means buy the saffron—costly as it is—and buy plain rice.

d. *Don't stockpile*. Don't buy the big economy size of any spoilable until you are sure you can use that quantity before it spoils. Also avoid buying large sizes of such items as spices that you might use within six months, but that lose potency. When you are tempted to tie up money in nonspoilables, ask yourself whether the money is not better off elsewhere—even at the savings bank.

e. *Beware the "new improved" product*. Any advertising tyro can tell you that "new" and "improved" are magically effective selling words. As a result, manufacturers are always making changes that allow them legitimately to put those words on the label. Try to discover what the novelty is. If it's only that a flaked soap, let us say, is now in granules; or the canned soup now includes a few noodles; or the facial tissue is perfumed—is it worth more money *to you*?

After these general rules, here are some specifics:

1. *Shopping lists and budgets*. Keep a piece of paper handy in the kitchen or some other convenient, fixed place, and write down everything you need before the need becomes desperate. (This should be a shared responsibility in the household—particularly if some products are more used by one than by another.) Keep a small notebook for your shopping lists, at least at the beginning.

(Later on any scrap of paper may do.) *Date the page in your notebook; copy out the shopping needs.* If possible, arrange your shopping list in a logical order: If you go to several shops, put the items available at each store together; if you go to the supermarket, group meats, cleaning products, canned goods in the sequence of the market layout.

To the needs add your wants: what you are going to get for meals in the next few days. If you live in a community where the week's specials are advertised in the paper, you can really plan ahead in detail. Or if you live near the supermarket, you can walk by, examine the posters in the window, and make up your shopping list accordingly. Most likely you will develop a rough-and-ready method: one definite meal plan (particularly if you entertain) and several possibilities to be explored at the market itself.

Write down what you spend on your shopping list. In most cases the total is all you really need. In special cases (when, for instance, you give a party, or when you have a house guest, or when you buy a sixteen-pound box of detergent) you might want to write down what the extra expense was all about.

Why all this? Because it is the quickest method by which to determine the pattern of what the bankers call your "cash flow." It allows you to gear your actual spending to the pattern in which your money comes in—x dollars a week from your job, let us say, plus y dollars once a month from Daddy. Once you have adjusted to your cash flow, you ought never to face four or five totally penniless days. Knowing where the money goes also allows you relatively painless cutbacks should the need arise.

If you discover, for instance, that you drink ten quarts of beer a week, you may decide that the saving is worth a trip to a wholesaler (many in big cities sell retail at substantial savings); or you may decide to drink wine and water. If you drink a lot of cola beverages, you might decide that buying plain soda, or even a siphon (about twenty dollars) plus gas cartridges to make your own soda, and buying the cola flavoring by the gallon, will save you a pretty penny.

I am certainly not urging scrimping and penny pinching for

its own sake. But one can frequently make oneself a lot richer, simply by stopping up loopholes in one's spending pattern.

2. *At the store–buy staples first:* coffee, beans, flour, toothpaste—all the stuff that requires no imagination and does not vary from week to week—should be gotten out of the way *first.* If there are two of you shopping, let one do the staples while the other addresses himself to the perishable, seasonable, variable items.

3. *Food buying.* This is truly difficult and makes strong strategists shudder with its geometrically multiplying options.

Assume that—through newspaper ads or window displays—you established that the supermarket has ground chuck and Idaho (baking) potatoes among its specials. You decide therefore that on Saturday night you will serve your guests (a total of six including you all) meatloaf, baked potatoes, tossed salad, and ice cream. The biggest expense will be the meatloaf, of which you plan to make extra for Monday sandwiches.

At the supermarket you discover, however, that there is no more ground chuck* and that the butcher who could grind some more has left for the day. The other meat special is standing rib roast. So, even though it is a special, it is beyond your means. Here are your options:

a. Buy ground steak instead of chuck. Although the price is $0.35 more a pound (and for the 3 pounds of meat you want, this adds up to $1.05), by making bulgur or rice instead of the potatoes (although they are on special, rice remains cheaper) and substituting a frozen cake (cheaper per serving) for ice cream, you make up the $1.05. (If it's winter, eliminating the tossed salad and buying some coleslaw should also save money.)

b. Buy roasting chicken instead of ground meat. The chicken, although cheaper per pound than chuck, will cost you only a little less per satisfactory serving. But (at today's prices) there should be enough of a difference for half a pound of bologna or liverwurst for those Monday sandwiches.

---

*In a decent supermarket there is enough of the weekend specials to last through closing Saturday, at least. If your supermarket consistently "runs out" of weekend specials by Thursday or Friday, they have specials as come-ons only. Complain to the chain headquarters, with a copy to Better Business Bureau, Consumer's Complaints, or whatever your city offers.

You get the picture. Remember there also will be days when there are mushrooms or endives at the market, and you will want to juggle your figures to allow for a luxury.

When buying food, get your proteins squared away first. They are by and large the costliest items on your food list, and the most important. Build the rest of your shopping around the proteins.

How to Save Money and How Not To

1. *Pick your stores carefully.* Try all the stores in your neighborhood. You may discover, as we did, a fantastic difference in quality between supermarkets, all within one small area.

Try *all* house brands at *all* supermarkets first. Nowhere does quality seem to vary as much as between house brands. And they are cheaper than the nationally advertised trademarked products.

2. *Pay more if you get more.* We buy meat at a butcher's. His quality is better, there is less fat weighed in, better aging, less shrinkage. Although his chicken breasts cost more per pound, he does not include the spine; so it evens out. And in actual use, his meat does not cost much more than at the supermarket, and it gives us greater satisfaction.

3. *Buy quality and quantity,* not *variety.* This applies only to seasonal items: always buy what is in season, or being featured. Buy peaches, not apples, in summer; and apples, not peaches, in winter. Even if the canned peas-and-carrots cost only a few cents more than a can of peas and a can of carrots, consider (if you can use the quantity) mixing the two yourself.

4. *Never buy quality you cannot use.* If you use paper towels for your face, of course get the softest, nicest, etc. But if it's only to wipe paint brushes or to wash the cat's feet, get the cheapest. If you are making stew, do not buy filet. Even if you were a millionaire, filet would be throwing out money, since it is a very soft, quickly cooked meat and in stew would turn gummy and nasty.

5. *Buy day-old bread and muffins and cake, but never cream cakes.* With all the preservatives in commercial baked goods, the whole notion of freshness is academic. Still, there are stores that

sell at remarkably low prices yesterday's bread, which is perfectly good, and even better than fresh for toasting.

In some towns commercial bakeries that sell packaged goods have day-old-bread stores which often go under euphemistic names. Here you may buy anything—except items whose wrappings have torn.

But if your local bakery simply has a shelf on which day-old products are kept to be sold at a discount, avoid buying pies or any kind of gooey cake that is likely to contain eggs or milk in the "gooey" part. Here food poisoning is a real risk. Iced cakes, on the other hand, are likely to be okay. An icing is crisp, crumbly, generally shiny and smooth—as opposed to fillings and toppings, which remain creamy and soft.

6. *Buy at bankruptcy-stock, distress-stock, or other salvage stores.* You find these stores in poorer neighborhoods. They exist, of course, for all lines of merchandise, but it is the grocery stores of this type we are concerned with. These stores buy up the leftover stock of stores going out of business, stores that have burned, as well as the distress stock of manufacturers—cans with improperly stuck-on labels or that have been badly dented. Remember that a dented can is safe, but one with a domed or bulging top (or bottom) is dangerous, since the doming is likely to be the result of gas pressure inside the can, and the gas due to putrifaction. Some of these stores supplement their stock by buying regular grocery stock; so not *all* their stuff is necessarily cheaper than elsewhere. Still, if you know the price of similar items at a regular grocery, try some of these "secondhand food" stores.

7. *Buy wilted vegetables for soup and stew.* The carrot with a spade mark, the broken celery stalk, the discouraged parsley, the tomato in the top layer of the case that got dropped—all these damaged vegetables are perfectly good to use. And a greengrocer is likely to let you have them extremely cheap because to him they are, as a rule, "unsalable." If you know your greengrocer, ask him to save these for you—likely as not he will, and for a few pennies too. As long as the vegetable is damaged, not spoiled, use it.

8. *Take advantage of weekend and holiday closings.* Many small stores do not really have good storage facilities and can be talked into letting you have spoilables at vastly reduced prices, smack before closing time on a weekend or before a holiday. I enjoyed a whole winter of mushrooms once by getting the leftovers of the week's supply Saturday evening from my neighborhood green-grocer at about one-fourth normal price. (For sauce they were fine.)

9. *Avoid bargains unless you are sure they* are *bargains.* Delicatessens frequently sell sausage ends, carp fins, salmon tails, and the like at vastly reduced prices. Some are generous in their cutting, and you get something besides a clot of plastic casing and a wad of string when you buy salami ends. Experiment: if most of the salmon tail is bone (which is heavy), it is probably not worthwhile. If there is a good portion of fish left when the bones are cleared away, you have a genuine bargain.

NOTE: Depending on the region, or even the part of the city, certain meat prices will be absurdly low. Kidney, lights (lung), skirt steak, oxtail virtually will be given away by some butchers because their clientele does not eat them (kidney, lights) or because, as only one comes with the carcass (skirt), it is not worth featuring.

NOTE: Specialized cheese stores frequently sell bags of ends, or crumbles of crumbly cheeses such as Caerphilly and Feta, at very reduced prices. Be suspicious here of lowered price on ends of *runny* cheeses. Sometimes they have gotten so aged that they have become too strong in flavor to eat.

10. *Cook with dry milk.* Dry skim milk is a great money saver. It costs one-third as much as whole milk, and the equation permits you to use butter as a finishing touch on soups (*inter al.*) cooked with dry skim milk, and still save money. For example, a cream soup for four costs $0.13 for milk (1 quart) if made with the powder and $0.34 if made with whole milk. A pound of sweet butter costs $0.90, or less than $0.015 per pat (64 per pound). A quart of soup made with dry skim milk, and with each of four servings enhanced by a pat of butter, still saves you a dime.

At time of writing, *whole dry milk* is just being introduced on the market. Considering what a tremendous part of the price of milk is perishability and transportation, the dry whole milk will in all likelihood have almost as good an effect on your budget as the skimmed milk.

Evaporated milk also is a money saver. Perhaps I'm prejudiced, but it always seems to me evaporated milk imparts a slight off-flavor, somehow overcome by sweetening—so I use evaporated milk in desserts.

11. *Buy the big economy size* only *if it will stay good to the end.* I buy dry skim milk in the twenty-quart package, with each quart sealed in foil. This costs more per quart than the loose milk, but experience has shown we do not use twenty quarts quickly enough to prevent moisture absorbed from the air from spoiling the milk. By getting the twenty quarts in foil, I still save money, however, over the four-quart loose size (which is all I can consume before spoilage).

Flour is likely to deteriorate from water-absorption and—despite the processers' efforts—to "develop" weevils.

Yogurt, cottage cheese, and similar products *if bought in the large size on the day they get to the store* easily keep a week. It is wise therefore to find out on what day delivery of these products is made. Unlike the mushrooms, the stuff may as well age in your fridge, while you take advantage of the economy of the larger size. (Dog and cat owners know that, even slightly high, milk products are a treat to pets.)

12. *Set up a shopping commune.* This is mostly a question of how much time you've got, and the time vs. money equation has to be worked out by each person for himself. I have read recently of wealthy New Yorkers who have set up cooperatives and thereby can frequent the wholesale markets and save dough. This works only if—as these people do—you have lots of time, and lots of cash, and cars, and so on.

But there is a modest in-between way of doing this too. You can get together with friendly neighbors and buy everything in the biggest size available at the supermarket. That way you can take advantage of the saving on rice in 25-pound bags, soap in 16-pound boxes, without tying up too much of your money. Divide it up either by weight (an old scale costs little) or by measure (an old coffee can does fine), keeping a separate measuring cup for the soap, *please*.

If you *do* have time and transportation, the purchase of nonperishable products from wholesalers may well be worth half a day. Toilet paper, paper napkins, shampoo can all be bought at wholesalers, jobbers, or suppliers to professionals at remarkable savings. We even have bought our dog food at a kennel supplier; they deliver free if you get 300 pounds. Obviously you cannot tie up $25 so easily. But a consultation with several dog-walkers in the park may allow you to pool resources and buy wholesale.

13. *Be skeptical of the distant bargain.* You must figure the cost of time, gas, tolls before you set out for the farmers' market twenty miles away. If—as it often does in summer—the market provides an entertainment as well as an opportunity to do your shopping and to get better quality, that is fine. But to travel a great distance—as the mother of a friend of ours will do—to get a bargain that is a bargain only because she ignores the cost of transportation, is a poor thought.

Also remember that while certain things will be cheaper in the country, let us say, you must figure some of your forays will end in disappointment. And you might be wiser to settle for a higher-priced but immediately available product in town. (Antique furniture and automobiles are cases in point.)

14. *Use time and money savers when they save time and money.* Garlic and onion powder are great money savers; unless you are making a dish that calls for several whole onions, use the powder. If the fresh, cut-up onion just sits in the refrigerator and spoils, you have wasted money.

If a frozen meat pie or a barbecued chicken allows you to eat at home on hectic days, and with wine or beer you will have a better meal for your money than if you eat out, get the convenience food, despite the fact that it is costlier than its equivalent made by your own hands.

If (on the other hand) eating breakfast out once a week permits you to go to the laundromat on a weekday—when there are fewer people—and thereby avoid the awful Saturday crush, that convenience, by making life happier, is in all probability worth the expense.

15. *Beware the ethnic label.* Some manufacturers and importers make a big deal out of the genuine ethnic quality of their imports. Marmalade made by Scots, cookies baked in Holland, salami made in Italy are not necessarily better or "more genuine" than the American-made counterpart. Experiment, but do not be fooled.

10 / Eggs: The Simply Perfect Food

Someday I'd like to write an ode to eggs. They simply are the greatest food. They can be prepared in countless ways, for any meal and occasion, and in no time at all.

Eggs are low in calories, high in protein, calcium, vitamin A, and other good things. Moreover, they do not *need* refrigeration. What spoils eggs is the absorption of air through their porous shells, which is why our grandmothers stored eggs in a sodium silicate solution. (I do not know how strong.) *Eggs do keep longer on ice, but try never to have so many they need to be kept there.*

Eggs are sold in grades and sizes. Although the government checks and controls these, even in the case of the highest-grade (AA) checking up on the flock, keep in mind this *does not* mean that the chickens are kept off antibiotics, hormones, or whatever else comes in commercial feed. Grade AA are supposed to be pretty near perfection. But what most stores carry is Grade A. Grade B consists of eggs with less perfectly shaped shells (but not cracked), sometimes blotched or marbled shells. They are/are not just as fresh as A's and just as good. But not as pretty. I have not seen Grade B eggs around in a long time, in New York, but saw some on sale in San Francisco. So look around.

Within grades, eggs are sold by size. New York State, for

one, regulates how much a dozen eggs must weigh to be classed *jumbo, regular,* and so on. It is hard to tell this weight difference with the naked eye; it can be as little as three ounces per dozen. But it should be there.

A few years ago a salmonella epidemic alerted people to the dangers of raw eggs; particularly raw eggs with damaged shells.* I no longer eat eggs raw at all, or buy cracked eggs except for baking—in which the very thorough cooking should kill any residual bug. But cracked eggs are an excellent buy.

Eggs sold as *cracked* are not necessarily shattered. They generally are perfectly nonleaky, but have a weakness in the shell.

The only way to tell the freshness of an egg is to crack its shell and pour the contents onto a flat dish.

A really fresh egg will keep its yolk centered in the rather stiff white, and the yolk will remain rounded in a pleasing hump, reminiscent of a supine woman's breast.

As the egg ages, the membrane that holds the yolk together (fresh yolk can actually be picked up by this skin) deteriorates, and the yolk flattens out. Next it slides off-center in the white. Later the membrane becomes so weak that the shock of cracking the shell breaks it, and the yolk makes a shapeless puddle inside the white. Should you ever—God forbid—get a rotten egg, you will see that the yolk has mingled with the white inside the shell into a stinking olive mess.

The color of the shell depends on the breed of chicken and has no effect on the taste. In some parts of the country white eggs are preferred, in other parts brown shells, and there may be a price difference between brown and white depending on the local preference.

The color of the yolk can vary from a lemon yellow to near orange. This too depends on the breed and also on what the chicken eats. The chicken's diet *does* affect egg flavor.

Abandon hope of getting really fresh eggs in the city. We have kept country-bought eggs four or more weeks, and they have

*The government bulletin *Keeping Foods Safe to Eat,* Department of Agriculture Home and Gardens Bulletin #162, goes into great detail about salmonella and other food poisonings.

still been fresher than most of what we buy in New York. (Although New York stores often advertise "Eggs brought in daily from New Jersey," they fail to add that the eggs come from storage plants.) Fair-to-middling fresh is what you will get; shop around and see which market sells eggs with the upstandingest yolks!

Remember that the best supplier can occasionally get a rotten egg in the batch. *Always* break each egg individually into a bowl or cup *before adding it to other eggs, or any mix.* One rotten egg can spoil a whole bowlful of stuff (other eggs, meatloaf, etc.).

Boiled Eggs

1. Have eggs at room temperature; otherwise the heat is likely to crack the shells, allowing the white to leak out (ugly but not unusable). Cover the eggs by half an inch of water set on medium flame, bring to a slow boil. Allow to boil one minute for soft-boiled eggs.

2. If eggs are cold, as from refrigerator, take a heavy needle, such as a darning needle, and make a quick, neat hole in the *wide end* of the egg. A hole just deep enough to go through the shell. It allows the air in the air hole (at the wide end) to escape and allows the egg proper to expand without cracking its shell.

3. *For hard-boiled eggs* cook the eggs ten minutes or more after the water starts to boil. Be sure the eggs are covered by at least half an inch of water. Hold the pan with eggs under running cold water or dunk in a bowl of ice cubes as soon as cooked. This makes them easier to peel.

Hard-boiled eggs can be peeled, and put in a jar, which is then filled with boiled and boiling cider vinegar to which a pinch of pickling spice, 1 teaspoon of prepared mustard, and ½ teaspoon of salt have been added. Pickled eggs are a fine snack and a good way to take advantage of egg bargains. I have kept them on ice for three or four weeks, but assume they keep longer yet—we just keep eating them up, as they get better every day.

Eggs can be kept warm by letting them sit in hot water. If the temperature of the water is less than 140°F, they will not go on cooking. If you have no thermometer—well, 140°F is damned uncomfortable but not painful to the finger.

Poached Eggs

Most cookbooks tell you to make a maelstrom in boiling water and drop a deshelled raw egg into the center, and then you get a poached egg. I have tried and tried this method, and all I get is a nasty yolk surrounded by disgusting-looking strings of white.

Recently a friend showed me how to do it right:

Bring salted water to a boil in a frying pan—1½ inch deep or so.

Break the egg into a cup or, better yet, a big spoon, and when the water boils, slip the egg(s) into the water as gently as you can, immediately turning the flame down so that the water just simmers. Remove the eggs when done, using a slotted spoon.

As wise as my friend is, and as good as these eggs are, they tend to be watery. So I still prefer egg poachers, which can be bought for a couple of dollars at a department store or through a mail-order house, or a frying pan that comes equipped with little poaching cups. You also can use custard cups.

In *all* cases, butter the little pan that will hold the egg; break the egg and pour it into the poacher. Sprinkle with salt and pepper. The poacher is now set into boiling water (or cold water that you will bring to a boil), and either the poacher is covered, or the whole saucepan with the poacher in it is lidded. Make sure the water level is not so high as to bubble water into the eggs. Cook over medium flame for a few minutes—till the white is solidly opaque.

Poached eggs can, of course, be eaten out of the poacher, but mostly are removed from their pans and served on toast.

Scrambled Eggs

Why so few people make these well is a puzzle, because there are only two rules: have the pan hot enough; know when to stop!

Break as many eggs as you need—following the rule to break each egg individually into a little bowl before adding to the big bowl. Beat the eggs thoroughly with a fork, chopsticks, egg beater, or whisk. *Thoroughly* means the yolks and whites are completely intermingled and the mixture has become fluid rather than "lazy" as raw eggs are. There will be—and should be—a slight amount of foam. Add a pinch of salt for each two eggs.

Heat a frying pan with 1 tablespoon of butter, or bacon fat, or lard in it for each two eggs. The size of the frying pan is important. A six- to nine-inch pan is fine for one to four eggs; but you either use a bigger pan for more eggs, or cook 'em in several batches. The reason is that too many eggs in too small a pan result in part of the eggs being overcooked (dry and rubbery) and the rest not done well.

On your first tries, use 1 tablespoon of fat for each two eggs. Later you may want to reduce the fat a little; different people like different proportions. You should, however, have enough fat to cover the bottom of the pan easily with a thin film, when you start.

When the pan and fat are so hot that a drop of water sizzles violently if you shake it in—this is long before the fat begins to smoke—pour in the eggs, turn the flame very low, and stir the eggs away from the sides of the frying pan. Scrambled eggs are dried, rather than cooked; as soon as part of the mix solidifies, stir it up so that an uncooked bit of egg has contact with the pan bottom. Remove the pan from the fire a moment *before* the eggs look done to you; the heat of the pan will go on cooking the eggs for several minutes, so dish them up as soon as you can. Sprinkle lightly with pepper before serving.

Don't—as I have seen people do—stir frantically all the while the eggs are cooking. The eggs come out an ugly mess, something like soggy popcorn. Stir around the edge once, pull the spoon across the middle of the pan twice, in a cross, count to ten slowly before stirring again.

Additions: Fried onions, bits of ham, leftover bacon, chervil, parsley, marjoram, garlic—all make nice additions to scrambled eggs. Add to the raw eggs, or sprinkle on the finished dish.

Omelets

I will probably be declared *persona non grata* in France for saying this, but there really is no great difference between scrambled eggs and omelets. The difference lies mostly with the pan. For scrambled eggs you use a pan where the eggs "stand" about ¾-inch deep in the pan. For an omelet you use a wider-diameter pan—for two eggs a 10-inch frying pan is right—because you want the eggs to cook quickly, with the bottom part turning golden while the top part turns custardy. If the pan is too small, the top part will still be liquid when the bottom has turned to rubber!

Beat your eggs a little longer than when scrambling. Work up a pleasant head of foam. Use 1 tablespoon of fat for each two eggs, or 3 tablespoons for a 12-inch pan. Again, what you want is a film of fat generously covering the bottom of the pan. Unlike scrambled eggs, omelets absorb just so much fat and no more.

Heat the pan with the fat till a drop of water will sizzle violently in it. (After a while you will be able to judge the heat without this method.) Pour *all* the egg mix into the pan at once; lower the flame to medium. As soon as the bottom layer of the omelet has solidified, lift the edge of the omelet (first at one side, then the other) to allow all the uncooked egg to run to the bottom of the pan. Continue this (working your way around the frying pan and tilting the pan a trifle if necessary) till all the egg mix has been "used." Now watch like a hawk: for the perfect omelet the bottom of the omelet should be a rusty golden color, while the center top (the last part to cook through) should have lost all its sheen. At that magic moment, serve the omelet posthaste. Nothing ruins omelets like a delay between stove and eating!

Additions: You can have waiting in a bowl chopped parsley, chives, chervil that you sprinkle onto your omelet before serving it.

You can have a bowl of grated or finely chopped cheese—Swiss or cheddar—which you sprinkle on top of your omelet when it is *half cooked* (no more raw egg, but the top still very wet and shiny).

Or you can have a previously prepared filling of finely cut

ham; a sauce of fried onions, tomato, green pepper (all cooked together with a little water, or tomato or vegetable juice, till the vegetables wilt); plain fried onions—any and all of which should be hot and are added to the omelet after it is cooked. When it is put on a plate (or serving plate), the filling is added quickly, and the omelet folded over.

Bauern Fruehstuck

This is one of the many possibilities of an omelet that has the filling incorporated in it. The name is German for "peasant breakfast," and that is what this is—a solid, sturdy breakfast dish that is as good for lunch or supper. I make it when we have leftover franks or potatoes.

Have: 2 eggs per person; 1 frankfurter or 2 slices of salami per person; 1 boiled potato per person; butter. The frankfurters and potatoes can well be leftovers from the day before. If they are, this takes but a few minutes to prepare; otherwise you must boil and peel the potatoes, and (if they contain pork) precook the franks.

Break the eggs into a bowl and beat them well. Add a little pepper.

Slice your potato and the sausage into bite-sized pieces. Heat some fat in the large frying pan, and add the potato and sausage when the fat is hot. Cook over medium flame, turning the slices with a spoon so that both sides brown. When the "bottom" side of each slice is halfway done, check that you have a sufficient coating of fat in the pan. If not, add about 1 tablespoon for each two eggs, then pour the eggs into the pan so that they surround and incorporate the potatoes and sausage slices.

Lift the edges of the omelet from all sides of the pan to allow the liquid egg that remains to run under. When the omelet is brown at the bottom, serve (without folding).

Some people like this pancake very thick. If you do, use the smaller frying pan, and put a lid on it after the egg has been poured in, to permit the egg to cook more quickly although it is thicker.

Variations: You can see that leftover ham, roast beef, tomatoes, peas can also be used in this dish—fried (except for the peas) to a good brown first, then covered with egg. I like it with leftover liver and onions, but that may be an acquired taste.

Sweet or Dessert Omelets

See page 201.

Fried Eggs

One thinks these are so easy, but ha! Most of what one gets is horrid, and I for one am willing to believe that frying eggs really was at some point the ultimate test of a chef.

And, apparently, the chefs cooked the egg with a candle that they centered right beneath the yolk. Because the secret of fried eggs is to get the yolk done without overcooking the white.

Use the smallest or most centered flame on your stove. Use a relatively small frying pan, so that the white has some thickness to it. Use 1 teaspoon of fat per egg. I cover the eggs for a few seconds while they are cooking, as I like the yolk quite hard. If you wish, turn the eggs over and fry both sides.

Baked Eggs

These are very nice, but there is no sense in lighting the oven just for some eggs. If, however, you are baking something else or have the oven on for heat, know that you can put eggs in a well-greased (1 teaspoon per egg) baking dish and bake eggs. The dish should be small enough so that the white is at least ½-inch thick in the baking dish. If you have some cream, add 1 tablespoon per egg; just float it on top of the egg after it is in the baking dish.

Remember, once more, that the hot dish will go on cooking

the eggs for several minutes after they come out of the oven. So remove from oven when *almost* done.

Variation: When the white has set, lay a slice of American cheese or Provolone on top of the eggs (1 slice per 2 eggs) and bake on till the cheese is melted. In this case, omit the cream even if you have it!

Another possibility, which I make occasionally for lunch or supper, is this, which is a very relaxing main course.

Baked Eggs De Luxe

Have: 2 eggs per person; 1 slice of cooked ham, or 3 slices of cooked but not crisped bacon per person; 1 slice of cheddar or Swiss cheese; 1 (#2) can of chopped spinach.

Light the oven, set to medium heat.

Drain the spinach thoroughly, squeezing out the water with a spoon. Cook the bacon till done but not "breakable." (Or brown the ham slightly on both sides.) Butter large custard cups, small baking dishes, or a 2-inch-deep foil cake pan (a 9-by-9-inch pan is fine for 8 eggs). Line the dishes with bacon (or ham); spoon the spinach in, making little nests into which you can drop the eggs.

If you are eating alone, use only part of the spinach; a #2 can is enough for four in this recipe, so divide the spinach accordingly. If you use all the spinach, it will still be cold when the rest of the dish is cooked. (Or, if you are a spinach fiend, preheat the spinach.)

Place the baking dishes in the oven. Watch carefully. When the eggs are almost done—the white at the center still transparent —cover each pair of eggs with a slice of cheese. By the time the cheese is melted, the dish is done. Ideally this is served with English muffins.

11 / Cheese: Or What to Eat till the Refrigerator Is Fixed

To like cheese is a great good fortune.

And, fortunately, there are so many varieties of cheese, just about anyone can find some to like.

One of the charms of cheese is that, like eggs, it does not really *need* refrigeration. While heat makes cheese sweat and will, after a while, turn it rancid (waxy in flavor) so that it must be discarded, all that hard cheese really needs is a cool place—a windowsill in winter, a bucket of cold water in summer. (Place the cheese in a sealed container before submersion!)

Cheese is an excellent food.

Hard cheeses are preferable for people in need of calories, while soft cheeses are the standby of dieters. The exception is cream cheese, which is the highest in fat and lowest in protein of any cheese and therefore should be considered a butter substitute rather than a cheese.

It has often been noted that the poor are frequently obese and eat lots of sugar and starch, which misleads fact-gatherers into concluding that sugar and starches are cheaper than proteins, and that poverty and a high-carbohydrate diet must go hand in hand. *This is simply not true.* You can eat an adequate and nonfattening diet even while very, very poor. And cheese is a keystone in this diet, partly because, as a highly concentrated food, a little of it goes a long way (few people can eat more than two ounces of cheese at a sitting), partly because fat and protein have a far greater stick-to-your-ribs quality than do carbohydrates.

The only kind of cheese you might avoid is the *spread* or *processed* cheese. These have undergone a preservation process which, according to Adelle Davis in *Let's Eat Right to Keep Fit*, ruins their value. I suppose this is a pity, as the cheeses in vending machines are convenient, and those little foil-wrapped packages quite tasty. But after reading Miss Davis, we struck processed cheeses (and other hydrogenated fats) off our shopping list.

Hard cheeses include the cheddars, Swiss, Muenster, Caerphilly, Dunlop, Feta, and so on. Roquefort, Danish blue, Stilton, Gorgonzola and other green or blue "molded" cheeses are also in this group. Runny cheeses, such as Camembert, Brie, and Limburger, should be classified in this group for their fat and protein content. These runny cheeses, however, contain about 10 percent more water than the solid hard cheeses, and this fact should be taken into account when you are pricing them. They also have a short life span; they go on aging, and very quickly overripen into such a strong flavor that few people can eat them (or stay in the same room with them—particularly Limburger).*

Soft cheeses are pot, cottage, and farmer's. According to a nice dairyman, pot cheese is the first step in making these soft cheeses. It is simply the curd. Cottage cheese comes next in the process and has had some cream added to it which gives a smoother flavor. Farmer's cheese is either pot or cottage with all the water squeezed out to mold it into a loaf. It is like bone-dry cream cheese in texture. There is only a 20-calorie difference per 100 grams (about 3½ ounces) between plain and creamed cottage cheese, so unless you are on an extremely rigid fat-free diet, get pot, cottage, or farmer's, according to flavor preference. Keep in mind that farmer's cheese has the least water content of these three and frequently is the best buy.

Ricotta—that delicious Italian cream cheese—used to be made of whey. Today it is made of whole or partly skimmed milk and has a bit less protein and about three times the fat of uncreamed cottage cheese. It also has about twice the calories and is more than twice the price. (I do not know why the price; for so popular a cheese it is very costly.)

Speaking of whey cheeses: there are some on the market, such as mysost. The ones I have seen have all been imported from Scandinavia. They are made by reducing whey over a very slow fire. Since whey contains a lot of sugar, the end product tastes less like cheese than like salty caramel. If you like it, it certainly is an interesting food.

---

*If you are stuck with overripe but not hopeless runny cheese, remove the rind, and mash the cheese with a small amount of cottage or cream cheese for a perfectly acceptable spread.

What to Do with Cheese

The frank answer is: *eat it!* Although a grand variety of recipes make cheese a more entertaining dish, cheese can be a meal in itself. A selection of two or three cheeses, accompanied by a dry red wine, is a perfect meal any time of the year.

While Americans usually eat bread or crackers with cheese, or ham, or apples, the Dutch eat Gouda and Edam (very like cheddar) with honey cake or spice cake. In the Mediterranean Feta and Bryndza (a sheep cheese) are eaten with figs, olives, or melon. In South America bland cheeses of the Muenster or Caerphilly type are eaten with guava paste (a jam cooked down to sliceable form).

Soft cheeses benefit from a slight chilling. The hard cheeses should be served at room temperature—by which I do not mean Biloxi in August, but a comfortable 60–65°F or so. Certainly *not* iced.

When you get bored with straight cheese, try one of these:

Liptauer

This recipe came from my father, who brought it back from the Russian front, German side, in World War I. I have since seen the recipe in cookbooks, but I am fascinated, somehow, by the origins of mine.

As you have them, add to one pound of cottage cheese: a 3-ounce can of anchovies, oil and all; ½ cup of capers (taste them first; if they are very salty, rinse them before adding); ½ cup of finely chopped onions, scallions, pickled onions, or fresh chives; enough mustard so you can taste it (if you use dry mustard, mix it with water and let it sit 10 minutes before adding). Add enough paprika for a good pink color.

You can chop the anchovies, onions, capers separately before adding—use a stainless knife—or you can chop as you mix. If you like, add some ketchup or pickles.

You can use farmer's cheese instead of cottage or pot, but add a little milk to make the mix creamy.

Liptauer is eaten on black bread, or as a salad.

Almost all the things your mother used for cheese dips can be added to plain cottage cheese to make it more exciting. You can add a bouillon cube dissolved in a little water (one cube per cup of cheese, just about does it); or dried onion soup; or chopped fresh chives and green onions; fried onions; green olives; capers; peppers. Chopped clams are fine: add them drained to cottage cheese, and with some liquid to farmer's cheese. Also try crushed, very crisp bacon.

Cheesecake: Sweet and Not So Sweet

Cheesecake is a generic term that includes anything from high-fat, very sweet desserts to lean, somewhat crumbly confections, to egg custards seasoned with salt and pepper that can be eaten as a meal by themselves—with or without sour cream atop—or instead of a vegetable with a meat course.

Good cheesecake is extremely hard to come by, and violently expensive into the bargain. I do not know why, as it is very simple to make, and if you feel like skipping the crust it is fine as a baked pudding.

Unless you are on a no-sugar diet, there's no good reason why you cannot eat a healthy chunk of cheesecake—even the sweet kind—as your lunch. It is actually a very good food.

1. *The rich, sweet cheesecake*

Buy: 1 pound ricotta or small-curd cottage cheese; 1 small (3-ounce) cream cheese; ½ pint sour cream; 4–6 eggs (depending on size). For crust: about 10 graham crackers; ¼ pound butter.

Have: sugar; vanilla, lemon juice, or rum; a 9″ diameter, 3″ deep (round) foil baking dish, or equivalent size in square.

Preheat your oven to 350°F—or adjust flame to medium heat.

To make crust (optional):

Place the ¼ pound of butter in a frying pan. Carefully melt

the butter. Do it in your heating oven with the door open (if the frying pan has an overproof handle), or do it atop the radiator in winter, or set the pan over hot water: you want to melt the butter without browning it at all.

While the butter is melting, put the crackers (if you buy a box with three packets in it, use one packet) in a plastic bag and close the bag tightly. Then with your fist, a rolling pin, or a heavy can, crush and bash the crackers into fine crumbs. Be careful not to punch holes in the bag. The crumbs should be pretty fine.

Stir the crumbs into the melted butter. If the butter hardens up while you are doing this, reheat gently. You want the crumbs to soak up the butter, but you don't want the crumbs to be soppy either.

When this is done, place your foil pan on a flat surface so it does not de-form during the next step. Which is to wipe the sides of the dish with a little grease (butter, lard, or oil) and then to pack the crumb mixture hard into the bottom of the pan so that it forms a solid, even crust of packed-in-tight crumbs. If you cannot push hard enough with your knuckles, use the bowl of a big spoon or the (freshly washed) bottom of a can.

If you omit crust, start here:

Preheat oven and grease pan (all of it) as above.

Mash the cream cheese with some sour cream to make a smooth sludge that will mix in easily with the other ingredients—you add all the cheese, and sour cream, stirring a lot. Add ½ cup of sugar and 1 teaspoon of vanilla or lemon juice or rum. Taste; adjust sweetness and flavoring to your taste. Then add the eggs, stirring till all is well mixed. Pour into dish or atop crumbs and set in the oven. Bake till the top is golden brown and a knife comes out "clean." (This latter instruction, which you find in many baking recipes, means that the knife will come out damp and perhaps with a few streaks of crumbs, but not coated with raw batter or cheese.)

NOTE: The danger with cheesecakes and custards is that over-cooking will make them separate, that is, curdle the mass, separating solids and liquid. This is not a disaster—the thing can be beaten smooth with a beater—but of course it will not have the solidity of a cheesecake; it will be more of a sauce. *To avoid this, avoid overcooking.* Sacrifice the brown top crust if the knife comes out clean (check after 30 minutes) before the crust is brown. *If you cannot regulate your oven accurately, keep heat on the low rather than on the high side.*

2. The nonsweet, lean cheesecake

I never can decide which I like better. You will be surprised that, without any salt in it, this cake has a salty taste.

Buy: 2 pounds cottage cheese; for crust, ¼ pound butter.

Have: 3 or 4 eggs (depending on size); 2 tablespoons flour, rice starch, potato starch, or cornstarch; 1 cup milk; for crust, 2 cups bread crumbs.

This is normally made without a crust. If you wish a crust, prepare as the graham cracker crust using the butter and bread crumbs.

Put the flour or starch in a bowl; slowly add the milk. *Slowly* so as to avoid lumps. Add the other ingredients. Beat well to mix thoroughly.

Pour into a greased dish and bake as above. Eat hot or cold.

NOTE: If you make this frequently (we do), it is worthwhile to buy a thick, preferably china, baking dish for it.

NOTE: *Cheesecake should be refrigerated at all times. It basically is a custard, and can spoil easily.*

The #1 cake above can be made unsweetened. Cake #2 can be sweetened, or used as a base for stewed fruit or berries. My husband likes the unsweetened cheesecake with maple syrup. And of course you can use honey instead of sugar as sweetener.

Whipped Ricotta or Cottage Cheese

If you have a blender, try blenderizing ricotta or cottage cheese. For the latter, add some sour cream. If you do not have a blender, force either cheese through a sieve, and beat very well. Add a little sugar or honey, and some vanilla. Chill thoroughly, and you have something even better than ice cream—a superb base for fruit, or a lovely dessert by itself.

Blintzes are without doubt the dreamboats of cheese creations (at least I have no doubts). To know how to make them is to be a better person. But since they are time consuming, I have put them under desserts, page 202, assuming that you will, at present, only make them for special occasions.

12 / Meat: The Most Important Item in Your Food Budget

There are a number of government classifications for meat. Prime is the highest rating. Prime meat, which you do not frequently find in the stores, is supposed to be richly marbled with fat—an advantage of limited use. Most stores carry choice meat, which again is of little help to the consumer, because so much of the quality and flavor of meat depends on its handling by the butcher: the care he gives the carcass, how he ages and refrigerates and carves it up.

In other words, a piece of good or standard meat (next grades down) that has been excellently cut up and aged is likely to taste better than a sloppily handled piece of choice or prime. You will have guessed by now that even in a chain store, the quality of meat can vary from branch to branch, and week to week.

Depending on the part of the anatomy a piece of meat comes from, it will be darker or lighter, the grain close and tight, or loose and sloppy-looking. Beef is bright red or even cordovan, veal and lamb pink, and pork tends toward a rococo gray-pink that is quite lovely.

Chicken can vary in color from an off-white to a pale gold. This depends on age and breed. But if the chicken has what looks like large freckles—roundish brown areas, which are generally leathery to the touch, the chicken has freezer burn (from improper wrapping in the cooler) and is best avoided. Liver, kidney, and lung vary tremendously in color. Mostly liver is a cordovan, as is kidney, while lung is pale purplish pink. But I have seen perfectly good liver that was a dark rust color, veal kidney that was dark rose, and lung that was much lighter than expected.

So while your eyes are a good guide to meat shopping, *your best bet is to use your nose and your touch.*

All meat when fresh has a pleasant fresh smell—or no detectable smell at all. *All* fresh meat feels moist but *never* slimy or sticky. The color may vary; there may be more or less fat, more open or closed grain—but the smell and the feel are the same for all.

What do you do when everything at the supermarket is prepackaged? Remember that the prepackaging is done for *their* convenience—and a real convenience it is, too. But it is *not* a fact of nature. So, after you have decided to buy a piece of meat, unwrap it; examine it—and if it is no good, consult the butcher about it. *Do not* put it back unwrapped in the case, as then the store will have something to fuss about. If you are in too much of a hurry to unwrap, check the wrappings. If they are clean and smell good, give it a try. If the wrappings are stained, if the tray is soaked with juices that are discolored and sticky to the touch, do not buy.

Note here, by the way, that markets (is this intentional?) generally package on the high side of what are normal "quantities." The half-pound package almost invariably contains 9 or even 10 ounces. The pound package generally contains 1¼ pounds. In many cases—as with chicken, chicken parts, or meat-with-bones—the store cannot help it: it would take too much time to try for surgical accuracy. But when you cannot use resulting leftovers, it is a bore, and I frequently end up with two "half-pound" packages because they add up to less overweight than the official "one-pound" package.

After a few expeditions to the different meat departments in place—one whose meat is fresh and well stored; whose specials are worthwhile; where only a logical amount of fat is weighed into the meat, and very little into the ground beef.

As I keep repeating, proteins are your major and most important food expenditure, and no amount of care in their procurement and preparation can be called exaggerated.

Meat Storage and Preparation

1. Till you know your refrigerator well, and unless it is a very new one, don't rely on the meat tray or drawer to hold the meat fresh indefinitely. I find I can keep really fresh meat two days in the refrigerator without loss of quality; I suggest you do not keep it longer.

2. Unwrap meat from its original packing as soon as you get it home—regardless of the type of wrapping. Rinse solid pieces of meat, wipe dry with a paper towel, rewrap in wax paper,* leaving the ends open for some air circulation. You also can use bowls or plastic containers with a loose paper cover.

3. If you have a large chunk of meat and intend to make stew, do not cut the meat up till you are ready to use it—unless you are marinating it.

4. *If for some reason you must keep the meat longer than two days, cook it—even if only partially (that is, not the full cooking time).* This gives it a new lease on life.

All of the above rules and regulations apply to poultry, liver, and tongue as well.

NOTE: Prepared meats—such as sausage of one kind or another—is much harder to judge by smell, as the spicing dominates any other odor, at least till active putrefaction has set in. Texture

---

*Wax paper has been replaced in many households by the more fashionable plastics and aluminum foils. It remains, however, a good *cheap* wrapping, and you should give it a try.

and appearance are your criteria here. Grayness, sliminess, stickiness are out. Also a leathery look (which you find in dry, salami-type sausages that are too old). There are dry, hard salamis, but these still have a healthy, slightly moist look; they are not wooden or leathery to the sight or touch.

With these meats freshness is extra-hard to detect as preservatives are generally part of the mix. Here you are thrown upon the mercy of the manufacturer and the store, and shopping around, carefully, is my best suggestion.

Stew, Pot Roast, and Meatballs

The vast majority of recipes for meat fall into this group. A meat chart will tell you why: only about 16 percent of a beef carcass is suitable for broiling; only 7 percent for dry roasting. The rest is best cooked in moist heat—and all these moist-heat cuts are also the cheapest.

Chuck, plate, round are the main cuts you will be buying. Flank, shank, arm (of which there is much less per carcass, hence less at the butcher's) are excellent, but generally these are what the butcher uses in ground beef and in stew meat that he prepackages.

My own "best buys" are chuck and round, but by all means try what the different stores prepackage as *ground beef* and *stew meat*. These can be—though not always, by any means—cheaper and better than chuck or round for these purposes, since stores often add steak and roast trimmings to these packages.

Pot roast, stew, and meatballs are the same basic thing. *Pot roast* is a single, large piece of meat cooked in liquid and sliced before serving. *Stew* is the same piece of meat, sliced fine before cooking, and prepared in the same way as pot roast. *Ground meat*, that is, meatballs or meatloaf, is the same kind of meat once more, minced this time for easiest serving. While meatballs are cooked in the same kind of sauce as pot roast or stew, meatloaf is baked and served, either with a sauce or dry.

But for all three the same cuts of meat are used, and fortunately these are inexpensive.*

Pot roast and stew are generally made of beef, veal, or lamb. Meatballs and meatloaf incorporate pork as a rule—up to one-third of the total amount of meat—to provide the fat that keeps them from being too dry. As pork is a fat meat, it is better suited for dry cooking—roasting or broiling, or frying (the latter quite indigestible unless the meat is allowed to render its own fat slowly, and cook itself in it). Chinese stews made of pork use only the leanest parts.

Keep in mind that pot roast takes the longest to cook, stew comes next, and meatballs really take no time at all. If, therefore, you have bought a pot roast but misjudged your time, cut the meat into stew. And if you have a grinder, you can convert stew meat into ground meat for still further time savings.

Basic Pot Roast

A pot roast should be between 2 and 4 pounds.

Have: salt, pepper, celery salt, parsley, soup cubes, oil or fat, (sugar), bay leaf and other spices.

Buy: 2 pounds of chuck or round; 2 carrots; 1 onion; 2 tomatoes.

Put your big saucepan on the stove, over a very low flame. Heat 3 tablespoons of fat slowly. Peel and chop your onion, add it to the hot but not smoking fat. Stir till brownish gold. Transfer the onions to another pan or onto a dish. Clean the carrots, slice a couple of times lengthwise into pencil-like strips. Add fat to the saucepan if needed, and fry the carrots lightly. Remove them to onion plate.

Wash and dry the meat. Raise the flame under the saucepan and fry the meat thoroughly on all sides. *The flame should be*

---

*No meat is actually cheap. Still, as nothing placates the appetite as well as meat, I insist that, meal per meal, meat does not cost more than other foods.

hot enough so that any liquid that comes out of the meat evaporates immediately. When the meat is a rich brown on all sides—this takes quite a while, like 10–15 minutes—add your onions and carrots and any liquid that has oozed out of them. If you are using fresh tomatoes, quarter them and add. (Break canned tomatoes in half with a spoon before adding.) Add 1 teaspoon of salt, some pepper, a crushed bay leaf, and one of the following: oregano, marjoram, thyme. (No more than a teaspoon of these for 2 pounds of meat.)

At the same time add *one* of the following: a bouillon cube dissolved in water, or wine, or beer; a mixture of wine and water and soy sauce; a bottle of stout (in which case no oregano, thyme, or marjoram); beer and 1 teaspoon of sugar (in which case no oregano, thyme, marjoram); leftover chicken soup, bouillon, or tomato or vegetable juice. Concoct enough liquid so that the meat is half covered with it.

Cover the pot and cook over a slow flame 2 hours or more. Check the amount of liquid every 30 minutes or so, turning the meat another-side-down when you check. Look more frequently if the lid does not fit your pot well (that is, if much steam escapes). Add water if necessary. *Do not keep adding wine or beer or other flavored liquids.* Cooking time depends on the toughness of the meat, its size and shape, and how well done you like it. Some people like pot roast that is virtually a flannel rag; others like it on the rarish side. Obviously, a flat piece of meat cooks more quickly that a cube. The first time out, cook till a fork goes in easily. Remove the cover when the meat is done, raise the flame, and allow the liquid to reduce to 2 cups. Adjust seasoning.

Variations

1. Just about any vegetable can be cooked with the pot roast. Add them at serving time minus the cooking time of the vegetable. (Let us say 30 minutes before dinner for potatoes, 5 minutes for frozen peas.)

2. An Italianate variation on pot roast is achieved by using a small can of tomato paste in the sauce and adding a few cloves of garlic (peeled). Use only water or bouillon as your basic cooking liquid.

3. For a Latin American variation, fry a cleaned, chopped

green pepper with the onions, and omit the carrots. Use only water as your basic cooking liquid and add 2 cups of tomatoes, or 1 small can of tomato sauce plus water to make 2 cups. Add 3/4 teaspoon ground cumin seed and chili powder to taste (about the same amount as the cumin seed—but commercial chili powders vary in strength). *Or* buy a commercially prepared chili or tamale sauce (the canned, not the ketchup type). This dish is great with canned kidney beans, whose liquid is used as part of the cooking liquid, the beans being added a few minutes before serving.

4. *Marinate the meat.* This requires no extra cooking time, but a 24-hour or more battle plan. Marination had two original purposes: to soften tough meat, and to minimize off-flavors—in the case of game the (I think odious) gaminess; in the case of not-very-fresh meat, the mustiness. These original purposes still serve, though really tough meat is uncommon these days. But if you have kept a piece of meat too long, wash it well in water and a dash of vinegar; trim the awful parts off, and marinate it. *You can, however, and please do, marinate perfectly good meat.* Select a bowl into which the meat fits snugly but without crowding, and has enough room to be covered by ¼-inch of liquid. If no pot is big enough, select the biggest, turn the meat at 4-hour intervals or so to give each side a soak.

A very good marinade is made with oregano, bay leaf, a chopped carrot, a chopped onion, a few cloves of garlic, and two or three cups of wine (red or white, but dry) into which 2 tablespoons of oil have been beaten. Turn the meat in it a couple of times. Use after 24–36 hours.

Sauerbraten is made of one-third wine (red or white, but dry), one-third vinegar (cider or white), and one-third water. This mixture is boiled up with 2 bay leaves, a chopped onion, 3 whole cloves or allspice (or ¼ teaspoon of the ground variety), and a pinch of thyme. Cool the marinade till you can stick your finger in it comfortably, and then pour it over the meat. Sauerbraten is generally marinated for several days, but I use it after 48 hours, turning the meat every once in a while.

A mock-Oriental marinade which I also use for pork chops and chicken is made of one-half sweet wine (sherry or Marsala—any-thing that tastes close to sake) and one-half soy sauce with ½ teaspoon of ginger, 1 or 2 cloves of peeled garlic. If you must use dry wine, add a bit of sugar.

When you are ready to cook your meat, drain thoroughly, dry the meat, and fry it on all sides like a normal pot roast. Use the marinade liquid, with the spices strained out, as your sauce for cooking. *Add only water if you need more liquid, or the sauce gets too strong.*

5. You also can start with basic pot roast and simply gussy up your gravy: thicken it with flour (page 207), or, add sour cream just before serving (never, never boil sour cream, as it curdles), or, be heavy-handed with the garlic and onions, and toss in a handful of black, Greek olives before serving. Explore!

Pitfalls of Pot Roast

1. *Overspicing*. While a combination of many flavors is good, take it easy. With most herbs and spices ½ teaspoon per 2 cups of liquid or volume is plenty; with some, ¼ teaspoon is enough. It would be nice if directions could be given, but several things affect the flavor intensity of spices and herbs—the original quality, the age, other spices with which they are being used, and the temperature at which the dish you are cooking is eaten. *Heat intensifies flavor.* Taste the food at the temperature it will be served, before adding any more flavorings. (On many jars and cans of spices you will find indications of the normal tolerance for that spice. Follow the directions the first few times.) Whatever you do, a light touch is best.

2. *Burning*. Keep the liquid level high, and *lift* the pot roast from time to time. Otherwise the part resting on the bottom may stick though there is liquid all around. (I do not know why this happens.)

3. *Cooking too fast*. If you must hurry, make stew. Or use a pressure cooker. The "secret" of pot roast is a slow, slow fire. Two pounds ought to take about two hours. (Figure 40 minutes per pound.)

4. *Greasy sauce*. Examine your meat before cooking it. If

it is very fat, cut out the biggest pieces of fat, even if you have to tie the meat into a chunk afterward with thick sewing thread or kite string (not jute rope, or any cord with glue in it). If the meat cannot be trimmed, try cooking it the day before, cooling it in the refrigerator overnight, and removing the fat that coagulates at the top. Or cool as much as possible and spoon off the liquid fat that rises.

5. *Meat tears instead of slicing.* Meat should be cut across the grain; but many cuts used for pot roast have the grain running every which way, and it is next to impossible to cut any but very small slices with the grain. If that is not the problem, is your knife sharp enough? Perhaps the meat is stringy or really cooked out—as well done as can be. If tearing bothers you, slice the meat when it is only partly cooked, finish cooking later. Or make the pot roast a day ahead of time, chill well, slice while it is very cold, and heat to serve. (My favorite method. See #4 above.)

Basic Stew

Have and *buy* as for pot roast.

Stew can be made in smaller quantities, but less than a pound seems a waste of time.

Prepare as for pot roast. Wash, dry, and trim meat. If you are cutting it into stew, do it after the washing and drying. Brown the meat, stirring all the time, so each side of each piece is browned.

Cook just long enough, stirring every 20 minutes or so and keeping the liquid level high.

Americans generally use large chunks of meat for stew—they subsequently slice the pieces as they eat. Europeans and Chinese seem to cut the meat much smaller. I prefer the latter method (which also cuts down cooking time) and cut my stew meat into bite-sized pieces so a knife is not needed at table.

Depending on the size of the pieces, a stew is done in 40 minutes to an hour. But a long slow simmer will do no harm, if you stir occasionally and watch the liquid level.

You can make all the variations as for pot roast, except the marinade. If you marinate small pieces of meat a long time, all the flavor goes out. You can, however, cut a marinated piece of meat into small pieces for quicker cooking.

Variations: Cook the stew in a slow oven, covering it very tightly with aluminum foil (don't let any moisture out) till it is done. Cover then with a biscuit or pie crust, and go on baking till the crust is done. (Be sure to cut a few holes in the crust for air vents. Use a crust mix.)

Steak and kidney pie. If you like kidneys, but an amount equal to your other meat. (Steak, by the way, is not used, despite the name.) Wash the kidneys in water and vinegar. Trim out all the fibers with a small, very sharp knife that you work along the middle of the kidney (much like a boning procedure). Slice the kidney across, trim out any fat or fiber that remains, and slice the meat small. Fry the kidney—preferably with butter—add it to the other stew meat, and proceed as with stew, using red wine, or wine and bouillon, as liquid. If the kidneys are tough—and I know no way of predicting this by looking—this may take a bit longer to cook than other stews. You can, but do not need to, cover with pie crust. You can also add diced carrots.

Meatballs #1 and #2

I will give you two quite different recipes for meatballs, only to show you how very, very small the differences are. The first recipe is for Italian-style meatballs. The second is for northern European ones, which are, I think, as good cold as hot, but not as good as the Italian ones for sandwiches.

General rules for meatballs: You can add more bread or cooked rice if you need to stretch the dish. Some people use so much bread that their meatballs are virtually bread puddings with meat added. Some bread or rice is a good idea to help retain juices, but 2 to 4 slices of bread per 3 pounds of meat is quite enough, I think.

Ground pork is extremely hard to obtain, because most butchers only have one meat grinder, and as they cannot clean it between grindings, they reserve it for beef for fear of giving raw-ground-beef fans a dose of raw pork with their *steak tartare*. (Trichinosis and all that.) Therefore in #1 use Italian sausage, either bought loose or decased at home. In #2 I use plain pork sausage—the least spiced I can find.

NOTE: *Never taste meatballs or meatloaf raw, once the pork has been added.*

Meatballs #1

Have: onion; 2 eggs; 2–4 slices of dried bread or old toast, or about 1 cup of cooked rice or cracker crumbs; garlic; fat (preferably oil); (ground Romano or Parmesan cheese).

Buy: 2 pounds ground beef or chuck; 1 pound sweet Italian sausage, or ½ pound sweet and ½ pound hot; tomato sauce or tomato paste.

Crumble and tear the bread as well as you can into a bowl. Or place the rice or crumbs into a bowl. Break the eggs into the bowl and stir well, crushing the bread. Add the decased sausage and the meat. If you wish, add ½ cup ground cheese. Mix the stuff well with your hands.

If you can, chill the mixture a while for greater ease in rolling the meatballs. Or you can dip your hands in cold water between rolling them. You can roll them all now, or roll as you fry.

Anyway, wash your hands at this point and chop your onion. Heat ¼ cup oil in your big saucepan, fry the onion, and remove to a plate. Put the meatballs in the pan, and stir them to cook on all sides. *The temptation here is to tilt the pan to roll the meatballs around. Don't do it. The fat can catch fire easily and cause a disaster.* Better uneven meatballs that a scorched face, I always say.

Remove the meatballs as they brown to leave plenty of stirring room. When all are done, return them to the pan with the onions and the tomato sauce or tomato paste. Add water so there is enough liquid for a thorough cooking.* Allow 30 minutes over a slow

---

*Unless a pot is tightly lidded, the part that's in the liquid cooks much more rapidly than what sticks out. One therefore must stir and turn stews, meatballs, pot roasts, and the like. An alternative is to use a small pot with just a bit of room at the sides, but enough depth to allow the whole stew to be submerged.

flame. Slice a meatball. It must be cooked through thoroughly before you can eat it, as this dish contains pork.

Tomato paste and sauce generally contain some spices. If you are using plain canned or fresh tomatoes, add some oregano and basil to the sauce as it cooks. Add as much garlic as you like.

Serve with spaghetti and noodles, and more grated cheese—or a liberal sprinkle of fresh, chopped parsley.

Meatballs #2

Have: Onion; allspice or nutmeg; butter; salt; pepper; 2–4 slices of dried bread, or cracker crumbs; (1 egg).

Buy: 2 pounds ground beef or chuck; ½ to 1 pound ground pork or plain port sausage; ½ pound sour cream or light cream.

Chop very vine half the onion if large, whole onion if small, and fry till golden brown in 2–3 tablespoons of butter. Drop the fried onion plus remaining fat into the bowl in which you'll mix the meat. Add meat and either the egg or ½ cup light cream. Rub the bread between your hands to reduce it to crumbs (a light pretoasting helps dry the bread to real crispness, or use old toast). Add ¼ teaspoon allspice or nutmeg, or add 3 whole allspices or a chip of nutmeg to the sauce later. Knead very well. Roll into small balls. For some reason, German and Swedish meatballs are made small; Italian, big.

Again, you can preroll the lot, or roll 'em as you fry (messier but quicker).

Fry them in butter with a dash of oil added. When all are fried, remove from pan. Add water and light cream to the saucepan, stir well to get up all the stick-ons at the bottom,* add enough water to make about 2 cups of liquid and whole allspice or nutmeg chip, if you did not have the ground. Return meatballs to pan, cover, cook slowly for 30 minutes.

If you got sour cream instead of light cream, cook the meatballs in water, reduce the water at the very end by boiling it away,

---

*This process, which is allegedly one of the backbones of French cuisine, is called *deglazing*. A term that conveys little. However, it is as good a word as any for the process of scraping and boiling up all the stuck-on goodness at the bottom of a frying or roasting pan with a little water and effort, and adding it to the sauce.

stir 1 teaspoon of paprika into the sour cream, and the sour cream into the sauce. *Be sure not to let the sauce boil after you have added sour cream.* If you must heat or reheat, you will have to do it by placing your lidded pot of meatballs over boiling water.

Variations: Try this once with a lemon white sauce, made as follows: Cook the meatballs in water or chicken stock. When they are done, remove all the liquid. Stir 2 teaspoons flour into a paste with a little milk, in a small pan, and *slowly* add all the meatball liquid. First add a teaspoon at a time. Then, when you have a thinnish liquid, add the rest more quickly. (We are trying to avoid lumps.) Add 2 teaspoons lemon juice (enough to taste) and cook the sauce 5 minutes over a slow flame, stirring all the time, mainly along sides and bottom, to prevent sticking. Add fresh, chopped parsley and pour over meatballs. Serve with boiled potatoes.

Add capers to a white sauce for which you have used the meatballs' own liquid. Add capers at the last moment, after turning off the flame. Capers turn bitter if boiled and should not be cooked. Serve with boiled potatoes.

Or you can skip other spices (except salt and pepper) all along, add a pinch of oregano and mint, and mix yogurt in at the last minute, *after* the flame is off (same reason as with sour cream). Serve with rice.

Both the preceding mixes can be used for meatloaf. In each case you can have a separate sauce to pour over the meatloaf.

NOTE: As meatloaf is cooked open in the oven, you should add some water to the mix, and ladle a tablespoon of water onto the loaf every 15 minutes or so. If you make a meatloaf with pork in it, you just bake it in a normal 4-by-4-by-9-inch pan for a *good hour.* Or you can precook the pork in water before adding to the mix and not worry about how long the meatloaf cooks in the oven. (I do the latter, when I'm cooking just for me, as I like rare meatloaf. My husband likes his very well done.) If you don't care about a crusty meatloaf, you can cover the pan with foil, tightly, and not bother with the watering.

NOTE: Always pack meatloaf loosely. Don't see how much you can squoosh into the pan.

NOTE: You don't need to use any bread or rice in meatballs

(or loaf) at all. The result will be drier and harder, but just as tasty.

NOTE: You don't need to use pork. The purpose of the pork is to incorporate some fat in the mix, that is rendered slowly throughout the cooking process, and makes a fluffier mass. But it is not essential, or there would be no kosher meatballs, would there?

Cabbage Rolls

A simple but time-consuming dish worth its weight in gold when you are cooking for a largish group.

Buy and *have* all the meatball ingredients for either recipe above. Precook the pork by either frying or boiling in a little water, which is then added to the meat mix. Prepare the meat mix as above.

Buy a large cabbage—white, green, or savoy. Not red. Trim and wash it. Place the cabbage in your largest pot, and pour 1 pint of boiling water over it. Turn up the flame as high as you can, cover the pot, and cook briskly until the leaves wilt. (Peek in after 5 minutes.) Wilting gives the leaves a transparent jade-like look, and makes them flexible so you can roll them without breaking. When the cabbage is wilted, remove it from the pot, cool it quickly under running cold water. (Save the cooking water.) Turn the cabbage bottom-up, and cut out the hard core (stem). When you become more expert, you will *core the cabbage before wilting it;* but at this stage of the game, you risk having the whole thing come apart on you if you core first and then misjudge how much time it takes to just wilt a cabbage.

Remove the leaves and pile them up. You will see they curl, saucer-like, in one direction. Fill the stem end of each leaf, allowing enough room so you can roll the thing up tidily. Work your way to the smaller leaves, using as many as you can. If you have leaves left over, shred them and cook along with the cabbage rolls. If you have meat left over, make some small meatballs and cook them with the rest.

Brown the cabbage rolls in a frying pan, slowly.

(From this point on you can cook the thing atop the stove, or in the oven.)

Return cabbage rolls (and also any possible meatballs and shredded cabbage) to main pot—that cabbage water you kept—and add tomato sauce (for #1 meat mix) or bouillon cubes (for #2 mix). In either case, add 1 teaspoon sugar. Have enough liquid in the pot so your rolls are covered two-thirds of the way. Cook 30 minutes atop stove, or 2 hours in medium oven. (The oven will give the top of the cabbage rolls a deep brown color and a caramely flavor some people adore.) Finish the #2 meatballs by adding sour cream just before serving.

Spaghetti Sauce

One of the nicest uses one can make of chopped meat is to turn it into spaghetti sauce. You can start from scratch, or you can prepare the meat and buy the tomato sauce (with or without mushrooms). In our area there are a lot of Italians, and many small groceries carry excellent tomato sauce made by small local manufacturers. This has fewer additives and higher quality than much of the mass-produced stuff.

For all spaghetti sauce you start with ¼ pound of meat per person. You take your biggest frying pan, and heat oil in it till it passes the water-drop test described previously. You then take the ground meat and crumble it into the fat. Do a bit at a time, and stir a lot. The point of this exercise is to fry each little grain of meat thoroughly on all sides (this prevents it from ever clustering up with other pieces). If you like garlic, fry a few cloves of it along with the meat, removing them when they get beyond the rust-brown stage.

If you are using commercial sauce, you simply add it to the meat once it is thoroughly browned, and cook it for half an hour or so, stirring and adding water occasionally. Do not fill your pan too full: the sauce will boil over, and cooked-on tomato sauce is one of the toughest things to remove from pan or stove.

You need about 1 pint of tomato sauce per pound of meat.

If you decide to make your own spaghetti sauce, you will need either a 2-pound can of tomatoes, a dozen fresh tomatoes, or a can of tomato paste (the smallest is fine).

With fresh tomatoes: either scorch them over a flame till the skin blisters, and peel them; scald them in boiling water, chill and peel; or stab them a few times (to allow the juices to come out more quickly), do not peel, and sieve the tomato sauce later to get the skins out. Peeled or unpeeled, put the tomatoes into a pot with a tight lid, placing a very little bit of water in the bottom of the pan. Cook as slowly as you can, mashing the tomatoes when they soften. Soon you will have something that looks like lumpy tomato juice. Add one or two bouillon cubes and a pinch of basil and of oregano. Stir well (sieve if necessary) before adding the tomatoes to the meat, or vice versa.

With canned tomatoes you can just add them and their own juice to the meat, seasoning with bouillon cubes, salt, pepper, oregano, basil.

With tomato paste, you must dissolve the paste with at least three times its volume in water; do it in a bowl before adding it to the meat. Many tomato pastes come seasoned, so read your label, and taste as you go along.

NOTE: There seems to be a great difference of opinion, or at least practice, about how tomatoish tomato sauce should be. Many Italian restaurants serve up a thick red gloop that reminds me of nothing so much as stage blood. The flavor of the meat is totally hidden. Possibly destroyed.

To my way of thinking, the meat should definitely dominate, so take heed of this: fresh or canned tomatoes let through the most meat flavor; then tomato sauce; the least meat flavor comes through with tomato paste—unless, of course, you dilute it very generously. So suit yourself.

Variations: Use red wine along with the tomatoes, or use it to dissolve the tomato paste. Cook an extra while to reduce the wine.

Add a laurel leaf; or juniper berries; or a shot of gin.

Add fresh, canned, or dried *Italian* mushrooms.

Spaghetti sauce can be made a day or two ahead of time and kept in the refrigerator. It can also be frozen; and it is not a bad idea to make enough for two weeks' use at a time, and sacrifice one ice tray to freezing the second part (cover ice tray well with foil). If you have a freezer, you can make a six-month supply in one sweep.

Need I add that the sauce is served over ravioli or spaghetti made according to directions on package?

Lasagne

Lasagne is actually a party dish. It is costly, very time-consuming to make, and utterly delicious. I am including it here because it seems logical to have it with the sauce—but it is not an everyday thing. It definitely is one of the costliest recipes in this book, but let me add that per person it is probably cheaper than a roast beef sandwich eaten out!

Before trying this recipe, see the section below, "Problems with lasagne."

Have: spaghetti sauce with meat (as above); a large baking dish; extra-heavy-weight aluminum foil; salt; pepper; oil (olive if possible).

Buy: lasagne noodles; mozzarella cheese; ricotta; grated Parmesan or Romano.*

Lasagne is a layer cake built up of noodles, ricotta, mozzarella, grated cheese, and sauce. During Lent one makes it with tomato sauce *sans* meat, or with a white sauce or canned cheddar cheese soup instead of the meat sauce (and a generous sprinkle of parsley is added to the sauce).

How much of each ingredient depends a lot on one's finances

---

*Both of these are Italian grating cheeses; there are one or two more grating cheeses available in Italian markets. I cannot tell the difference in flavor between them and buy—trust me—the cheapest.

and figure. I put in just enough noodles to *be* there, and go easy on the mozzarella. When I've been fat and my wallet thin, I have used cottage cheese instead of ricotta—but it is not as good.

For the skinny and wealthy I would say 1 pound of ricotta, a mozzarella the size of a large orange, and ⅔ cup of grated cheese to 1 pound lasagne noodles.

1. Prepare your meat/tomato sauce.

2. In your largest cookpot boil a large amount of water. Add 1 tablespoon of oil; this keeps the noodles from sticking together. If your baking dish is 9 by 9 inches, the noodles will be too long, and you might as well break them in half before cooking them. When the water boils like mad, stick the noodles in, one at a time. Despite the oil in the water, the noodles will stick together unless immersed one by one and not crowded. Cook the noodles till you can take one out and bite clear through it, meeting a consistent toughness but no hard spots. (This is the famous Italian *al dente*, that is, "to the tooth," or "toothy.") Remove the pot with the noodles, set in sink, and run cold water over the noodles. (This is safer and easier than trying to get the noodles into a colander and then quick-cooling them.)

3. Pour a little oil into the bottom of your foil pan.

4. If you are crazy about garlic, stir some fresh crushed or chopped cloves (1 or 2 only) into the ricotta. Chop the mozzarella into ¼-inch pieces.

5. Spread a layer of noodles at the bottom of the dish. Make this layer at least 2 but not more than 5 noodles thick. Smear with 1 tablespoon of oil. Spread ricotta about ¼-inch thick on top of the noodles. Sprinkle with some mozzarella. Pour over this a generous portion of sauce. Sprinkle with grated cheese. Top with another layer of noodles; even 1 noodle deep is enough, but judge how many noodles you have to use up. Add a little oil, then the ricotta, etc. *The top layer should be sauce*.

6. Place a layer of heavy foil beneath the dish in your oven. Make sure the foil extends 4 inches or so in each direction. Lasagne spatters a lot, and the foil will save you a lot of work later.

Bake in low oven slowly till very hot, then raise the temperature till the whole thing is actively bubbling. This will take at least 40 minutes. If you have a very ancient oven that always is too hot, leave the door open for the first 20 minutes or so.

Serve with salad and red wine. This dish cannot be made for fewer than four people.

Problems with lasagne: Read before you ever make it!

1. *If you can't afford the ingredients:* You can substitute cottage cheese for ricotta; that saves you a bit. But you cannot substitute the other cheeses. So it is wiser to skip lasagne for a better day.

2. *If the noodles stick together:* The water was not boiling fiercely enough; there was not enough oil in the water; the noodles were not added one at a time; too many noodles in too small a pot (do in two batches next time).

3. *If the noodles are soggy in the final lasagne:* You overcooked them in the first place. Remember they go on cooking in the oven.

4. *If the lasagne is too dry:* Your sauce was not liquid enough to begin with—it should be like thick paint—or it dried out too much. If you fear this, add a couple of tablespoons of water to the lasagne as it bakes, or cover it for the first 20 minutes or so (with foil). This will add to the bubbling over, so be sure about the foil underneath.

5. *If the lasagne is too salty:* This is likeliest to happen when you use commercial sauce. Go very easy on salt; the cheeses supply a lot of salt, and as you are cooking them down and heating them up, you are intensifying all the flavors.

6. *If you have leftovers:* All your problems should be so easy! Leftover lasagne can easily be reheated in the oven, if well covered so it cannot dry out. If you also have leftover sauce, you can cut the lasagne up into small cubes and reheat in a saucepan with the sauce. If you have too many noodles, cut them fine, mix with butter and a bit of parsley, heat in oven, serve with stew. If you have ricotta left, eat it plain as lunch, or sweetened for dessert. If you have sauce left, incorporate it in a stew or soup, or use it as any spaghetti sauce. Mozzarella can be made into melted-cheese sandwiches. Grated cheese keeps "forever" in a tightly closed glass jar.

Winter Beef (or Lamb)

A delicate dish, whose charm lies in prettiness. (Also see

Pot-au-feu, a close kin, page 00.) Uses winter vegetables, and the oven heats the house; hence the name. Slice and cut carefully; use a pretty baking dish if you can.

Have: salt; pepper; butter; dry white wine (dry vermouth is okay).

Buy: 2 pounds chuck, brisket, or lean lamb (no bones); 1 pound onions or 1 package frozen small white onions (no sauce); 8 nice carrots or 1 package frozen carrots (1 pound); 2 potatoes (boiling type).

Slice the meat as evenly as you can into fine slices (¼-inch). Peel and slice the potatoes, and clean and slice onions and carrots, if you are using fresh instead of frozen. Make thin, almost transparent slices. Place a layer of meat in the baking dish, top with each vegetable in turn, add meat, then more vegetables, finishing with a layer of meat.

Pour in ½ cup white wine and ½ cup water. If the dish is not filled with liquid to about ¾ inch from the top, add a bit more water, a bit more wine.

Cover the dish with foil, cook in slow oven (300° F) for 1 hour. Taste juice, add salt and pepper to taste. Add water if necessary. Keep cover off, cook till the potatoes test "done" to a fork. Serve in soup plates with plenty of broth.

NOTE: Much depends on how thin you slice; lumps of potato will take up to 2 hours to be done.

This is actually a stew made without browning the meat first. It can be spiced with thyme, marjoram, bay leaf—but just plain it has a delicacy that is very comforting indeed.

Sixth Street Liver

I once subsisted a whole winter on this, and it still holds a special place in my heart. That is the only reason it is included. Otherwise—besides teaching you how to cook liver—it has little to recommend it, since liver, which once was dirt cheap, is now fairly expensive. So the agonizing cheapness of this dish—which besides its nutritional merits was its chief charm—has faded away. Still, here it is.

Have: Some fat; salt; pepper.

Buy: 1 pound liver; 1 pound sauerkraut; 1 onion; 1 can tomato soup.

How to cook liver. If you like liver, and I love it, it can be a delicacy—*if properly cooked.* Liver has no fat in it, so to prevent it from turning into shoe leather while being cooked, one must cook very carefully and provide some fat. If you fry liver, this is no problem; use as little fat as possible, but add as necessary. If you broil liver, you must first grease the outside or place a piece of raw bacon on top (between broiler flame and liver) to grease-as-you-go.

Wash and dry liver, and prepare as above. If you fry (my preferred method), heat the pan thoroughly, put in fat to cover bottom smoothly, place liver in, and as soon as bottom side is seared, turn the liver over. Cook 5 minutes on this side, turn back, cook 5 minutes more (for a slice ½-inch thick and thoroughly nonfrozen). There should be just a hint of pinkness left in liver after cooking.

When the liver is done, remove to a plate. Put the sauerkraut in a colander, rinse thoroughly, remove as much water as you can, and set aside. Fry the onion (in slices) in the liver pan, add the sauerkraut, and after the sauerkraut begins to fry, immediately add the tomato soup. Stir thoroughly, add the liver just to heat up, and serve—ideally with a lot of rye bread and butter.

Chicken Livers and Pork Chops

Chicken livers have become (proportionally) cheaper since I was a child; pork chops have risen dramatically in price. Chicken livers are cooked exactly like the beef liver above, except that one stirs them with a spoon as they are chunky if not sliced. Chicken livers are too good to use in Sixth Street Liver but are lovely with scrambled eggs, and even lovelier if at the end of the frying you pour ¼ cup of bourbon into the pan to make gravy. Half a pound of chicken livers is enough for a person's main course, so it is not as costly as you think. Serve with mashed potatoes and fried onions.

I put pork chops here because they too are quick-fried like liver. Only they have enough fat not to require any in addition. Cut off the excess fat from the chops, leave it in the pan to grease it. Sear one side, turn, sear and fry the other 5 minutes, turn, cook other side 5 minutes. *Cut into a chop: pork must be cooked so no trace of pink remains.* The addition of bourbon at the end of the cooking period is fine. Or, with pork, you can add onion and sauerkraut, as for Sixth Street Liver, but use bouillon as your liquid instead of tomato soup.

About Chicken Fat, Lard, and Bacon Drippings

These maligned fats have well-documented defenders. (I am with those who feel we eat far more fat than we should for the sedentary lives we lead, and that it is *fat*—particularly rancid and/or hydrogenated fats—one should go easy on, without picking on animal fat as a special culprit.)

Anyway, even anti-animal-fat arguers say some good things for chicken fat, and it is a good thing to use if you don't eat pork. It can be bought at kosher butchers. A little goes a long way, and it is a fine flavoring.

Lard (the unprocessed kind is very hard to find these days) is also a good cooking fat and can, unlike chicken fat, go into sweet dishes (such as pie crust).

Bacon drippings are fine for frying, browning meat, and other unsweet cookery. Be sure to refrigerate the bacon fat as soon as it is rendered. Do not let it sit around and become rancid—which it does very quickly on the back of the stove.

A Kind Word for Your Dog and Cat

Dog books I've read have pointed out that most dogs receive

less fat than they should in their diets. Apparently because people have to go easy on fat, it is assumed dogs must too, and dog diets are lower in the stuff than is really nice for the pups. The books recommend you give your normal-weight dog some extra fat. Mine get drippings, skimmings, and fresh beef (no uncooked pork) fat. My cats have had the same, and all have been healthy and full-coated.

Chicken

After I do my Ode to Eggs, I shall do one for chicken.

Chicken is the poor man's meat. It also is the dieter's meat, and the housewife's friend. It is nutritionally excellent; it is easy to prepare; and it can be prepared in so many ways one could eat it for a week at every meal and still not be bored.

Unless I roast or stew the chicken, I buy only the parts we like. In our case this is breasts. We do not eat the backs, necks, or legs with any great liking, so the slightly extra expense is compensated by not having anything hateful to eat. Since I have a generous freezer, I stock up on breasts when they are on special, which they frequently are.

Opinion varies about when chicken is done. I like it when the juice is still faintly pink and the meat still has a blush. My husband prefers it *thoroughly* done, with the juices yellowish and the meat almond-white. On a whole chicken one tests doneness in two ways: (1) by articulating the thigh muscle by wiggling the leg (if it moves easily, the chicken is done), (2) by cutting between the thigh and body and checking visually if the chicken is done.

Broiled or Fried Chicken Parts

This is the 20-minute supper or dinner that makes one wonder how convenient convenience foods really are.

Have: salt; pepper; spices; fat.

Buy: whatever chicken parts you like. Figure ½ pound of breast, ¾ pound of legs and thighs, per person.

Rinse and dry chicken. Place in your ovenproof frying pan or in an aluminum-foil baking dish under broiler, about 10 inches from flame. *Place skin side up (toward flame)*. Add 1 tablespoon of fat to pan. Broil 10 minutes. Salt, pepper, and season skin side. Turn skin side down and broil 10 more minutes. Season the underside, turn skin side up once more, and finish browning the skin. *Do not put the chicken too close to flame.* It will burn the skin without cooking the meat. The secret is to get the meat cooked and the skin brown at the same time.

Add a little water, sherry, white wine, or cream to the juices in the pan to serve with the broiled chicken.

Frying is much the same process. Fry in butter and oil mixed: skin side down first, meat side down, and skin down once more. Season as above.

I find that it is better to season chicken as one goes along, since it gives off a lot of juice which tends to "rinse' the seasoning off. Almost any spice enhances chicken: Oregano, marjoram, thyme, garlic, lemon, ginger, paprika—all in turn make fine chicken seasoning.

If you like poultry sweetened, try dissolving a tablespoon of apple, guava, or currant jelly in hot water, stirring it into the juices before serving.

Marinated Chicken (or Pork)

An excellent dish for those days when you have only a little time to fix dinner. It does, however, require planning ahead.

Have: soy sauce, sherry, or white wine; sugar or honey; (powdered ginger); (garlic); salt; pepper; oil.

Chicken and pork have many traits in common—a bland, delicate taste, a particular talent for going well with other foods. This dish is one of many in which one can substitute for the other *with the clear understanding that pork must be thoroughly cooked through and through, and cannot be tasted until done.*

Buy: those chicken parts you like best. Have the butcher chop them up into small (1½-inch) pieces for you, or get breasts, which are easy to bone and cut up.

Or buy lean pork and cut into neat slivers.

The night before, mix marinade: one-third oil, one-third soy sauce, one-third sherry or white wine. If the wine is dry, add a small amount of sugar or honey. Beat the sauce to mix it well. Pour over the meat, stir to cover all sides. Refrigerate. Stir and turn at least once more. Two or three times is better. You may notice that the sauce "expands" with time and becomes cloudy. This is the result of the meat yielding up its own juices and is perfectly all right.

At dinner time prepare quick-cooking rice according to directions. (If you are *not* in a hurry, make normal rice!) Heat ⅓ cup oil in your big frying pan, and after patting the meat dry on a paper towel, drop it into the pan piece by piece. Stir, and turn, working quickly so that the meat cooks on all sides without overcooking (more a worry with chicken than with pork).

When the meat is browned on all sides, lower the flame and add the whole marinade. Allow the sauce to cook at a slow simmer, until the chicken is almost cooked or the pork done. Turn the flame up and reduce the sauce as quickly as you can, stirring and turning the meat every few minutes.

An excellent dish to serve with canned or fresh Tofu* or Chinese or Japanese vegetables which can be heated up in the sauce.

If you like ginger and/or garlic, add them at the last minute before serving.

Variation: Use white wine, lemon juice, and oil as a marinade for chicken. Serve not with rice, but with richly buttered crisp French bread.

For the pork, try marinating it in pure cider that has been boiled down to half its volume and cooled before being used in a marinade.

---

*Tofu, or soy bean curd is a delicious food, and good for one as well. It can be bought canned, fresh, dried, and in powder form, like pudding. A Chinese or Japanese restaurant can tell you where to buy it, should no Asiatic grocery be handy.

Coq au Vin

This opens the door to an infinite number of dishes. It is simplicity itself, cheap, and perfectly lovely. Nobody agrees at all on how this is made, so feel absolutely free. The basic elements seem to be chicken (or capon, or rooster, but of course if you change the name you can use rabbit), wine (white or red or both), onion.

Have: 2 onions; 1 pint wine (*not* vermouth); butter; thyme or marjoram.

Buy: chicken; (vegetables).

The chicken must be cut into serving-size portions. Wash, dry. If you like, sprinkle the chicken gently with flour, as though you were talcuming a baby. Use rice flour, soy bean, or white. This is not necessary but will lead to a thicker sauce with more luxurious texture.

Method #1

Heat a generous amount of butter in your big frying pan. Brown the chicken on all sides in it. Remove chicken to a casserole. Add a little water or bouillon to the pan and stir to dissolve all the stuck-ons at the bottom. Pour the pan gravy into the casserole. Add onion, wine, salt, pepper, herbs. Cover and cook in slow oven for 1½ hours. Open, allow the sauce to cook away so that about ¾ cup remains—enough so each diner has a few spoons to mash a boiled potato in.

Method #2

Fry your chicken in a saucepan, removing done pieces to a plate while you fry the others. Add all ingredients as above to the saucepan, and cook on top of the stove. With this method you have only one pot to clean, but the chicken requires much closer watching and an occasional stir.

Variations: For #1 or #2.

Fry the onion (when you fry the chicken).

Add mushrooms.

Add mushrooms and tomatoes (or tomato spaghetti sauce).

Use wine and spaghetti sauce.

Add small carrots; peas and carrots; white onions; potatoes.

Add summer squash.

Add lima beans.

Tug Hill Chicken

The first weeks we had the farm we cooked on a gasoline stove, and we made this *a lot*. It probably has a fancy name in some fancy cookbook. As I noted elsewhere, one of the charms of inventing dishes is that one rarely invents them at all, just rediscovers some classic dish. And it always delights me when I've "invented" a classic—much as it delighted the Bourgeois Gentleman when he discovered he was speaking prose!

Have: salt; pepper; hot pepper; onion salt or powder; butter or bacon fat; (sherry or soy sauce).

Buy: 1 chicken breast per person, or 3 for two; 1 can condensed cheddar cheese soup *or* mushroom soup (*not* barley mushroom).

Heat just enough fat in your big frying pan to grease the bottom thoroughly. Rinse and dry the chicken breasts. Fry them slowly skin side down till the skin is golden. Turn them skin side up.

Open the soup and pour into a bowl. Beat with a fork, which makes it more liquid. Add sherry or soy sauce—about 2 tablespoons. Add enough water to make the soup a very thick liquid; about ½ cup is right for most brands. Pour soup over chicken and cook *slowly,* covered, 20 minutes. Season. Serve over rice.

Variations: Use condensed chicken noodle soup and serve with more noodles.

Serve over rice and peas mixed, or peas and carrots. The cheese-chicken is fine with cauliflower.

NOTE: Leftover sauce, diluted a bit more, is a fine soup for another day.

Lemon Chicken

A good, basically simple, summer dish.

The quantities here are figured for 4 large chicken breasts. Exactness is not important. What you are aiming at is boned chicken breasts neatly sitting in a small amount of rich, lemony sauce.

Have: 1 can chicken soup, or enough cubes to make 8 ounces chicken soup; salt; pepper; thyme; 2 egg yolks.

Buy: chicken breasts; fresh parsley; 2 large lemons; or 1 lemon plus some lemon juice.

Wash the chicken. Put into pot.

Wash lemon or lemons. You want ½ lemon to decorate the chicken with before serving. You want the yellow rind off the second half. So peel the lemon-half carefully, then squeeze its juice over the chicken. If you are using only fresh lemons, squeeze the juice of the second lemon over the chicken as well. If you are using prepared juice, add 2 tablespoons to the pot.

Add the 8 ounces of bouillon, 2 or 3 healthy sprigs of washed parsley, a pinch of thyme, salt and pepper. Have enough liquid to rise 2 inches in pot. Add water if necessary.

Cover the pot. Simmer for 20 minutes or until chicken is cooked.

Remove chicken. Refrigerate. Strain and measure the liquid. Taste. Add water (or dry white wine), or water mixed with lemon juice, to make 8 ounces. Taste again. Season. Cool. (If you have too much liquid, reduce, then cool.)

When the chicken soup is cool, beat 2 egg yolks into it. Beat good and hard so that the egg yolks are really dissolved. Heat gently—either over a double boiler, or on the tiniest flame you have—stirring constantly, scraping sides and bottom well. Do not allow to boil. As soon as the liquid thickens, remove from fire. *Do not go on cooking the sauce after it starts thickening. The heat of the pot will go on cooking it.* Keep on stirring for a minute after the pot is off fire.

Pour over the chicken breasts and chill thoroughly.

If you have time, or are putting on the dog, skin the chicken breasts and neatly (your fingers are the best tools) bone the breasts before pouring the sauce on. The meat may not come off in one piece, but that does not matter.

Chop up some more parsley—the leaves only, not the stems

—and sprinkle over the chicken just before serving. Cut the lemon half into slices, decorate the plate. (Have enough slices so each person can have one to squeeze over his portion.)

NOTE: What do you do with leftover whites? Unless you have a freezer and are saving up for an angel food cake, the simplest use for leftover whites is to have scrambled eggs the next day for breakfast and incorporate them. We do the same with leftover yolks.

13 / Fish: The Costliest Protein

It is a grave pity fish is so expensive, since it is one of the healthiest of foods. Most hearty eaters can consume a much larger portion of fish than of meat.　Two people can easily demolish a fish that—head, guts, tail, and all—weighed four pounds. And, even with fillets, one figures one pound per person, if nothing else of substance is included in the meal.

Even frozen fillets and fish steaks cost too much. Tuna is over a dollar per pound for the cheapest. Sardines, salmon, and so on all cost a lot. The only reasonably priced fish left is canned mackerel, whose somewhat oily flavor is similar to that of the cheaper sardines—the ones packed in tomato sauce or mustard.

If you are a fish lover—we are—you may have to limit your indulgence to eating fish when invited out to dinner, or to the rare occasions when fish is on special.

It used to be the fish lover had another resource—off to lake or beach or river with a line and hook. This, as you know, is no longer a safe procedure. Before you eat the fish you catch, you should check with a local authority, such as the Board of Health, to see that fish caught in those waters is safe to eat.

Composition of Foods indicates fish has a higher water, lower fat content, by and large, than meat. This may be the reason for the difference in satisfactory portion.

A second problem with fish is that it is troublesome to prepare. Fried fish—breaded or plain—is a delicacy. But the smell that frying fish produces is one of the most penetrating and lasting that can emanate from the kitchen. Unless you have a ventilated range hood or can run a whirlwind through the house once you are through frying, you *literally* risk having to dry-clean clothes or wash them to get the smell out. Breading fish (which means either dipping it in a batter, or first in beaten egg and then in flour) "stretches" it and saves money. But the smell of frying fish is a nuisance to be avoided.

There are a few products on the market which allow you to "fry" fish in the oven. I have tried them and find they have very little to contribute to the kitchen. Baked fish is very nice in its own right, and fried fish is too, and this hybrid process is not as good, and costlier, than either.

On to buying fish.

Most of what you can get is frozen packaged fish. Those of you in seaports or large cities *should be able* to get fresh fish. *But do not think that because a fish has head and tail it is fresh.* It may have been frozen in its lifelike entirety, and defrozen by the fishmonger. And the fish lying filleted and loose may also have been frozen and then defrozen by the seller. The only way to be sure is to stick the fish in a bowl of water. If it floats, it's fresh. There is little one can *do* about it, except to check out whether the fishmonger tells the truth. Frozen fish is not as good as fresh. There are no two ways about it.

Assuming you find a fresh fish—it should look healthy. Its skin should be a bit sticky, but not at all slimy, its gills will be bright red—actually anything between orange and liver red, but *bright*. Its eyes will be convex and sincerely shiny. And above all, there will be almost no smell. This is no fooling. People often are prejudiced against fish because of the offensive smell of fish markets. This strong smell is the smell of decaying fish, and unpleasant it certainly is. But a fresh fish smells slightly marine, and that is *all*.

Fish is sold in three ways: *whole*, in which case you pay for the head, tail, fins, and generally guts, which are weighed in; *steaks,* available only for bigger fish, which are slices cut perpendicularly through the spine (and you do pay for the skin and that bit of bone); and *fillets,* pure meat, cut lengthwise along the spine, after the removal of the skin.

For baking, steaks are prettier, because easier to serve. For frying, steaks are tastier, because thicker (fillets are *unavoidably* thin). But generally fillets are cheapest, because the fish is filleted before shipping and the saving in transportation offsets the originally higher cost.

Fresh fish should be rinsed once or twice in water to which lemon juice or vinegar has been added. Frozen fish can be used as is.

About raw fish: Check your local health department. As excellent as raw fish is, I am wary of it, and do not eat fish or shellfish without checking first that it is safe.

Baked Fish

Buy: 1 pound fish for two people. Get cod, flounder, or haddock. Any lean fish is fine, but these are generally the cheapest.

Have: butter; lemon juice; salt; pepper; thyme or marjoram; oil.

Heat the oven as hot as possible for at least 10 minutes before the fish goes in. You want this heat in order to evaporate instantly the water the fish gives off in cooking.

Rinse the fish as above; pat dry with paper towels.

Choose a heavy baking dish; your big fireproof-handled frying pan is fine. If you use foil, line the foil pan with heavy-gauge foil.

Pour enough oil into the pan to coat the bottom generously. Tilt the pan, and pour back any excess above a teaspoon. Place the fish in the pan; season with a sprinkle of pepper and thyme; place in the oven. After 7 minutes for filets or 10 for steaks, test for doneness, as follows.

Remove the pan from the oven, take a wooden toothpick or a wooden match whittled to a fine point, and stick it in the middle of the fish. Push down gently so you can look into the fish. Raw fish has a translucent, pinkish look. As fish cooks, it becomes opaque much as egg white does. Cooked fish looks milky, totally opaque. For *fish steaks*, stick the toothpick near the spine to check. If the fish separates easily from the bone, it is cooked. For *whole fish*, poke the toothpick gently parallel to the spine at the back. If the bone is loose, the fish is done.

Most people overcook fish. So test too early rather than too late. The fish will go on cooking a while out of the oven, as long as it remains in your hot pan.

If the fish is not quite done when you test, return to the oven and turn off the heat. Let the fish cook another minute or two before rechecking.

Never check fish or anything else that is baking without removing the whole pan from the oven. Tilting things on an oven shelf is a good way to get a serious burn.

While the fish is cooking, you can prepare a sauce—mustard or horseradish, or simply melt two or three inches of butter off a ¼-pound stick in a saucepan. Do it over as low a flame as possible; if there is room in your oven, do it in the oven. When the butter is melted, but not the least brown, remove from heat and beat in 1 tablespoon of lemon juice and a bit of salt. Pour over each portion of fish as you serve it.

This baked fish is quite bland and best served with mashed or boiled potatoes.

Variations

1. Marinate the fish in white wine or soy sauce, or white wine and soy sauce, before cooking. Bake in the marinade.

2. Get a can of chile sauce—not the stuff that is bottled like ketchup, but the mix of peppers and tomatoes used in Latin cooking. Bake the fish in the sauce. Particularly good for fat fish, the tuna-bonito-mackerel family.

Chowder

In case you've wondered, the dictionary says this comes from the French *chaudière*, a cooking pot. Why is this not under soups?

Because a true chowder is a fish stew, a main course, and not the thin pap available in cans or restaurants. I first tasted real chowder at the home of a Vermonter whose ancestors came from the shore. What a revelation!

Buy: 2 pounds flounder, or cod, or haddock; or 1½ pounds dried salt cod (see below); 2 to 4 boiling potatoes; 2 large onions; 1 quart milk.

Have: 2 or 3 slices of bacon or a piece of salt pork about 2 by 2 inches; salt; pepper; celery salt; (soup greens); butter.

Wash the fish if fresh. Thaw at least partially if frozen. Peel and chop the onion. Cut the salt pork or bacon into small pieces. Place the pork in your large saucepan and heat very gently to render the fat. When the fat starts to accumulate, add the onions and fry to a golden brown. Meanwhile peel and slice your potatoes. The slices should be as thin as possible. If you have a peeler, use it for slicing the spuds.

Add the potatoes to the frying pork and onions. Do it carefully. Whenever you add anything wet to hot fat, the fat sputters and can cause bad burns. Stir the lot so the potatoes get browned a bit. Add a little extra fat if necessary.

With your fingers, tear the fish into small chunks. Add them to the pot and go on stirring. Do this over a slow flame, and be prepared to add a bit of butter or bacon fat if anything looks like it might scorch. Stir enough to "circulate" the ingredients. The fish soon will start giving up its own juice. Now start adding your milk a bit at a time. As you have guessed, the starch from the potatoes makes a binder for the milk, and a very thin white sauce. Add the dried soup greens if you have them. Cook *below* boiling till the potatoes are done and the fish is totally opaque. Season with salt, pepper, and celery salt. Serve in bowls with a good pat of butter afloat in each.

NOTE: The reason for slicing the potatoes so thin is to be sure they cook without the fish overcooking.

This dish does not take much over 20 minutes to make. But it does require attention. After the addition of the milk it should not boil, or the milk will most likely separate. Not a tragedy, but not as pretty.

Variation: Use clam juice to cook with; or use the liquid from a can of chopped clams as part of your liquid, adding the clams at the last minute. You can of course, you lucky thing, add lobster and/or shrimp. Or add cream.

Chowder II

Fish stews are found wherever there are fishermen. And the chowder given below is the Mediterranean type, called Bouillabaisse or Sopa de Pescada in fancier books. But it is essentially a fish stew. When meats such as sharp sausages and chicken are added, it becomes a *paella,* which is essentially a fish and meat stew, seasoned with saffron and served on a bed of rice.

The only "trouble" with this type of chowder is that it cannot be made in small quantities. I've never managed to make it for less than six as a main course. If one likes the dish as much as I do, the leftover problem is quickly solved: it reheats perfectly the next day!

Buy: as wide an assortment of lean fish as possible: pike, sea bass, cod—any seagoing fish is fine. Go very easy on (or omit) mackerel, tuna, sardines, or other "fat fish." These have a very strong flavor and will dominate your stew quite unpleasantly.

Assemble your fish for variety. Be shameless: ask the man for usable scraps—the hard-to-sell tail off the cod, the lonely perch—whatever he has that can go cheap.

If you buy only cleaned fish, ask for a few heads, tails, and spines.

If you can get cleaned squid and octopus, buy some too.

Also buy: a #2 can of tomatoes, preferably the Italian (pear-shaped) kind, or 2 pounds of tomatoes; (canned peas); (soup greens).

Have: (olive) oil; garlic; (soup greens); a bouillon cube; basil; onion; a bay leaf; salt; pepper; parsley.

Wash your fish and sort it. All heads and tails and bones go into a pot, are covered with water and cooked for a good half hour.

Take the rest of the fish and cut or break into smallish chunks.

In your large saucepan heat ½ cup of oil—olive preferred. Drop in 4 or 5 cloves of peeled garlic. (Smack the garlic hard with something like a can or the side of a cleaver, and the skin comes off easily.) Keep an eye on the oil. When the garlic is browned on both sides, the oil is hot enough so you can add the onion—chopped or quartered—and the fish. Drop everything in, give a good stir or two, then add your tomatoes or, if the tomatoes are fresh, tomatoes plus 2 cups of water. Add soup greens if you have them, a bay leaf, a bouillon cube, ½ teaspoon basil (or two fresh leaves), and pepper.

Cover the pot and let simmer very gently for 20 minutes.

Meanwhile strain the liquid from the head-and-tail pot and add to your main chowder.

Authenticity fiends cook head and bones together with the main soup. I *never* do, because the result is a dish that is no fun to eat. It stops all table talk because everyone is busy picking bones out of his mouth. If you are very frugal, you can pick usable meat off the head and tail bones and add them to your main chowder too. Anyway, I just add the liquid.

Variations

1. Add mussels and clams; canned is easier. (See note below.)

2. Add saffron. Saffron—the pistil of some rare flower that has to be hand-picked—is worth its weight in gold. Fortunately the pistils are light, and two or three add flavor to a whole dish. Use only a pinch; it is very strong. If you prefer, put the pistils in a spoon with a flameproof handle (and bowl of course) and hold over a flame till the saffron darkens. I have never found much difference in flavor between toasted and untoasted saffron, but some cookbooks swear by the toasting.

3. Add leftover chicken with or without broth. Add leftover ham. Cut meats small.

4. Serve with rice, Spanish rice, or pasta (the small shapes are best).

5. Serve with lavish amounts of toasted, buttered Italian bread.

Dried Salt Cod

Bacalao, as it is called in the Puerto Rican stores, comes in several qualities. Bonier and saltier is cheaper. It also comes in neat little boxes much like those that dominoes, or cigars, come in. This is the way you find it at supermarkets. Any salt cod is perfectly usable instead of fresh, but certainly not cheaper. Especially because it is a lot of work.

Dried salt cod must be rehydrated and rinsed. The night before using it, cover the fish with cold water, and change the water three or four times. Every hour or so. Change by lifting the fish out of the water; don't pour the water over the fish, or you will be dousing it with all the salt that you have painstakingly soaked out. Leave the bowl with the fish in the sink overnight under a tiny trickle of cold water. Next day taste the water at the *bottom* of the bowl. If it is still salty, you must rinse the fish some more. When you are satisfied the fish is rinsed enough, you can use it in a chowder, bake it in oil, or just plain cook it in a small amount of water, and serve with oil into which some fresh garlic has been crushed.

NOTE: No matter what you do, the fish will remain very salty. That is why I use it only in chowders and omit all salt.

Mussels and Clams

Once upon a time you could go to any beach without a *No Trespassing* sign, and dig and dive for clams and mussels. Last year on the outer frontiers of Canada I dug oysters with a friend, and we both commented that we might be the last generation able to do so.

The waters have become so polluted, I warn you *not* to eat clams or mussels or oysters off the beach without first checking the local authorities to ask if their mollusks are safe to eat.

When you buy at a fishmonger's, you are taking some chance. But professional fishermen are in it for a living, and the Coast Guard *inter al.* tells them where the shellfish are safe. I think they stick to the guidelines pretty well.

After pollution, the big problem with clams and mussels is sand. Clams are very sandy. After you get them, and check that each shell is closed tight as a clam, soak the clams in cold water to which salt and some cornmeal have been added. Scrub the clams with a stiff brush, and soak in two or three changes of water (always with the salt and meal, which help catch the sand). Soak at least an hour each time; preferably give the clams a last soak of several hours.

You can add clams directly to your dish, or place them in a saucepan alone, cover, heat slowly till they open, then add to the main dish (it is customary to add the shell too, leaving the clam inside), and strain the juice they relinquish, when they open, into the main dish.

To strain: line a strainer with filter paper, a paper towel, a piece of clean unbleached muslin, or the like. Anything that will catch the sand.

Mussels frequently come equipped with a "beard" of tiny shells and seaweed. Also a "dead" mussel shell may be sealed tightly around a shellful of sand. So first rinse the mussels, then pull off the beards and test the edge of each mussel with a knife.

After the scrubbing, proceed as with clams, though you do not have to soak them more than an hour or two. Around here they are much cleaner.*

Fish Loaf

You've wondered when I'd come along with a recipe from my mother. Here it is, a staple of my childhood diet and a staple of my current one.

It can be eaten hot or cold, and it makes a fine sandwich filling, particularly on rye bread with mayonnaise, mustard, and/ or ketchup. It is also fairly quick to prepare. As with a meatloaf, you can make the mix the night before.

Buy: 2 pounds of flounder fillets or cod fillets.

Have: butter; eggs; stale white bread or wheat germ or cracker crumbs; salt; pepper; onions; parsley.

---

*How dirty mollusks are seems to depend on variety and region. The point is that one must get all the sand out or it will spoil the food.

Preheat the oven to 350°F. Boil a little water.

Peel and chop the onion. Soak 2 or 3 slices of white bread, or ½ or ¾ cup crumbs, in a little milk. Fry the onions to a golden color in 2 tablespoons butter. Place fish in your pan and add 1 cup of boiling water. (Never add cold water to a hot pan; that way lies accelerated warping.) There should be enough water to go ½ inch deep in the pan. Cover, and let the fish steam 5 minutes. It does not have to be cooked through and through. Just cooked enough so you can mash it all up. Place fish and crumbs, bread, or wheat germ in a bowl with the water, onions, and all, and let cool. When you can touch it comfortably, knead in 2 eggs, 1 teaspoon parsley, 1/2 teaspoon salt, and pepper. Mix well, and pack loosely in a foil pan. Bake till a knife comes out clean and the top is golden brown.

Serve with mashed or boiled potatoes, topped with a bit more fried onion.

Variation: Use 1 pound canned mackerel instead of the second pound of fish. Pick the bones out first, and use the liquid as some of your cooking water.

Tuna

I refuse to believe that any American child doesn't know how to mix tuna with mayonnaise and a bit of celery to make tuna salad.

But I must include a perfectly awful dish (soothing though) that was very popular after World War II. So many of us were so happy in that naive, idealistic, and now-much-maligned era, that we smile at the mere mention of it. *Tuna fish casserole* is to us what *pizza* may someday be to you. So I include it.

A thick white sauce is made, or canned mushroom soup (not barley mushroom, but plain cream of) is used with only half the dilution called for on the can. Drained tuna is mashed into this and mixed with about 2 cups of boiled noodles per can of fish. Sometimes, drained canned peas are added. The mix is placed in a greased ovenproof dish and baked till golden brown. *Pace!*

Boiled Fish

This goes for any lean fish.

Make a court bouillon by cooking a generous portion of soup greens for 30 minutes in water. (A court bouillon has nothing to do with kings, or judges, but with shortcuts: it is a fake bouillon, or *short*cut one, made with vegetables only.)

You can use dry white wine (vermouth is okay) or wine and water as your liquid. Place the cleaned fish in a frying pan, pour the strained liquid over it, adding a bit more liquid if the liquid is not ½ inch deep in the pan. Cover lightly, and cook as slowly as you can, checking every five minutes for doneness.

Not an exciting dish, but excellent with a Mornay sauce, or a white sauce enhanced by capers, or tarragon, or mustard, or (cold) with *aïoli*.

14 / Vegetables and Fruit: Summer Soldiers, Winter Luxuries

I've had a miserable time getting into this chapter, because the whole area of produce, farming, and the cities triggers the Cassandra in me, and I find myself lecturing on organic gardening and alternate life styles, and on how our scientific megalomania will ultimately reduce us to cretins. Our bodies cannot mutate and evolve at the pace required by what our computer-aided brains concoct. (Even if we could, would we be *better*? And surely, in this age of destruction, that is the only issue.) We must accept that bread goes stale; fats turn rancid; healthy fruit may shelter a worm. We cannot go on assuming that just because something was invented by well-intentioned men, it is good; that just because thousands have not died on the spot from additive X, thousands won't suffer dreadfully in twenty years because they ingested the stuff in infancy and the reaction is a delayed one.

But this is not the place to lecture.

What I want to tell you is that almost everything you find in the shops—particularly in cities with no nearby vegetable farms —has been mutated, cross-bred, hormonized, sprayed, and chemically fertilized, *not for nutritional value, but for uniformity of size, long shelf life, prettiness, and endurance through cold storage and travel.* Many delicious varieties of vegetable—such as the fragile Boston or Bibb lettuces, and the "ugly" romaines—are hard to find, although they're better sources of vitamin A and much finer in flavor than the ubiquitous iceberg varieties. The ever-present McIntosh apple has only one-fourth or one-fifth the vitamin C of the rare Northern Spy or Baldwin. And so on.

Some fruit varieties have been abandoned commercially because they do not ripen all their fruit at once but require the harvesters to make two or more trips through the orchard!

If the breeders and growers are to blame, it is only to the limited extent of giving in to pressures. It is the public that is at fault for allowing itself to believe that one can have everything for nothing. As my husband says, one not only gets what one pays for, but *someone* always pays for what one gets!

The most miserable part of the scientific delusion is that the public was not only promised perfect, even-sized, brightly colored fruit and vegetables at any and all seasons, and in any and all locales, but that they were told it would be *cheap.*

But a single trip to a greengrocer in winter shows you tomatoes costlier than chicken breasts, or a mingy salad "worth" four or five eggs!

Because our problem is the same as that of poor countries—enough calories but not enough protein—we must concentrate on protein in our food buying.

This is easily done, since for one to fifteen cents a day you can get all the vitamins (and minerals) you want or need. Cost depends on whether one takes multi-vitamins put out by the large pharmaceutical houses, or individual one-per-vitamin pills made by small manufacturers from organic or natural sources. Size of dosage makes less of a price difference than manufacturer or source.

Do I suggest not a leaf pass your lips all winter? Never! Loss of pleasure alone forbids that. But I think you might eat all the produce you can in summer, making vegetables (along with milk) your main source of carbohydrates, and cut back in winter.

I am convinced we are much better adapted to seasonal eating patterns than we have been led to believe. We are, after all, descended from hunters, fishermen, and fruit gatherers, and no doubt our genetic patterns reflect their realities. I think climate control and uniform year-round diet have done nothing for us and may yet be found to account for the rise in tension diseases, which reflect *something* amiss in what we are doing to our bodies.

But no matter my opinion. If you plan *any* major change in your diet—like turning vegetarian on the one hand, or going on an all-protein diet on the other—*consult a physician specialized in nutrition.*

Speaking of vegetarians: vegetarians are not immune to vitamin deficiencies, and particularly those who drink alcohol may need supplements in the B family. Check with a good doctor.

NOTE: *My fruits-and-vegetables-last-in-off-season stance excludes legumes, raw nuts, and seeds, which are high in protein and a good value.*

Off to the greengrocer's!

A vegetable or fruit is *a living thing.* Once cut from its root or picked off the tree, it begins to die. Careful storage can delay this sad decline, to a very limited extent only.

So the first criterion in produce-buying is to learn to recognize that fresh, healthy, vital look—exactly what you seek when buying flowers.

Greens, such as lettuce, endive, celery, string beans, watercress, should be crisp and their fibers brittle. Some greens, such as Bibb lettuce (!), are rather limp by nature, but the fibrous part of the leaf—its veins—are brittle and crisp when fresh. A bean should not bend, but break with a snap. (Hence the name "snap bean" which is used instead of "string bean" by many people.) Celery should be inflexible. The more and the thicker the fibers, the more rigid the leaves. A lettuce leaf should pull off the head with a crisp sound, nothing like the whirr of a tissue being pulled from a dispenser box.

Color may vary, but the fresher the vegetable the more radiant the color—the closer to spring, the farthest from fall.

As vegetables lie about the greengrocer's shop, he is likely to do three bad things to them. The first cannot be helped: he exposes them to light. But sprinkling them with water—to give a dewy look and revive flagging spirits—destroys vitamins. And trimming off outer leaves that "have had it" is plain deception.

Let's go back to lettuce (and such) a moment. These vegetables grow around a "core" or "heart" much the way roses do. The core is smack above the root or stem. The outer leaves are lower down on the stem, darker in color, and more heavily veined than the inner leaves. The outer leaves (which are formed earlier in the growth of the plant) also fade first. And the greengrocer is likely to pull them off, exposing more and more stem. If you turn a lettuce upside down, you should see an earth-stained scar flush with the outer leaves. If the scar at the bottom is very clean, the greengrocer may well have trimmed the stem to hide the fact that he's removed leaves. The lettuce may be on its last legs.

The big exception to the "outer leaves should be there" is cabbage. The outer leaves of cabbage are so tough and fibrous that even romantics feed them to poultry and pigs.* cabbage, by the way, comes in three varieties: *white* or *green,* which are almost identical, and best known in this country; *red,* actually purple, and used in German or Scandinavian cooking; and *savoy,* a little-known, curly-leaved, somewhat loose-headed, bright green variety. Broccoli and brussels sprouts are cabbages too, but different rules apply. *Broccoli* should be crisp and dark green, without a trace of yellow in the buds. (Some broccoli are purplish at the buds, which is okay; just make sure there's no yellow. Yellow indicates too-long-in-the-field, beginning to bloom.) Brussels sprouts should be tightly wrapped, hard, firm. You should be unable to pull off a leaf without tearing it.

Smaller greens, such as watercress, parsley, scallions, are also selected for their fresh look and bright color. An easy way to tell how long they've been lying around is to check the tightness of the string that holds them in bunches. These strings are put on

---

*Even organically raised cabbage has to be trimmed of its outer leaves, which are the likeliest to be attacked by cabbage worms.

by the wholesaler or grower, and as some of the bunch gives up the ghost, the greengrocer is likely to pull out the dead leaves. But he will not rewrap the string, and a slack string warns you not to buy!

Root Vegetables and Potatoes

While we *all* know the potato is not a root vegetable, we will put it here because it shares so many root characteristics.

All carrots, turnips, parsnips, radishes, beets, and potatoes should be firm, crisp, and smell good. The skin should be free of slime and unbroken. Mushiness, dullness, wrinkling, or flexibility indicates old age. From a nutritional point of view this is not as bad here as with leafy vegetables, because root vegetables are never very strong in the perishable vitamin area. (Beet and turnip tops or greens are far richer in vitamins than the roots.) Caloric value is undiminished by storage, and the older turnips and beets and carrots can be well used in soups and stews.

You will occasionally find turnips—particularly rutabagas—covered with paraffin. Since all the root vegetables seem to age by dehydration and lose both looks and texture, the paraffin is applied to prevent evaporation. I have never heard any reason not to use the coated turnips, but they must, of course, be peeled.

Potatoes come in a number of shapes, sizes, and even colors —red, white, and yellowish—but basically one buys them either for boiling or for baking. The boiling varieties are also used in stews, for home fries, mashed potatoes, and so on. The baking type is purely for baking. Potatoes should be smooth, and while a few dark spots are permissible, eyes or sprouts are not. Green potatoes have been improperly stored and should not be used.

Turnip tops, beet tops (or greens), mustard greens, collards, dandelion greens, chicory, Swiss chard, spinach are all excellent vegetables.* The last three, when *picked* young, are lovely raw, in salads. The trouble is that, except for spinach, these greens

---

*There seems to be evidence that fertilizer and/or pesticides leave dangerous residues in the leaves of some vegetables. My adjective *excellent* is limited to the vegetable itself, and not to the "additives" that may be in it.

are, I gather, considered *ethnic foods* or regional ones. In New York City chicory and dandelion greens are found only in Italian stores, and the others in black and/or Puerto Rican areas. But if you find them, use 'em. They are delicious.

Tomatoes

One can wax Proustian or Nabokovian about the tomatoes of one's youth, those globes of acidulous sweetness that burst beneath one's teeth, bringing shrieks from nearby adults about spots on one's pinafore. . . . I thought tomatoes like that were gone with the fine, dry, sunny, laughing summers of my childhood, till I rediscovered them in the garden of friends. Lately I have grown some of my own, which is chancy, as the Tug Hill climate is pretty poor.

When I am in town I wait till the end of summer, when Italian shops are likely to have home-grown tomatoes. These can be recognized by their irregular shape, bright color, and dustiness. In many towns there are nearby gardeners who raise tomatoes, and generally it is not too hard to find some good ones for sale.

Quite frankly, I never buy the hothouse or boxed or crated tomatoes, unless in a fit of wastefulness. For cooking I use either frozen tomatoes,* canned ones, or juice.

If you *must* buy tomatoes, all the rules for fruit selection apply.

Eggplant, Squash, Cucumbers, and Such

These are all mysterious plants, seductive in shape and color, delicious when good, and terribly hard to choose well; so any magic

---

*I have never frozen whole tomatoes, which I hear can be done. We quarter fresh, good tomatoes, cook quickly into a stew, strain, and freeze in ice cube trays. The cubes are then deep-frozen in plastic bags, to be used whenever tomato is called for.

applies. They all should be tight in their skins, free of bruises, with a clean, dry stem scar and a good color. But there is no guarantee that the meat inside won't taste spongy or wooden.

Eggplants are "safer" when small. The large ones may have been on the vine too long. The operative word is *may*. (I have grown delicious huge eggplants.) The same goes for the rest of the lot. Too-slow growth (an unfavorable summer) or too-long-on-the-vine may have overripened the big ones.

Cucumbers are sold in two varieties: the smallish, rounder *pickling* ones, which are generally sold fully ripe, *that is,* almost yellow, and the *salad* kind, which are sold when dark green (still) and are frequently waxed, to prevent dehydration. If the cuke looks awfully shiny, peel it before using.

The summer squash—yellow and green varieties both—are more likely to be good if small. They should be hard, have a dead ring when you hit them, and fit tightly into their skins. Summer squash, by the way, is the *vegetable marrow* of British novels, in case you've wondered.

Winter squash is meant to be stored. And while some are better than others, I have never really found a bad one—unless damaged in shipping, which shows on the outside.

Onions come in two major varieties: sweet, and regular or cooking. The sweet—Spanish, salad, hamburger, Bermuda—can be white or purple and are for eating raw. They are very large, sometimes weighing a pound each, costlier than the cooking onion, and like all onions do not keep well once cut into. If you buy one and cannot use it all at once, use the leftover in cooking. The purple ones stain, so avoid putting them in "pale" dishes.

There are a number of varieties of cooking onions, mostly with ochre, pale rust, or manilla-envelope-colored skins. Onions are cheap, and medium-sized ones have the best flavor. In onions "medium size" is about that of an egg or lemon.

From Thanksgiving to New Year's very small white onions are sold, for cooking as creamed onions. Delicious as these are, they are expensive. Be careful that the greengrocer does not substitute small-sized cooking onions for these white ones, or give (and charge you for) the creaming onions when you agreed to smaller regular ones.

Never buy a sprouting onion. If you buy a bagful and get one sprouter, okay, use it first, and quickly. But an onion loses flavor when it sprouts, and you should avoid any onions showing even a bit of green at the top.

All I have said about vegetables seems ominous. There are so many varieties, and it takes time to learn the signs of quality. But since you are unlikely to like *all* varieties, you will soon discover how to select the best of the kinds you like. I repeat again and once more—and not for the last time—use your nose, your hands, and your eyes—particularly your nose.

Fruit

All of the above applies as well to fruit.

The rosy-cheeked look has been bred into so many varieties that totally unripe or already spoiling fruit still bears the blush of health.

On the other hand, aroma is not deceptive. Hold a fruit in your cupped hands for a moment. A slow count of 30 is fine. Then see what it smells like, and decide whether to buy.

Pinching fruit, that classical "method" of selection, releases some juices, and thus some fragrance. But it really destroys the fruit, so don't pinch even a peach you've decided to buy, unless you are going to eat it on the spot.

Apples are best brought small or medium-sized. Biggies tend to be pulpy. Except for the small, speckled brass-colored eating apples I know only as *goldens*, and a few cooking apples such as Romes and pippins, most apples are shiny, with a very satiny skin. I distrust *too* shiny apples. If the man's had time to polish them, his shop's not busy. If business is slow, the merchandise is, quite likely, stale.

Cooking apples are the ones used in baking and for sauce. They are less juicy, more meaty, but should not taste floury. They should be very hard and crisp, something like a raw potato. In cooking apples "medium size" is fairly large—about the size of a tennis ball. Cooking-apple varieties bear huge fruit.

Believe it or not, I have nothing to say about pears. It's been years since I've bought a good pear at market. What we have gotten has been watery, hard, tasteless, and a waste of money. We have, in fall, bought some small pears (mostly Seckels) at roadside stands, and I have canned these; they are superb. In town we stick to buying dried pears. But criteria for pear selection are the same as for apples.

Oranges are of two kinds: the eating and the juicing kind. The eating orange has a thick, spongy skin, and is relatively fibrous, so you can easily divide it into sections. The eating orange may or may not be seedless. The skin, although spongy, should be tight. The juice orange is not as pretty. It has a thin, tight, rather shiny skin and a not-so-pretty color. Sometimes the skin has streaky wooden lines, which never seem to affect flavor. I like to eat juice oranges, because of their juiciness, and cut them much like grapefruit.

Grapefruit and *lemons* also come in thick-and thin-skinned varieties. The thin-skinned are smaller in both cases.

Tangelos and *tangerines* may or may not fit snugly into their skins. I have seen some with skins as loose as a hound's that have been fine and tasty, and some with tight shiny skins that have been wooden inside.

I must confess I've never found an infallible way of telling the quality of citrus. The skin is so aromatic, one's nose is not much help as a guide to the inside. Perhaps there is no real way, which would explain why so many fruit vendors exhibit halved citrus to show the customers what's inside. My advice is to bring your penknife and peel and eat an orange on the spot before buying a lot. With grapefruit I don't bother because we only buy one or two at a time anyway, and if it is pulpy it can always be broiled (about five minutes, with a teaspoon of honey atop).

At the height of summer *peaches* and *plums* become abundant. For some ever-puzzling reason, peaches arrive rocky and unripe and the plums on their last legs. Both come in a variety of shapes and colors. A good peach or plum is firm and strongly perfumed. Neither should be soft and squooshy. Look in the plums' basket. If there's a lot of brown mush and traces of moisture, they are likely to be overripe and you are seeing traces of the dear departed.

The safest fruit to buy is the banana! Here skin color really indicates ripeness, and ripeness is 98 percent synonymous with flavor. The commercial "when they are flecked with brown and have a golden hue" speaks true, but what you possibly did not know is how well the banana compares with the apple for vitamin content.

Banana, mango, and papaya are the only fruits I've ever "met" that really do ripen after you get them home. They are the only fruits I buy unripe.

Yes, there are red bananas, and sheer bliss they are too, but rare in Northern climes. Cooking bananas, huge green things called *plantains,* are hard, green, and ugly, and baked with sugar and butter too good for words. In New York plantains are only found in shops frequented by Southerners or Latin Americans.

How to Buy Fruit

I confess to a *frisson* of anxiety. Even if you follow my every word, you will from time to time have a fiasco. So do I. And the person who claims to be infallible in fruit selection is, I think, not to be trusted!

1. *Find a good store and stick to it.* There *are* stores *and* supermarkets that take pride in good, fresh produce. Do not be seduced away by "bargains." Support your local honest merchant!

2. *Unwrap plastic trays!* If you must shop where all fruit and vegetables come prewrapped by the store in plastic, *unwrap.* You cannot sniff fruit, or check for bruises unless you do. You have every right to examine and check what you are buying. You also are under no obligation to take four apples just because four come wrapped up together and there is nothing smaller. You can take only what you want. *You should not do this* with produce

wrapped by the grower, who has printed the quantity on the wrapper, or where your unwrapping makes the contents unsalable.*

3. *Turn little baskets upside down into paper bags.* Berries and small items such as cherry tomatoes and brussels sprouts frequently are sold in small baskets, with the prettiest on the top. Have a good look at what's below before you buy.

4. *Buy only what's in season.* Use newspaper ads and columns as an indication. Be wary. Shoppers' guides and weekend bargain columns often are pure PR for local growers or stores. They reflect bargains, not necessarily quality.

Preparation of Fruits and Vegetables

1. Unwrap, wash, dry, and store in cool, dark place. Do this as rapidly as possible.

2. Peeling and scraping are a problem. On the one hand, the peel or skin contains a lot of the more important nutrients. On the other, spraying mainly contaminates the skin, and the loss of vitamins is less of a threat to you than the presence of poisons. I peel commercial fruit, but never the organically grown. Bigger turnips and carrots and beets must be scraped; the younger are quite edible in their paper-thin skins.

Whatever scraping, peeling, and dicing needs to be done, do it as close to cooking and eating time as possible. Peel fruit at the table.

3. The secret of cooking vegetables is to do it quickly, with a minimum of water. Never throw out the water. Save it to drink cold for breakfast; with an added bouillon cube, hot, with dinner; or use it in making soup or stew. *Never* let vegetables or fruit sit in water.

---

*There are people who unwrap meats and substitute the wrappings of a cheap cut for those of a costly one, thus giving themselves fraudulent bargains. With meat it takes an expert to identify a cut. And if you unwrap but do not buy, you must return the package to a clerk for rewrapping. But with fruit anyone can tell what's what, and if anyone grumbles at your open-and-look technique, grumble back and buy elsewhere.

Cooking Vegetables

1. *Ideal for spinach, chicory, beet or turnip greens–any of the thin-leaved vegetables.*

Pour a tablespoon of oil in your bigger frying pan. Add a shake of garlic salt. Just before you are ready to serve, heat the pan, drop the leafy vegetable into the pan, stir so all the leaves wilt. Add a few spoons of water if necessary, go on stirring, and when the leaves are totally wilted, serve. This whole process takes about two minutes.

2. *For cabbage, Chinese cabbage, broccoli, and vegetables that require more than a few seconds to cook.*

My second choice (after eating these raw) is to put them in a stew or omelet, so I do not have to worry about losing vitamins in the cooking water.

If I cook these alone, I heat a pan and add some fat as above, omit the garlic, and after stir-fry-cooking the vegetable half a minute or so, add ½ cup of bouillon to cook for a few more minutes. Ideally the bouillon evaporates, but if not, it is fine to drink. Five minutes is the outside cooking time for any but root vegetables or big potatoes.

3. Root vegetables such as potatoes and parsnips and turnips really should be cooked in stews. Otherwise give them 1 inch or so of water, and boil lidded at top speed till a knife stabs in easily. A pressure cooker is a great vitamin- and time-saver here. Potato water (from peeled potatoes, please) is ideal to mix with dry milk powder for any yeast baking.

Ratatouille

This lovely recipe—as good hot as cold—is a summer favorite. It uses a bit of this and that, and is most versatile.

Assemble: a few ripe tomatoes (not overripe); an eggplant; onions; summer squash or zucchini; a fistful of fresh parsley, preferably Italian; a lemon.

Have: olive oil; a clove or two of garlic; salt; pepper; (grated cheese).

Peel your tomatoes. Either impale them on a long-handled fork and hold over a flame, peeling off the blistered skin, or dip in boiling water for a minute, dip in ice water, and then peel.

Heat ¼ cup of olive oil in your big frying pan, and fry two cloves of peeled garlic till they are brown. Remove the garlic. To the *slowly* cooking oil add your tomatoes, and slice in your onion and squash. (Zucchini does not need peeling, but summer squash does, so peel it first.) Let these vegetables cook themselves down into a purée, stir them a lot, add more oil if necessary. Remove them to another dish.

Peel and dice the eggplant. Heat a little more oil in your pan, and fry the eggplant over a high flame till it is browned on all sides. Lower flame immediately, return other vegetables to the pan, and cook a few minutes longer. Taste. Add salt and pepper.

If you serve this hot, sprinkle with chopped parsley, and give everyone a slice of lemon to put on. Or omit lemon and give 'em grated cheese.

If you serve it cold (preferably the day after making it), mix the chopped parsley in after the dish is cold, and add the lemon juice straight to the salad.

Green Salads

What goes into a salad is almost infinite in variety, and I for one like the American salads that incorporate fruit with the greens. It is a bit harder for me to get used to salads that have a fistful of seeds, raisins, or wheat germ tossed in, but I think that is more the dictate of my mind than of my palate.

As a friend of mine said, tossing a whole bunch of parsley into a salad, where I would have used a twig or two: *In a salad anything goes!*

You can use commercial dressings, preferably those from the health food store. But it is so much cheaper to mix your own, even if you resort to packets of mixed spices to give "French" or "Italian" flavor.

Ciceil's Dressing: How Simple, How Good!

Ceil mixes all her (washed, well-dried) greens, then pours enough oil to coat everything with a thin film. Any oil that accumulates at the bottom of the bowl gets poured back into the bottle. Ceil next adds vinegar and herbs and tosses and tastes as she goes. A fine procedure, that produces a splendid salad. Its only limitation is that one can't use it when making just a little bit of salad, because the tossing-and-tasting will consume too much!

My Dressing

We use regular oil for cooking because those virtues that are lost by processing the oil would be lost in cooking anyway. For salad we use unprocessed olive oil, which we keep in the refrigerator. There, of course, it kind of solidifies, so a small bottle is taken out ahead of time for table use.

For dressing I mix two parts olive oil, one part wine vinegar (or homemade cider vinegar), one part lemon juice, with a dash of mustard stirred in. (If I don't use prepared mustard, I premix the mustard powder with water before adding.) I keep the jar of dressing in the refrigerator but take it out shortly before I make my salad, so the oil thaws. I pour the dressing over the salad and return extra dressing to the bottle. I taste, add seasonings and, if the salad needs it, a bit more oil or a bit more vinegar—the latter if the salad is rich in bland ingredients such as avocado.

Sour Cream

Sour cream and raw vegetables is an Eastern European delicacy (you can order it at many Jewish restaurants), and sour cream—plain, or with dill, capers, or a bit of mustard—is a marvelous dressing for all except pure avocado (too rich).

Other Possibilities

Half sour cream, half commercial mayonnaise.
Half sour cream, half prepared dressing.
Sour cream with a bit of blue cheese mashed in.
Any dressing, with ketchup added.
Sour cream, sugar, and dill (superb on cucumbers).
Yogurt instead of sour cream.
Any dressing with chopped pickles, chopped anchovies, anchovy paste, or capers added.

NOTE: Oregano, basil, chervil, thyme, tarragon, marjoram all make excellent salad spices. The tendency is to overseason salads, a great pity when you have good greens, but necessary if you are using iceberg lettuce. I prefer to season my vinegar.

Herb or Spice Vinegar

1. Clean fresh herbs thoroughly and break up small enough so they can be stuffed in a bottle or jar.
2. Rinse jar with boiling water, and stuff with herbs.
3. Bring a proper amount of good vinegar (white or cider) to a boil, pour it over the herbs in the jar. Seal tightly. Let sit as long as possible. When half the vinegar is used, you can "extend" with more vinegar. But don't do more than once, or the herb flavor gets too weak.

Use very sparingly, mixed into salad along with wine vinegar.
4. If you use dried herbs, you do exactly the same thing. Place a few spoonfuls in a bottle, pour boiled vinegar over them piping hot.

15 / Baking: A Reckless Way to Spend an Afternoon

About baking. *Don't.*
Baking is a time-consuming extravagance, uneconomical for the small household (unless you have a deep freeze), and it "forces"

you to consume far larger quantities of carbohydrates and cooked fats than are good for you.

Telling you this makes me feel like a mother deploying for her children the reasons they should avoid premarital sex. The arguments are perfect; they convince no one.

Two more points:

I have it on expert authority that cookie and cake mixes are more economical than mixing one's own, because you must consider the outlay for ingredients which you cannot use up in a single baking (spices, baking powder).

If you *must* bake your own bread (and I think bread from the health food store, though costly, is a better deal), try to do it on a co-op basis with a few other home-baked-bread buffs. The *only* way to keep costs down is to buy ingredients in big enough quantities to get a price break. Good flour, the kind you want to use, goes rancid very quickly. Unless you can use it in big quantities or by the sack, and use it before it spoils, you have to buy-as-you-use, which (along with the fuel cost of an underfilled oven) skyrockets the price.

Bread

Since I'm a master at accepting defeat without humiliation, let me start with bread.

The basis of our* kind of bread is baker's yeast. (There are other kinds, such as brewer's.) To thrive it needs moisture and a constant temperature of 80–85°F. Excess heat kills it and coolness slows it down so it does not do its work at the proper rate.

Besides yeast, bread needs the right kind of flour† and flour blends to have the proper texture. The main material you'll need

---

*The *matzot* of the Bible that did not have time to rise were, in all probability, sourdough breads. Sourdough breads are made by allowing the flour/liquid mix to ferment on its own. Sourdough baking requires skill and experience. Don't mess with it (and a mess it can be) till you've mastered yeast baking.

†Particularly to vegetarians I recommend U.S. Department of Agriculture booklet ARS 61-7, *Cottonseed Flour, Peanut Flour, and Soy Flour*. It contains both family-sized and institutional recipes in which these high-protein flours are used as additives or substitutes for wheat flour. Some nonbaking recipes are found here too. I have never tried the recipes, but Department of Agriculture booklets are very reliable and good.

is *hard wheat flour,* also sold as *bread* flour. *Soft wheat* or *cake* flour gives too crumbly a texture for sliceable bread. *All-purpose* flour, a mix of soft and hard wheat, can be used, but it is better for cakes or breads such as challah that have lots of eggs.

Bread *must* be kneaded to develop proper texture. Avoid recipes that skip kneading. Again, fine for cakes, poor for breads. The rest periods called for in yeast recipes are *necessary.* Do not deprive your bread dough of them in the hope of speeding things up.

Basic Bread Procedure (for All Breads)

1. *Prepare a work space.* Bread baking is sticky and dusty, and really needs space. Spread newspaper under your table, or be prepared to wet-mop the floor later. Set out all your ingredients and tools. Have a damp towel ready to wipe your hands. Your work surface should be at least 2 by 2 feet, without cracks or crevices. Consider investing in a breadboard or making one (plywood edged with a tightly fitted molding).

2. If you are using dry yeast, prepare it according to package directions. If using fresh yeast, dissolve it in *lukewarm* water. Mix the dissolved yeast with 1 or 2 tablespoons of sugar or honey and ⅛ cup of flour. This mix, called a starter, should be prepared hours ahead of time, or if your place is cold, even the night before. European baking books always call for this starter, and I always use it, because it gets the yeast working before it is mixed with all the other ingredients. The starter should be foamy and bubbly before use.

3. Melt the fat and cool it. Measure your basic flour, mix it with other flours. Set aside a small bowl with extra flour for dusting. Assemble all ingredients you will need, and all tools.

4. Unless you are following other directions, proceed as follows.

Mix eggs, milk, melted fat, all liquid ingredients. Add the starter.

This mix will now look like a tan sludge, and the starter will have stopped looking like dirty soapsuds.

Mix all your flours together in a big bowl (when you get good, you can mix them on your board and add the liquid to a well, or crater, in the middle), and start adding your liquid. Using your hand, mix and knead, getting all the flour wet. If the resulting mix is soupy, add more flour. If it's like concrete, and some flour is still unwet, add a bit more liquid. The mix should feel like a baby's bottom—malleable, soft, but retaining shape.

Flour your board and dump the dough onto it.

Scrape your sticky hands with a dull knife, or wash them and dry them well. Dust your hands with flour, and start kneading your dough. It should become more and more elastic, but when it becomes hard to work, let it rest five or ten minutes. Knead for a total of twenty minutes. The dough should be shiny, with little blisters inside. If, as you knead, the dough becomes too sticky and adheres to the board, sprinkle a bit more flour.

Put the dough in a large oiled bowl, and turn the dough so that the top is greased too (with oil picked up when it was at the bottom). Cover the bowl with a wet but not dripping towel. Set aside to rise till double in volume. *Be sure* the bowl is big enough so the dough can grow. *Be sure* the wet towel does not dry. (I cover my wet towels with a wet newspaper.)

How can you tell if the dough has *really* doubled? You can't! But when it appears to have doubled, poke it gently at the top. If the dent made by your finger remains, the dough is ready.

5. Dump the dough onto the freshly cleaned and floured board. Sprinkle the dough with whatever salt is called for—also any nuts, raisins, seeds you want. Knead about five minutes. Divide the dough into greased pans, which again must allow enough room for the dough to double in size.

6. When the dough has risen (as above), bake.

Basic Bread Recipe

The flours you use, the kind of fat, whether you use sugar or honey, milk or water or eggs—all this affects the dough. So all one can tell you is that basically:

You use 1 package of dry yeast for 1 pound or 4 cups flour.

You use 1 cup of liquid and 1 tablespoon fat. You use 1 tablespoon sweetening (in your starter) and 1 teaspoon salt.

If you use eggs, you substitute them by volume for the liquid. (Put the eggs in your measuring cup, subtract their volume from the liquid.)

If you use a lot of raisins, nuts, oats, or nonwheat flour, you may have to increase the amount of yeast. Doubling it is quite safe to start. *Doubling it may, however, speed up the rising process and affect the texture.* If you are developing your own recipe—as you probably will—keep records, including how hot the kitchen was.

If you do not have bread pans, you will need a harder dough—that is, more flour—to permit you to make sausage-type rolls which you bake side by side on cookie sheets.

Some people grease the top of bread before baking; some butter the top right after baking. My own preference is to brush each loaf lightly with very salty water during baking—while the crust is still light (but already hard).

Notes on Bread

Some sugar is necessary to make the yeast work. If you must, leave it out, but be prepared for a poorer texture and a longer rising period.

Salt must not come directly in contact with yeast. That is why I generally add it only after the first rising.

It is getting more and more difficult to get bread flour at general stores. Get it from a reliable mail-order house or a health food store. Even if you get white flour, get the kind that still has the wheat germ. This type gets rancid quickly, so do not try to stock it at home.

While commercial bakeries do well with wheatless breads, I have never had decent results in a home oven with any mix that had less than one-half wheat.

You can test bread with a knife stab, as one does cakes. But the pro *taps* the bread with an experienced finger. A hollow sound means it's done.

The biggest problem is RISING! The ideal is, no doubt, to bake in August for the rest of the year. But that can only be done if one has a deep freeze. Ingenuity is called for, and here are a few suggestions:

Half-fill a sink with body-temperature water. Place your dough bowl on an inverted pot just *above* the water. Cover the sink with newspaper to keep the heat in.

Place the dough bowl on a chair near the radiator or near the oven. *Do not* place on top of anything hotter than body temperature, because yeast fails at 120°F gets killed at 140°F.

To kill two birds, etc., do as I did in my cold-water flat. Run yourself a real hot tub, lock yourself in the bathroom—you in the tub, the dough bowl nearby. Both of you will thrive in the moist heat.

We are told French peasants stick the dough bowl into their eiderdowns when they get up in the morning, leave them there to rise all day. I suppose that in a real crisis an electric blanket will do as well?

It can happen that your dough rises too much, too fast. Best step is kneading in more flour.

Once you've mastered yeast baking, you will find it a lot of fun, easier, and more challenging than baking-powder baking. Yeast baking is really a skill of touch and sight, and not conquered in a day.

Panettone, or Would You Believe Challah?

An egg-endowed bread or cake, which can be made with all-purpose flour. Equally good for *challah** (the traditional Sabbath bread) or *panettone*, an Italian Christmas cake.

Buy: undegermed white flour, or all-purpose flour; 1 package yeast.

For panettone: a small jar candied fruit peel; 1 thick-skinned lemon, or a jar of dried lemon peel; raisins.

---

*Hundred-percent-authentic challah has neither milk nor butter in it, since it is served with meat as well as dairy meals. See Appendix, page 228.

Have: milk; butter; eggs; sugar or honey.

Premix the yeast as directed on package. Or dissolve yeast in a few spoons of body-temperature water, add 1 tablespoon sugar or honey, 1 or 2 tablespoons flour. Set aside till bubbly. (The mix should be fairly liquid.)

Heat ¾ cup milk, or use dry milk powder and warm water. Allow ½ cup (¼ pound) butter to dissolve in the warm milk.

Rinse a big bowl with hot water, dry.

Measure into the bowl 3 cups flour, and for panettone 3 tablespoons sugar or honey. Mix in 2 eggs and the milk and butter mixture, which, I repeat, should be just body temperature.

Now add your starter and mix real well.

Cover the bowl and set aside for about 1½ hours—till doubled in bulk. This mix is too soft for the poking test, so volume will have to do.

For panettone: Blend the candied fruit and enough raisins to make 1 cup. Add the scraped peel of 1 thick-skinned lemon, or 1 teaspoon dried lemon peel (unless the package suggests a different equivalent). Add 1 teaspoon salt. Prepare a floured board (see page 165) and dump the risen dough on it. Knead it well. If it sticks to your fingers after the first turn or so, add a little more flour.

Knead thoroughly, adding as little extra flour as possible. This dough remains sloppy, and spreads when allowed to sit. After a few minutes of thorough kneading, knead in the fruit/lemon/salt mix.

For challah you just knead the straight dough and add only 1½ teaspoons salt.

Place well-kneaded dough in well-greased form or forms. (The lump of dough should not fill pan more than halfway.) Allow to rise till the dough reaches edge of pan top. Bake in preheated 350°F oven. Baking will take from 40 to 50 minutes, depending on size of pan.

For a glossy crust, you can beat an egg yolk with a very little water and brush it lightly on the breads before baking.

Either way this is very good, keeps well in a closed tin, but it cannot be sliced thinner than about half an inch!

Cakes

Cake recipes are truly endless. The variations are relatively small. While measuring is essential, and accuracy desirable, there is a certain amount of possible flexibility. The first recipe I give, for *Ruhrkuchen*—a cake that was baked each week when I was a child, and happily consumed week in, week out, forever it seems—is a perfect example.

I have baked this cake with and without raisins; using orange juice and rum (or brandy) instead of milk or for part of the milk; dividing the recipe (once mixed) into two batches and adding 2 ounces of melted chocolate (or 3 tablespoons Dutch cocoa) to one half to achieve a marble cake; I have baked this as cupcakes, loaves, and squares—and always it is fine.

Ruhrkuchen

First, read "Testing for Doneness" and "Disasters" (see page 173).

Buy: flour (cake or all-purpose); butter.

Have: milk; eggs; baking powder; vanilla extract; (rum or brandy); sugar.

Allow ⅔ cup butter to get to room temperature,* that is, soft and creamy. Place it in a large bowl, and stir in 1½ cups sugar and 2½ cups flour into which you have mixed 3 teaspoons of baking powder. When you have mixed in about half the flour/sugar mix, start adding 1⅛ cups liquid—milk, milk and rum, milk and brandy, or orange juice—into which you have beaten 3 eggs. Add 1 teaspoon vanilla. Stir and beat the completed mixture really till your arm aches, or at least till the mix is light, smooth, and shiny.

Pour into a buttered form (a regular loaf form 9 by 4 by 3 inches, or any form that will hold that amount while leaving 1 inch at the top) and bake in preheated 325°F oven for half an

---

*While for yeast cakes butter is frequently melted, *never* melt the fat in a baking-powder or sponge cake recipe *unless* the recipe says so. You will ruin your mix and get a cake like lead!

hour, or till a knife comes out clean. (One of the joys of this cake is that it does well even in a poor oven, with slightly higher or lower temperature.)

To make a marble cake: When the dough is thoroughly mixed, divide into two bowls. Add 2 ounces melted chocolate or 3 table-spoons Dutch cocoa to one bowl, mix thoroughly, then recombine with other half *and do not mix thoroughly.* Pour the streaky mix into a baking pan—and out comes a streaky (marbled) cake.

NOTE: Do not ever interrupt the making of a baking-powder cake. Double-acting baking powder (the kind now most commonly sold and the only one to get) works two (!) ways: (1) It raises the dough as soon as it (the powder) becomes moist; (2) it raises the dough when heated. So any delay allows the gases formed by moisture alone to escape and become useless. You cannot well add more baking powder, because too much ruins the flavor of the cake.

NOTE: Some recipes will call for beating the egg whites separately. I have never found this makes any real difference except in very heavy cakes, such as the chocolate cake that follows. A thorough beating (at least 200 solid strokes, but no more than 275) seems to be sufficient with modern ingredients.

Chocolate Cake

As far as I know I invented this rich, lovely cake. At least I invented it for myself, when one day I decided to push chocolatiness to its limits.

First, read "Testing for Doneness" and "Disasters" just below.

Buy: 6 ounces of the best eating bittersweet chocolate you can find; butter; all-purpose flour.

Have: eggs; baking powder; baking soda; sugar; rum or vanilla flavor; buttermilk or milk.

Preheat your oven and grease a pan (9 by 9 by 2 inches, or equivalent).

Melt the chocolate over hot water or near the radiator, or melt it in a pan of hot water (double boiler style) in your heating oven. Meanwhile measure out ¾ cup butter and allow to get to room temperature.

Remove the chocolate (from its pan of hot water, or the oven) and stir in 1 tablespoon or so of the measured-out butter, and ¼ cup warm water. Set aside.

Separate 3 eggs.

Dump the butter and the egg yolks into a large bowl and start beating. Add 1½ cups sugar, and beat 100 strokes. Add the chocolate mix, and start adding (little by little) 2¼ cups flour into which you have mixed 1 teaspoon baking soda and ½ teaspoon baking powder. Alternately to the flour, add 1 cup buttermilk. (If you use regular milk you do not need baking soda, but instead use 1½ teaspoons baking powder only.)

Stir in 1 teaspoon vanilla extract or rum flavoring.

Beat the egg whites till stiff.

This is a simple enough process, but try to get someone to show you. When you first beat egg whites, you get foam. After a while the foam turns opaque. It then becomes stiff enough so you can make it hold peaks, much as you can make shampoo peaks on your head when washing your hair. After this stage the shine disappears and the egg whites take on a styrofoam look. They are now so stiff they are hard to mix in with other ingredients. This stage is called *dry*. Most recipes say *stiff but not dry*, which means you stop before the shine disappears. Actually, when egg whites are at their peak, you can turn the bowl upside down and they stay put. Don't try this yet!

If you overbeat eggs a lot, they turn liquid again and refuse to become stiff—ever, as far as I know.

In most recipes it matters less if you underbeat a bit than if you overbeat. Do not try recipes that use only egg whites as leavening (no baking powder) till you are in perfect control of the beating of the whites.

When the whites in this recipe are stiff but still shiny, pour one-fourth or so of the whites into the chocolate mix and stir well. Then dump in the rest of the whites and *fold in*.

Folding in means burying as much of the foam in the chocolate mix as possible without losing the air. Use a flattish spoon or rubber spatula, go down the side of the bowl furthest from you, bring the spoon toward you along the bottom of the bowl and up the side nearest you, across the top, and down again at the far side just next to where you dipped down before. After you have done this three or four times, you will no longer see buried masses of white, just a few pebble-sized bits that are unincorporated.

Pour the mix into a very big pan or two smaller ones. I use two 9-by-4-by-3-inch pans or a big Bundt (doughnut-shaped) form, or the 9-by-9-by-2-inch. This cake rises a lot, and you must leave a fair amount of clearance at the top.

NOTE: Here is a recipe I do not recommend halving.

Bake at 350°F for 30 minutes.

NOTE: Testing for doneness.

The classical way of testing a cake is to stab it with a toothpick, or a fine knife point, smack in the center. Either the pick should turn out clean, or some crumbs will stick to it, *but no more liquid or goo*. In a well-regulated oven the state of the crust reveals the state of the inside, because by the time the recipe's mix has been baked in the proper pan, for the proper time, at the proper temperature, the crust as well as the inside is perfect.

But any substitution in ingredients, or a poorly regulated oven, or an odd-sized pan—or even baking a cake in cupcake tins (perfectly feasible)—will affect (in the last case shorten) baking time. So after three-fourths of the baking time called for, check with a toothpick or knife.

Please remember, you are not rehearsing *Julius Caesar*—be very gentle, and quick. *Do not* leave the oven door open unnecessarily, and *do not slam it* in closing.

Allow seven minutes between testings.

If, when you test, the cake is almost done (just a tiny trace of liquid), turn the oven off, and let the cake sit in the cooling oven for ten minutes, test again, and then remove the cake.

NOTE: *Always remove a cake from the oven immediately upon completion of baking,* unless your recipe calls for something else.

Disasters: Read this before you begin to bake.

A bad crack in the middle of your cake. Oven too hot to begin with, or irregular.

A shiny, sticky streak in the cake. Poor mixing, too-slow baking, irregular heating of oven.

A sticky, gummy, gooey cake. Too much sugar; too much

liquid (as when you forget to cut back on milk when you use honey instead of sugar). Maybe you forgot the baking powder. Maybe the baking powder was too old, or the flour past its prime.

Cake rises too much, overflows pan. Too much baking powder, too little flour. Or simply you filled cake pan more than two-thirds full. Particularly with narrow, deep pans (like loaf tins) you must leave room at the top.

Cake rises a lot while baking, caves in while cooling. Same as above. Beating the egg whites when the recipe does not call for it may also cause this disaster.

Prevention

Buy the smallest packages of baking powder possible; do not use after three months.

Use the flour and the type of sugar called for in the recipe, at least the first few times. Make your substitutions one at a time, so you know where to pin the blame if something goes wrong.

Bake in the middle of your oven. Do not slam the oven door. Do not peek in before three-fourths of the time allowed for baking in the recipe.

Use fresh flour. Flour need not be moldy to have gone bad. It can develop trouble without smell. Do not keep flour more than a few months, even in a dry place.

Use medium-sized eggs. Jumbos or pullet eggs are fine once you know what volume of eggs the recipe wants. First time out, measure the eggs in your measuring cup, then note on your recipe for later changes.

Honey or Syrup for Sugar

Ciceil tells me that an ancient cookbook she has reveals that while you substitute the same amount of honey for the same amount of sugar—that is, 1 tablespoon honey for 1 tablespoon sugar—in a cake, if you use honey for sugar you reduce your other liquid by one-fourth. (Egg counts as liquid.) This formula means that a cake that calls for 1 cup sugar and 1 cup milk gets 1 cup honey and ¾ cup milk. We cannot guarantee this formula, but give it a careful try. Same for molasses or maple syrup.

Breakfast Foods and Instant Snacks

Baking is a *good idea*, I think, in the convenience food line—if you bake yourself "instant breakfasts" and snacks that, with a glass of milk or yogurt, provide a quick, cheap meal. Here you not only save money but gain nutrition, and if you don't know by now that the coffee cart is a Trojan horse, there's no hope for you.

Many doctors and nutritionists claim snacking is better for us than three meals *if* the snack foods are well chosen. The anti-snacking campaign is not directed at the meal, but at the ghastly plastic junk foods most people snack on.

Here are a few suggestions as basics you can embroider on.

Oatmeal Raisin Cookies

Makes 4 or 5 dozen.

Buy: oats and white flour at the health food store;* ½ pound each seedless raisins and unroasted, unsalted nut meats; ½ pound sweet butter.

Have: sugar or honey; milk powder; baking soda; eggs.

Allow the butter to get to room temperature. Combine 2 cups oats, 2 cups flour, ⅛ ½ cup milk powder, 2-3 cups chopped nuts, and raisins into a big bowl or saucepan.

Add 1 teaspoon baking soda if using sugar, 1½ teaspoons if using honey.

Mix the dry ingredients well.

Cream the butter and eggs. Add the honey or sugar.

Add the dry to the wet ingredients. Mix well. If you are using

---

*I've heard of people buying oats, molasses, bran, and so on at feed stores. I'd buy and eat anything out of our feed mill, but this is my personal nuttiness and not a recommendation. I would not recommend this willy-nilly.

†You can "enrich" flours by adding nonwheat flour to wheat flour. I add ⅛ cup wheat germ to each cup of flour. Since soy flour, rye, and such are less standardized than the commercial stuff, check the wrappings as a guide and go easy at first. Try your own blends first on cookies; it's safer, because less can go wrong.

honey, you may have to add some more flour. Measure the flour, and if you use more than ¼ cup, add ¼ teaspoon baking soda for each ½ cup flour.

You can chill this mix (which should be quite stiff), then, after an hour, roll and slice it like a salami and bake the slices. Or you can roll balls in your hands and place the balls on a greased cookie sheet, flattening them with your hand. You also can use two soup spoons to "ladle" the mix onto a cookie sheet. Grease the baking tin well, allow 2 inches between cookies the first time (depending on how thick and how big you make the cookies, they will spread more or less in baking). Bake 8 minutes at 375°F.

NOTE: Because cookies do not really have to rise, very little can go wrong with their baking. If the oven is too hot and the cookies too thick, they may burn on the outside while the inside is still raw. But that is easily adjusted, and even a tyro can prescribe cookie cures.

Unbaked Fruit Bars

I am putting these here as a prelude to baked fruit bars. This recipe is so easy that my four-year-old niece apparently made it all alone, *after* my sister chopped the stuff up.

Buy several of the following ingredients: figs; pitted dates; dried apricots; dried peaches; dried pears; pitted prunes; raisins; unsalted, unroasted nut meats. (Use about one-third nuts to two-thirds fruit.)

Have: carob flour or Dutch (or instant) cocoa or *ground* nuts; orange, apple, prune, fig, or cranberry juice (nothing too acid like grapefruit). If no fruit juice is available, use sherry or brandy or rum—or, in a pinch, water.

With a large, sharp knife or a meat grinder, chop the fruits and nuts as finely as possible. Work the mass well together, and chop or grind till you have a homogeneous mass that sticks together. If the mass remains too crumbly, add some liquid (juice or liquor) a teaspoon at a time.

When the mass stays together when you take an egg-sized lump and squeeze it, roll bits of the mass in your palms tightly, then roll on a plate sprinkled with cocoa, carob flour, or ground nuts. This coating will prevent the fruit bars from sticking together. Wrap individually, or store between layers of waxed paper in a tightly lidded box in the refrigerator.

With my universal recommendation (a hard-boiled egg) or yogurt or cottage cheese or milk, here's lunch or supper.

Baked Fruit Bars

Buy: ½ pound each of raisins and unroasted, unsalted nut meats. (There are about 3 cups in a pound, in case you are using supplies on hand.)

Have: undegermed flour or all-purpose flour plus wheat germ; butter; sugar or honey; orange or pineapple juice; an egg; baking soda; cinnamon.

Allow ¼ pound butter to get to room temperature. If you are using honey, measure the volume of 1 egg; if it is more than ¼ cup, reduce the honey content accordingly. Honey, egg, and juice together should be equal to 1 cup honey plus 1 egg. Add honey or sugar to the butter, stir well. Add egg and ¼ cup juice if needed. Add 2½ cups flour (or flour and wheat germ), 1 teaspoon soda if using sugar, 1½ teaspoons soda if using honey, ½ teaspoon cinnamon. Work in 3 cups of raisins and chopped nuts. You can use chopped, dry, or candied fruit such as pineapples, figs, dates, currants. Turkish or Greek figs, which come on a string, are best "plumped" by a brief soaking in hot water. Otherwise they're murder to chop. Work the mass well; it should not stick to your hands. Pat into greased forms, about ¾ inch deep in each form. Bake 10 to 12 minutes in a slow oven (325°F). You can roll this out, my original notes say, and bake on cookie sheet, but why bother?

Banana Bars

Yes, one can replace bananas in banana bread/bar recipes with applesauce, and vice-versa. But only once one has had the original recipe well in hand to adjust variations in consistency as found in applesauce.

Buy 2 bananas. Allow to ripen well.

Have: flour (undegermed, or with wheat germ added); sugar; cinnamon, nutmeg, or allspice; 2 eggs; ¼ pound butter; milk; baking powder.

Mash the bananas thoroughly. Measure to 1 cup. A bit more, a bit less is no tragedy, but it should be no more than ⅛ cup off.

Allow the butter to get to room temperature; cream it with 1 cup sugar. Add 2 eggs, and begin to add (little by little) 2 cups flour into which 1½ teaspoons baking powder have been mixed. Alternately add 1 cup bananas and ½ cup milk (if you used exactly 1 cup bananas—otherwise a bit more or less milk to balance the lack or excess of banana, which sort of counts as a liquid here). Add 1 teaspoon of whatever spice you are using. Pour and spread into a greased form (your big frying pan with the fireproof handle will do) and bake about 30 minutes at 325°F. Cut into squares.

About Molasses Cookies

I have never been convinced of the merits of molasses as a nutritional marvel. It does provide some vitamins and calcium (sugar does not), but there are less carbohydrate-rich sources of these (besides which at least one vitamin is destroyed in cooking). But if you like molasses you can use it in any plain cookie recipe, replacing some of the sugar with molasses instead of replacing it with honey. If you use molasses, try brown sugar for a change.

Ciceil's Breakfast Food

It contains grains, though unbaked, and where else should I put it? Cheaper, much better than what you buy, but cheaper *only* if you really use it big. Otherwise buy a premixed type at the health food store.

Ratio is 7 parts dry to 1 part wet. Raisins are neutral. Add lots.

Dries: % *part each:* sesame seeds; pumpkin seeds; sunflower seeds (all seeds shelled); shredded coconut. *1 part each:* oats; wheat germ; soy grits; bran; nut meats (chopped).

Wets: equal amounts of honey and good oil (not olive in this case) mixed.

Set the honey/oil mix in a bowl in warm water, stirring till they blend well.

Mix all your dry ingredients, measuring them into a big bowl so you know how much oil/honey to add to keep the 7 to 1 ratio. Add the honey/oil mix. Some people then spread the whole thing on a tray in a slow, slow (open-door) oven to dry. Others (including C.) just mix real well, put up in tight-lidded jar, keep in refrigerator. (Take out only a small amount the night before for breakfast. You don't want the oils from nuts and oil/honey mix to turn rancid.)

Additional Baking Notes

1. You will be tempted to sift together a whole batch of flour and wheat germ or other flours. *Don't.* The whole reason some soul invented degermed flour was that the wheat germ goes rancid and spoils the flour. Store any whole, undegermed flour (or meal) in the refrigerator. If you use all-purpose or commercial cake flour, do not premix. Keep wheat germ tightly sealed in refrigerator till ready to use.

2. *Sifting.* Today flours and such are so super-refined that I never sift my dry ingredients together. I only sift lumpy things like brown sugar. Exception: when I'm making cakes that are hardly stirred at all, like angel-food. Breathing flour is just as bad for you as breathing other dust.

3. *If you don't sift, be super-careful not to pack your dry ingredients down in spoon or cup. Ladle in as loosely as possible.*

4. Even with a new oven, an oven thermometer is a good investment. More so for cake baking than for bread. The cheapest breaks down as quickly as the fanciest; get the cheapest. About $1.25.

5. When Marie Antoinette said, "If the people have no bread, let them eat cake," she was not just displaying a weird, naive sense of humor. She did not mean Dobos Torte, or Baba au Rhum.

What she *did* mean was that they should eat the flour with which professional bakers strew their ovens so they can bake without tins or pans. (Pizza ovens are still dusted that way.) For this unsound nutritional advice, she paid dearly. One hopes it is a lesson to all who tout junk foods.

A Word about Cornmeal

Much has been written recently against wheat and its gluten. Cornmeal—the undegermed, whole, stone-ground kind—has had a renaissance.

Certainly the corn breads of the South are a delicacy and deserve a place of honor among baked goods. Certainly the softer corn breads—which are baked like casseroles—are as good a substitute for potatoes or pasta as you will find (as is the cornmeal mush or polenta I describe below). And corn makes a splendid hot cereal.

But except for a supremacy in vitamin A that becomes negligible at the per-serving level, I neither see where cornmeal has it over wheat nutritionally, nor (as long as undegermed, etc. cornmeal and undegermed, etc. wheat flour are only to be had at health food stores) can I detect a saving.

Polenta, however, on its own merits, is a useful dish. Although it takes about an hour to make a dish of polenta, it can be stored for days and sliced to be fried, or reheated in a stew, or steamed, or baked. It is ready to eat in minutes.

Polenta

Cooking polenta is a two-stage affair. First the cornmeal is mixed with water and cooked *over a direct flame*. Like all starchy substances, it burns easily, tastes horrid if burned, and must be watched and stirred constantly to prevent burning. Hence the second step: when the mush has cooked 3 minutes at a slow boil, the whole pot is put *over, not in,* hot water, covered and steamed for 30 minutes. During this half-hour it gets stirred frequently—like every 5 minutes.

Stir 1 cup water into 1 cup cornmeal in a saucepan or in the top of a double boiler.

When the mix is smooth, cook it over a *low* direct flame, stirring constantly. When it bubbles, cook 3 minutes more. If, as you stir, the mix gets too stiff, add hot water, measuring (a guess does well) what you add and subtracting that from the second batch of water.

After the 3 minutes are up, stir 3 cups of hot water into the mix, place the pot over boiling water, cover, cook 30 minutes more with frequent stirrings. Check when you stir that the hot water below has not boiled away!

Dump the cooked polenta into a form and, when cold, slice it.

Variations

You can, after the first cooking, stir butter into the mix. You can add butter and grated cheese after the second cooking. (This will soften the polenta a bit.)

You can use plain polenta, or the butter-and-cheese-enriched one in casseroles, slicing the polenta and building lasagna-style layers with cheese and tomatoes, or sausage, or meat sauce, etc.

In case of need, polenta can be sliced, fried, and eaten with syrup or honey. It is what poor people call *filling.*

But the main use of polenta in your kitchen is as a rice or pasta or potato substitute. The slices can be heated in stew, or in soup, and are ready in minutes.

16 / Soups: Justice to Old Standbys

Soup is power to the people. Although there are effete soups and fancy ones, soup is a peasant dish, to be eaten casually, with stockinged feet planted under a rustic table. Soup is the *pièce de résistance* of artists in garrets and rebels in cellars and ought to occupy a place in your repertoire.

There are three basic kinds of soup:

Broths, which are the clear liquid in which something has been boiled. They are, obviously, fairly rich in vitamins if made of vegetables rich in water-soluble vitamins, but otherwise have little to recommend them except as a low-calorie drink, or as a basis of other soups or of sauces (in which case they are renamed *stocks*).

Cream soups, which are really white sauces mixed with a pureed (that is, mashed) vegetable. In so far as cream soups are rich in milk and butter, and enriched by the vitamins of any vegetable they contain, they are a good meal in themselves. In so far as they are fairly delicate—they must not boil—they are a bit of a chore.

Soups, which are the one-pot, one-plate meals I so highly recommend. These are really thinnish stews (each diner is entitled to one cup of liquid in his plate!), and actually many cookbooks still list goulash as goulash *soup*. Most stews began as such soups, and here protein and vegetables are cooked together to blend their flavors and nutrients, and make a sturdy, any-time-of-day meal.

A Few Friendly Remarks about Soup

1. Do not sneer at broths just because they are sissies. A special on chicken wings and backs, a batch of fish heads and tails, a gift of soup bones (*always* invent yourself a dog when you go to a butcher)—all can be the start of a broth that you stash in the refrigerator (or freeze in the ice tray) to be used as a base for a real soup later. In fact, if you do not own a real big pot, you may find it easier to make real soup in two stages—first the broth, then the soup.

2. Leftover soup, of the full-blooded kind described later, can be made into a cream soup. If there is fair amount of starch

in the first soup, you do not need to make a white sauce; simply add butter and milk to the leftover.

3. In soup-making a blender is a great boon. But three or four dollars at a rummage sale is all it's worth. Otherwise invest in a sieve, or a pureer—a sieve equipped with a blade and a crank that turns the blade, a combination which forces the contents through the sieve. These are also called food mills and, in fancy stores, *passe-vites*. They come in a variety of styles and should not be confused with ricers in which *pressure and pressure alone* forces the substance through the sieve. You need and want something that crushes and grinds. (Ricers are used to make mashed potatoes.)

4. Soup takes quite a while to make, and cannot be made in small quantities. Figure about 2 quarts, which will feed 4 to 5 people. Soup keeps well in a lidded jar in the refrigerator and can be frozen in a foil-covered ice tray, where it will keep a few weeks.

5. The basic winter soup I suggest leans heavily on dried vegetables. These, *dry*, contain about 340–350 calories per 100 grams (3½ ounces ±) and rate for protein contents like this: *Lentils* have 25 grams of protein per 100 grams, followed in decreasing order by peas, cowpeas, beans, and lima beans. Buckwheat is about 12 grams of protein per 100 grams, followed in decreasing order by bulgar, barley, and brown rice. Cream-style or other canned corn is of course *wet*, so cream-style's 82 calories and 2.1 grams of protein are less inadequate than one first thinks if one considers water content (over 70 percent). *Barley and rice* are not particular protein contributors and do little for flavor, so I would omit them from most soups and keep them as fillers for broths. *Buckwheat* has a strong flavor, and unless you are kinky for kasha (the name of buckwheat groats, which is what most stores have), go lightly.

Winter Soup I

Buy or have: lentils; beans; dried split or whole peas; canned or frozen corn; canned tomatoes; fresh or freeze-dried soup greens;

any assortment of winter vegetables; 2 pounds of chuck, brisket, shank, or "soup meat"; soup bones; 1 or 2 bouillon cubes; salt; pepper.

Set all dried vegetables aside, in a bowl of water. Let them soak a few hours or overnight.* Do not use the canned tomatoes or corn yet.

Rinse your meat, wash and prepare the soup greens and winter vegetables: carrots, onions, turnips, parsnips, potatoes. Dice the vegetables. With soup, you see, you do not mind losing the vitamins into the water.

Assemble the meat, the rinsed bones (carefully inspected for splinters and bone grit), the vegetables (you may want to fry the onions first for extra flavor) in a pot, cover with water, and boil slowly for about 40 minutes. Test the meat for doneness. You want it cooked, but not overcooked. Remove the meat to a deep plate (it will leak juices a while, which you want to salvage). Go on cooking the bones and vegetables for another hour. Throughout the cooking of the meat and bones, remove scum that rises to the top and discard (your dog will love it).

If you wish, set aside a cup or so of broth for reheating the meat, in case you want to serve it as boiled beef. Or you can cool the meat and marinate it in a mix of one part oil, two parts white vinegar, plus a dash of water and lots of chopped parsley and green onion, and serve cold at another meal.

Add your presoaked vegetables to the pot, and cook very slowly for about an hour. One cup of a dried legume gives 2½ to 3 cups of a soaked one and ends as 5 to 6 cups of soup. So go easy. Cook until the vegetables have lost their identity, checking continually to see that there is enough liquid. I cannot tell you exactly how much liquid you should have, because much depends on the vegetables you use, and also on the number of soup bones (that is, how strong your broth is). Add (canned tomatoes or canned corn) if you like. Flavor with salt and pepper, add a little hot pepper, and a bouillon cube or two.

---

*Some packages read that you do not need to presoak. Do it anyway. These dried vegetables soak up an inordinate amount of liquid, and it is much easier to presoak than to watch like a hawk that the soup isn't burning.

You can serve this soup alone, as a main course, accompanied by cheese.

You can reheat the meat in the soup and serve both thick soup and thickly sliced meat all together in bowls.

Or, as suggested above, you can serve the soup first, then the meat as a separate course.

Winter Soup II

Here the same idea is followed except that the soaked vegetables are cooked together with the meat, without the separate step of making a broth first. The meat will be discolored and rather gray as a result of a total of two hours of cooking with vegetables, and cannot well be served separately afterward. The meat becomes saturated with vegetable flavors and tastes quite different from the boiled beef above. But it is not as pretty, and certainly is never rare.

Winter Soup III

Hamburger is used instead of soup meat, and procedure is the same as for Soup II. So you do not have the problem of the unsightly meat. *Be sure* to break the hamburger up, and to crush any lumps that form in the cooking.

You also may fry the hamburger in a large skillet (with or without onions) before adding to the soup. Stir and mash till all the little grounds are individually fried or browned. Then they will not aggregate into lumps in the pot.

Borscht

The thin red fluid found in bottles as borscht—slightly sweet, and delicious as a summer drink, with or without sour cream—is Polish borscht. The other Slavs make a thick cabbage-and-beet soup, and that is borscht as we eat it.

Buy: a 2- or 3-pound white, green, or red cabbage (not savoy), or a 2-pound can of sauerkraut; an assortment of beets, carrots, onions, winter turnips; (potatoes); 2 pounds of chuck, shank, arm, or other soup meat.*

Beets and cabbage should dominate this mix. Proceed as in Soup I or II. If you use cabbage, you can quarter and core it, or shred it. If you use sauerkraut, be sure to drain and rinse several times before use. You can fry the onions or use them plain. You are free to use canned beets, but not pickled or Harvard style. (Some people do add a spoonful of vinegar to borschts, before serving. Try it, you may like it.)

Add potatoes just their cooking time before serving. Do not overcook them.

This soup makes a good vehicle for kielbasa or frankfurters—in which case you do not need meat, only bones.

Serve with lots of sour cream and rye bread or pumpernickel.

Other Combinations

Of course, all the above soups can be made out of one ingredient only. Kidney beans, tomatoes, and some onion and hot pepper prepared by method III is the basic chili con carne. Dried split peas, fried onion, and stock from a boiled ham are the basis of split pea soup. Since you are unlikely to have the ham, try the butcher for ham bones, or get a Polish sausage like kielbasa as your meat. (Pork shoulders or Daisy hams, also good in this, are very costly these days.) Fried onions, broth, and potatoes, cooked till the potatoes fall apart, is very good, if not nutritionally marvelous.

It would be unfair not to add the Brazilian black bean soup whose black beans are hard to find here, except in Puerto Rican

---

*If lucky, you can buy shank with the meat still on the bone. This is ideal for a soup of any kind, particularly this one. You then figure a total of about 3 or 4 pounds of bone and meat combined.

stores. Soak the beans well, cook for a long time with strips of bacon and soup meat. (Most Brazilians are too poor to cook this with anything except lard and perhaps some jerky.) Add some fried onions if you wish. This is served over steamed rice, sprinkled with manioc flour, and decorated with sliced hard-boiled eggs and orange slices.

Onion Soup

Onion soup is a beef broth in which onions—fried to golden perfection—have been added for a brief boil.

Generally the soup, once cooked, is ladled into individual, ovenproof bowls; grated Swiss, Parmesan, or Romano cheese is sprinkled on top; and the bowls are placed under the broiler till the cheese melts into a little island.

Why people rave about this dish as though it were a masterpiece of culinary skill is beyond me. Especially since few people have ever tasted good onion soup, because, as you realize, this soup is mostly faked. People use mixes or tinned consommé; and restaurants seem to use frozen onion.

To make it well, slowly fry 3 or 4 finely chopped onions per person in plenty of butter till just golden. Not a minute more.

Use a really strong homemade beef broth. Cook the broth and the onions just a few minutes together. Use a bit of broth to boil out the last bit of butter in the frying pan, and mix that into the rest.

If you cannot do the melted-cheese-under-the-broiler bit, plain cheese grated and sprinkled atop is fine. You can toast bread, put a slice of cheese on the bread, melt the cheese under the broiler, and float the toast, or melt the cheese atop the toast under the broiler.

You can also make open-faced melted cheese sandwiches separately and then float them atop your onion soup.

Dried mushrooms: There are, as you know, two kinds. The Italian, which are most common (although not always grown in

Italy), are used for cream soups. The Russian or Eastern European, found in Jewish, Polish, other Eastern European stores, are strong in flavor, used in borscht, in mushroom barley soup, with buckwheat groats, but never in Italian food. *All dried mushrooms are expensive*—but thank God a little goes a long way. We buy ours at wholesalers, and if you are in a big city, check your Yellow Pages. *All dried mushrooms are sandy* (the Eastern ones more so I think) and must be washed carefully before using (unless you like sand in your food).

Place the mushrooms in a lot of cold water. Allow to soak about three hours. *Fish out the mushrooms*, rinse under running water, soak in fresh water (being sure to wipe all sand out of the soaking bowl before refilling). Soak for about 20 minutes, fish out, check the bowl for sand (use your fingers, don't try to see it), and repeat the process till the mushrooms are clean.

You fish out the mushrooms because, if you pour the water out over them, you will just be resanding them. No fooling.

If you have filter paper, you can strain the wash water and use it, but I do not think this worthwhile.

A Last Word on Soup

The simplest soup is made by assembling a few leaves of this, a few roots of that from your garden, simmering the bouquet till just soft, adding some milk, cream, or milk powder, or some homemade stock, topping with a dab of butter, and eating with a slab of homemade bread. I wish it upon you, soon.

Pavese

Ideal for invalids, perfect for supper.

Take good broth, chicken or beef, preferably homemade. Bring to a boil.

Wash an egg thoroughly, beat it well into a soup plate, pour the soup atop. You are using the boiling soup to cook your egg, so beat the egg well so that the soup's heat gets to it.

Makes one serving. You can use 2 eggs per serving, but that is rather thick. You can sprinkle with cheese.

Cream Soups

Prepare a white sauce as follows (also see page 207).

Melt 1 tablespoon butter till just melted. Remove from flame and add 1 tablespoon flour or 1½ tablespoons potato starch (cornstarch is too delicate). Flour is the best to use for soup. Beat the butter and flour well together, return to a *very* small flame, and beat some more. Remove from stove again, add 1 tablespoon hot water from tap. Always get rid of any lumps that form as you go along, and do so immediately. Add 2 cups of milk, any type will do, pouring very gradually (again to prevent lumps). Heating the milk is a lump preventative, but care will spare you an extra pot to wash.

The white sauce has to cook at least ten minutes without boiling for all flour taste to be totally gone. You can do this now, or after you've added the vegetable, or just before serving.

When your sauce is ready, you can proceed many ways:

1. Add canned or home-cooked shrimp meat or crab meat. I like very small canned Japanese shrimp. Of course you use the liquid in the can.

2. Add diced chicken and a little broth. (You can use the meat from the wings and backs with which you made broth for something else.) Add a little curry powder for variation.

3. Cook any leafy vegetable, chop it up, and add it, water and all.

4. Use any chopped frozen vegetable you fancy, cooking it directly in the white sauce.

5. Use a canned vegetable. Here you may have to reduce (boil down) the liquid, because you do not want to thin out your soup.

6. You can halve the fat in the original white sauce and add a good cup of grated cheese—about half mild (Muenster or cheddar), half sharp like Provolone, Romano, Parmesan.

You can chop or puree (mash) all vegetables or just some, or part of the whole.

Do not allow soup to boil, and stir frequently if not constantly over low flame while heating.

Croutons: Stale (not spoiled or moldy, just dried), flat (as opposed to French or Italian) white bread is sliced, diced, fried in lots of butter, with or without onions, and floated atop soup. Delicious, fattening.

17 / Desserts: The Easiest Way to Get a Reputation as a Genius Cook

In memory, if not, alas, in life, the last *is* first. Which may explain why dessert is most frequently singled out for praise, and longest remembered, when people reminisce about a dinner party.

So the easiest way to pull the simplest meal into glory is to serve *only* dessert, or to make dessert the big feature of your meal.

Your first step must be to *plan* dessert and to plan the meal around it. Allow for the dessert in your budgeting, rather than simply buying "something or other" with change left from more important groceries.

You must plan dessert not only financially, but nutritionally. If you want a really sweet dessert, avoid starches and sugars (carbohydrates) throughout the meal. If you are planning on cheeses, cut back elsewhere on fat. And so on.

The desserts that are best for you are fruit and cheese, fruit and nuts, and seeds. The cheese can be hard (a blue cheese, a cheddar type, a Tilsit, Muenster, or Kummel) or soft (Camembert, Brie, Limburger, Liederkranz); all are excellent with apples, pears, and nuts. The milder-flavored varieties go superbly with melo;. and figs. You can also serve cottage cheese or ricotta (try combining them in equal portions) with berries, with stewed fruit, or with ground nuts and honey.

Next in line come desserts high in protein—full of milk and eggs. But they require work. When you make these yourself, from scratch, you can keep the sugar content way down, using honey or maple syrup instead of refined sugar. Gelatin desserts are easy to make out of pure gelatin and fruit juice.

You will see that I list store-bought pudding mixes among my ingredients. More and more of these are now at health food stores, and I have located at least one (imported) pudding mix that has only acceptable ingredients.

Last on the list of desserts—and we *don't* want to discuss it—are the gooey, puffed-up confections, full of every synthetic and artificial pseudo-food product known, and which have gained such tremendous popularity on the market. There is nothing I can say for these. If you are desperate for a sweet, get some ice cream, preferably from one of the stores that still use only natural fruit and flavorings, without additives.

Stewed Fruit, Pears Hélène, and So On

When fresh fruit is abundant, and good, nothing is better. Perhaps a dollop of whipped cream makes the berries a bit more luxurious; maybe a drop or two of almond liqueur or kirsch over the freshly peeled peaches gives a feeling of sophistication that the peaches alone do not have.

But when fruit is not abundant, then what?

Stewed dried fruit is the answer. Assemble a variety of dried apples, pears, apricots, peaches, currants, raisins, figs—*not dates*—at the health food store. (NOTE: One of the big manufacturers has recently started to put out dried fruits that say clearly "Refrigerate after opening" on the package. This is the *good* kind, and you can buy it at the supermarket.) You can also get dried *candied* pineapple.

Rinse the fruit (not the candied pineapple) and soak in a large bowl. Use just enough water to come halfway up the fruit. Check after an hour or so, mix the fruit up, add water if necessary. When all the fruit is "plumped," place it in a saucepan with 1 cup or more of water. There should be about 1 cup of liquid for every 2 cups of cooked fruit. If you want, add prune, cranberry, apricot, or orange juice instead of more water. Add ½ lemon, skin and all, to the pot. You may want to add some cinnamon or cardamom. Bring to a boil over a low flame, and allow to cook about five minutes—till all the fruit has been thoroughly heated and the liquid has turned slightly syrupy.

As so often in these recipes, because you choose the ingredients, you will have to decide how much liquid is needed. You want enough so that each serving is wet and so that any fruit you store (in a lidded jar) is kept well damp. Obviously the really hard Greek or Turkish figs absorb more water than the plump California ones, and so on.

If you have candied fruit or dates, add them after the cooking. Chill, serve.

Stewed fruit keeps quite well in a tightly lidded jar, but do not try to keep it more than four or five days. It loses flavor.

Stewing is also the answer to damaged fresh fruit. For instance, suppose that you get stuck with pears that are not ripe, or that have brown marks inside (I think these come from a nip of frost, or a fungus) although the skin is fine. Or you are called away over the weekend, and the apples you left behind have developed ugly brown spots.

Peel the fruit and cook it. A small amount of red wine is fine with pears—cook till the pears are soft, then remove from flame and sweeten. Pears are also excellent cooked in very strong coffee—straight, black coffee, and sweetened after cooking. Cinnamon is the common spice for fruit, so if you like it, add it, sparingly. (The first time out, add the cinnamon to the cooled fruit. You will be able to judge the intensity better.) Cardamom can also be used.

You can, believe it or not, cook pears in plain water with a bit of vanilla, and then serve them, cooled, with chocolate sauce.

I do not like Pears Hélène but they should serve as a shiny example of How Far One Can Go With Fruit!

Apples are a cinch. Peel them, slice them thin, place in a buttered form in which they are stacked 2 inches deep, add more butter, a few spoonfuls of honey, and bake till translucent. Use a slow oven. You need not use cooking applies for this; table apples will do.

If you want to get fancier, and to have a more substantial dessert, try apple pudding cake.

Apple Pudding Cake

Buy: 5 cooking apples (about 2 pounds); brown sugar.

Have: butter; sugar; eggs; lemon rind; flour; baking powder.

Allow ¼ pound butter to get to room temperature. Add 3 well-beaten eggs alternately with ½ cup sugar and 1½ cups cake flour or all-purpose flour that you have mixed with 1½ teaspoons baking powder. Add the grated rind of 1 lemon, or the equivalent in freeze-dried lemon peel (found among the spices at the grocer's). Quickly peel your apples, add them to the dough (which will be quite liquid), and spread in a baking form or casserole. Bake 60 minutes at 325°F. While cake is still hot—just after it gets out of the oven—sprinkle with brown sugar. Serve hot or cold.

Peaches, plums, and apricots that are unripe when you get them, or have gotten a bit depressed in your keep, can be peeled and stewed. Peaches must first be dunked in boiling water, fished out as soon as their skin balloons, dunked in cold water, and then peeled. (The skin comes off very easily this way.)

Superannuated berries are a big problem. The best solution is to incorporate them in a gelatin dessert, *but* here if *one* strawberry in a basket has gotten moldy it can spoil the flavor of the whole dessert. You really must examine each berry carefully, sniff it, and double, triple check.

A Note on Cider

If, like me, you love cider and buy the unpasteurized kind, you will sooner or later have some that you have to get rid of before it spoils. (If it turns moldy, strain it and taste. Mold forms at the top a while before the cider itself changes flavor. Boil the cider and refrigerate.)

You can reduce it by half in volume (measure before, measure after) over a slow fire, and use the cider as your liquid in a gelatin dessert.

Or you can reduce the cider, and proceed as follows.

Peel a sufficient number of cooking apples. Chop small. Place in a baking dish and cover with reduced cider. Dot with butter, and sprinkle with brown sugar. Bake slowly till you have a homogeneous, translucent mass. A wonderful hot dessert, and fine with ham or chicken.

Custards, Puddings, and Such Trifles

Milk desserts fall into a number of categories: custards, which rely on egg yolks to thicken the milk; puddings, which are *very* thick white sauces, really, that is, milk thickened with starch; desserts such as ice creams in which freezing is the "thickening" agent; or Bavarians, in which gelatin is used to stiffen milk or cream or eggs.

Then there also are *trifles* and *fools*, in which pure whipped cream or thin custard or pudding is mixed with fruit and served well chilled on a bed of some dry cake such as sponge or macaroons (generally soaked first in sweet wine).

The charm of these desserts is that they are cheap if one does not use cream, and can be varied according to need or season. One can have *just* the custard (or cream) and fruit (*fool*) or just fruit and wine-soaked cake (closer to a *trifle*) or mix the fruit with the custard or pudding and crumbs—one can do almost anything! The dessert takes very little time to prepare, particularly if one uses a mix; it can be served in a large bowl, in individual cups, or in V-shaped glasses.

One last word: Pudding is to custard what a sense of humor is to wit. On the other hand, puddings are a lot easier to make because less can go wrong.

Pudding

Have: 2 cups milk (3 if this pudding is to go in a trifle); cornstarch; sugar or honey; vanilla extract. If you use dry milk, strengthen it by using only three-fourths the called-for amount of water.

Measure your milk into a small saucepan or the top of a double boiler.

In a bowl mix 3 tablespoons of cornstarch with milk spooned out from the measured quantity. Add the milk to the starch, gradually, and mix very well into a thin liquid. Add 1 or 2 tablespoons sugar or honey.

Bring the rest of the milk to a boil. Stir in ¼ to ½ cup sugar or honey. Remove instantly from the fire. Pour in the starch mix slowly, gradually, carefully.

Place the little saucepan in the one of boiling water (that is, put the top of the double boiler on the bottom), and stirring *constantly,* cook 10 minutes. Add ½ teaspoon vanilla. Cover, cook 5 more minutes, being sure there is enough water below.

Pour pudding into bowls or big bowl.

For chocolate pudding, either add 3 tablespoons Dutch cocoa to the starch mix, or melt 2 ounces chocolate in the cooking milk. (Stir as you melt. Chocolate will settle at the bottom till fully dissolved.)

NOTE: You can use other starches, such as potato or rice, but these vary so much that you either experiment or use a type that gives directions on the package. I use a rice flour bought at a Japanese store as exact substitute for cornstarch, but have had rice flours that require twice the amount of a cornstarch recipe.

Custard

Have: 4 eggs; sugar; 2 cups milk; (vanilla extract).

Bring 2 inches of water to boil in your big saucepan, or bottom of a double boiler.

In a small saucepan (or top of double boiler) beat 4 eggs

thoroughly and beat in the milk. If you will eat this plain, add ½ teaspoon vanilla extract. If you will use as base for trifle, omit the vanilla. Add 2 tablespoons sugar. Place the small saucepan in the big one, just above water level (place top on bottom of double boiler above water level). Cook, stirring, till the mixture thickens to the consistency of mayonnaise or shaving foam. If you are going to eat this plain, pour into a bowl or individual dishes. If you will use with a fool or trifle, cool slightly and add the fruit slowly to the custard—or pour the custard over the cake and then, when cool, add fruit on top.

As you no doubt guessed, some wise person early decided to combine the delicacy of custard with the safety of pudding. These creams are mostly used for fillings, but are ideal for trifles as well.

This recipe calls for folding in egg whites, a process in which your spoon describes a motion rather like wrapping a balloon in ribbon. It is more fully described on page 100.

Crème Custard

Have: 4 eggs; sugar; milk; almond or vanilla extract; cake or all-purpose flour.

Separate 4 eggs. Beat the yolks with ½ cup sugar till very well blended and light in color. Beat in 1½ tablespoons flour, and beat till well blended.

Bring 2 cups of milk to a boil, remove from fire,* and stir in the egg yolk mix gradually, slowly, carefully. Cook over the lowest possible flame, stirring constantly till it thickens. (You can also do this atop a double boiler. But the flour—instead of corn-starch—should allow some extra leeway with heat.) If you only have a thin-bottomed pan, place an asbestos plate above the flame.†

When the mixture thickens, cook a few minutes—till all flour

---

*The gas burner, though turned off, and the electric ring, though disconnected, continue to give off heat. It is better to remove the pot entirely from the burner.

·†You will need these metal-bound asbestos disks only if you make quite delicate egg-involving mixes. But these are a good investment also for you who keep a pan warm while waiting for someone to get home for supper!

taste is gone. Remove from fire and stir in ½ teaspoon vanilla or almond extract. Beat the egg whites stiff but not dry (see page 172) while the yolk mix cools to body temperature. Stir one-fourth of the egg whites into the yolk, then fold that mixture carefully into the remaining whites. Chill.

This can be used in a trifle, but you do not need such a delicate concoction in a mix. It is wiser to use this crème alone, accompanied perhaps by some really good macaroons.

How to Make a Trifle

Assemble your ingredients. Some two-day-old ladyfingers or sponge cake; or some macaroons or plain cookies. If you cannot get oldies, light your oven at the lowest setting, place the cake inside with the door open, and leave 30 minutes.

Have: 4 or 5 peaches, peeled; some plums you have brought to a boil in 1 cup water to 1 pound plums, cooled, pitted (or perhaps a package, generally ½ pound or 10 ounces unsweetened berries);* a can of gooseberries; canned apricots. Any mix of these you fancy. Bananas. A handful of nut meats.

Slice your cake into 1-inch slices, or make a 1-inch layer of big crumbs of cookies at the bottom of a big bowl or small individual bowls. Spoon on some orange liqueur mixed half-and-half with water, or some Madeira, Marsala, or a *good,* and I mean imported, sweet port. (These wines are not expensive, if you buy house brands, and a bottle lasts forever!)

Allow the cake to soak up the booze at least an hour. Make your pudding, custard, or crème, and add by pouring it atop the cake.

Right before serving, add the fruit—syrup and all. If you use fresh fruit, there won't be any syrup, but a few drops of grenadine or a bit more wine will give the delightfully sloppy texture this dessert is cherished for.

NOTE: When you add acid foods (in this case rhubarb or goose-

*Although boysenberries, blackberries, and dark grapes can be used, they do tend to give the trifle a rather eerie purple color!

berries) to nonacid ones—custard or pudding—*you must* add the acid very slowly, carefully, and gradually to the nonacid, or it all curdles. (No effect on flavor, but a blow to looks and pride.)

Baked Custard

A heavenly, simple dessert that is also a perfect breakfast food.

Have: 4 eggs; 2 to 2½ cups whole milk (or dry skim milk mixed up with only three-fourths the called-for amount of water); vanilla extract; 2 or 3 tablespoons honey or sugar.

Preheat your oven to 325°F.

Prepare an ovenproof dish into which you can fit a 1-quart ovenproof bowl. Fit the bowl into the outer dish, which you fill with hot water to 1 inch from the rim of the smaller bowl. Set the big dish with the water into the oven to preheat. (Only the big dish. You still need the little one.) These dishes need not be elaborate. I use a big and little mixing bowl. A cake tin will do.

Heat the milk till it begins to bead at the edges of the pot. Heat it very, very slowly. While it heats, thoroughly beat 4 eggs in the 1-quart bowl. Gradually, carefully, slowly add the hot milk to the eggs, beating them all the time. (This is easier if done by two people—one pouring, one beating.) Add sugar and ½ teaspoon vanilla extract, which you'd omit if you use honey. Set the bowl with the mix in the bowl in the oven, and bake 1½ hours or till a knife comes out clean, that is, with only a film of moisture on it, when you insert the tip ¾ inch into the center. Remove the custard immediately from the pan of water and the oven, and chill.

NOTE: The baking time is affected by shape of your baking dish. Ideally a custard should be as wide as it is deep.

NOTE: If you have a pressure cooker, you can cover the mix with a double layer of foil tied on really well, and place it on a rack (an inverted saucer will do) in your pressure cooker. Fill the cooker halfway up the custard pot with hot water, close, cook

15 minutes after 15 pounds pressure is reached. Cool immediately (following directions of pressure cooker manufacturer) to release pressure. Remove and chill custard.

This custard tastes good in a trifle, but is too stiff to be my custard-of-preference.

Lilly's Egg Cognac

Lilly is a superb cook, with all the generosity and the rich imagination of great cooks. This is one of the recipes she gave me when I married—to start me off right. (She also made marvelous cakes for the wedding and managed to find heart-shaped pans to do them in!)

Buy: smallest container of heavy cream.

Have: 5 egg yolks; sugar; brandy.

You can always use the cream elsewhere. For this you need only 2 ounces (1/4 cup).

Boil and cool the cream. Beat the yolks with ⅓ to ½ cup sugar. Stir in the cream. Return the mix to the saucepan, and *stirring all the time,* cook over lowest possible flame (don't boil) till mix thickens. Remove from flame and add ¾ cup brandy.

The recipe says this keeps a long time on ice. Not among us! Serve like ice cream.

Mint Ice Cream

Expensive, delicious, cool as can be. Not difficult to make.

Buy: 2 containers (16 ounces) heavy cream; peppermint sticks (you'll need 1 cup crushed); 1 large can evaporated milk (1-⅔ cups).

Smash the mint sticks fine; pea-sized or smaller. Scald the milk (that is, bring just to a boil) over low flame, add mints, and let them dissolve. Stir once or twice as the mix cools. Add 2 cups heavy (whipping) cream *unwhipped.* Stir well. Freeze in ice cube trays till firm. When firm, put in bowl, beat till fluffy, return to trays, freeze till firm, return to bowl for a second beating, then freeze solid. Makes about 1½ pints of very rich ice cream.

Bavarian—In This Case Raspberry

A Bavarian—and there are many varieties—is a dessert in which whipped cream is given body by gelatin. Basically one uses the amount of liquid called for by the gelatin recipe, substituting fruit for part of the liquid. The amount of cream can be increased or decreased, but I stick to 1 cup (that is, 1 small container).

Buy: 1 package frozen raspberries; 1 small container (8 ounces) heavy cream; gelatin.

Defreeze the frozen raspberries and use the juice as your liquid in preparing the gelatin according to the manufacturer's directions. Usually gelatin is dissolved in cold liquid, and this mix is poured into boiling liquid and stirred a few minutes till thoroughly dissolved. When the raspberry juice–gelatin mix is cooked, cool it to room temperature. Whip the cream. (It must be well chilled, so on a scorching day place your whipping bowl inside a bowl of ice while beating.) Mix it into the raspberry-gelatin mix. Add all the fruit, or reserve one-fourth for decoration. Chill in icebox.

NOTE: Whipped cream—with no sugar added—does not get stiffer than shaving foam. Sometimes, despite proper chilling, it will not even get there. The great advantage of Bavarians is that it does not matter too much if the cream is not stiff. *But* then you have to stir the mass a few times as it sets, or the fruit will settle out at the bottom.

NOTE: Bavarians are usually served unmolded. But there is no need to unmold, if you put it in a transparent bowl or individual glasses so one can appreciate the always pretty color.

To unmold, one tops the mold with a serving plate, dips the mold about halfway into hot water, counts to ten, lifts it out, and flips the whole thing, serving plate down, mold up. The heat will have loosened the mold from the Bavarian, which will settle on the plate, and allow the mold to be lifted off. You also can turn the thing upside down (mold above, plate below) first, and use steaming towels to loosen the mass.

Variations: Any number come to mind. Some favorites: 1 cup strong coffee as the liquid for the gelatin (most gelatins call for 2 to 2½ cups of total liquid, and the cream accounts for 1 cup) and crushed macaroons strewed in. About 3 ounces of the best bittersweet eating chocolate dissolved in the water. Dried apricots cooked with enough water to make 1 cup of liquid mashed and incorporated in a slightly lemon-flavored gelatin mix. *Just remember, if you use canned or frozen sweetened fruit, you need no extra sugar.*

Whipped Cream, Sour Cream, and Other Decadent Delights

I don't inveigh against light, sour, or whipped cream for two reasons. First, from personal experience, I find the high-protein/some-fat/low-carbohydrate school of weight control to be correct. (By *personal* I mean for *my* physical self, which makes it as impossible for me to recommend the method, as to speak against it.) Second, 1 cup of cream, when whipped, becomes 2 cups. The same guy who'll eat a half-pint of ice cream by himself is unlikely to consume that amount of cream dispersed in a Bavarian. Sour or light cream, lightly ladled onto fruit, would be a menace only to those on religiously antifat diets. And cream gives a morale-boosting feeling of luxury at small cost. Last, while ice cream and other commercial desserts may be laden with additives, cream is pure.

The next two dishes, *omelette soufflée* and blintzes, have great versatility and can be, alone, breakfast, brunch, or supper. I put them under desserts to show how nutritionally acceptable desserts can be, and how you can build a meal around dessert.

Omelette Soufflée

The plain omelet described earlier is made of the whole egg.

Here the white and yolk are scrupulously separated, the white beaten stiff but not dry, and the prebeaten yolk folded in. Because the beating adds such volume, you'll need a large (10-inch or more) frying pan to cook a two-egg omelet.

For dessert a two-egg omelet serves two people.

Separate the eggs, beat the whites with a pinch of salt. Beat the yolks to break them up, and make them runny. Fold the yolks into the whites. Meanwhile gently heat 2 tablespoons (¼ stick) of butter in your frying pan, and when it begins to bubble, pour the eggs in and lower your flame as much as possible. Lift the edges of the omelet to allow excess egg to run under.

When the edges of the omelet are brown, the inside should still have a silken sheen of moisture. (If it is still sopping, turn off the flame entirely and let the pan sit a moment.) Spoon a tablespoon of jelly or preserves onto the omelet (currant, strawberry, guava, peach, apricot) and slide onto a serving plate. Fold in two. Serve. (My omelets always seem to fold themselves as I slide them out. Hence I fill them in the pan.)

NOTE: If you have butter left in the pan, keep it for the next day. Extra butter is a form of insurance in omelet making.

NOTE: Once you're a pro, you can do 4 eggs in a 12-inch pan. The thicker the better, for this omelet.

NOTE: You realize, of course, that a sweet filling is optional and that preheated peas, minced ham, minced chicken with mushrooms are lovely, grand, and impressive too—but not for dessert.

Blintzes

Blintzes are crêpes, and what we call blintzes are not to be confused with blinis, which are made with buckwheat flour. Blintzes are fried on one side, filled, rolled, refried. Crêpes are cooked on both sides, then filled.

The main problem with blintzes is that they require time, space, and strategy. The batter should be mixed the night before if possible, but at least three hours ahead. A large, clean work surface must be prepared to receive the blintzes prior to filling and rolling. The cheese mix must be ready. The great charm of blintzes is that the pancakes can be made, filled, and rolled a day ahead of time and then cooked at the last minute.

Considering the work involved, you will not be shocked by my saying that it is not worthwhile to make less than this quantity, which is a main course for four (as at breakfast) or a dessert for six.

Buy: 1 pound cottage cheese; ½ pint sour cream.

Have: 2 eggs; milk; cake or all-purpose flour; sugar; butter; lemon juice.

Beat the 2 eggs, add 1 cup milk and 1 cup flour. Melt 2 tablespoons (¼ stick) butter and stir the melted butter into the batter. Refrigerate at least three hours. At this point most of the butter will have risen to the top in a thin sheet. Crush the butter with a fork and beat the batter very well. If you have a beater or a blender, use it.

You can also mix eggs, milk, and flour, let stand overnight, and add the melted butter before you make the blintzes next day. I have tried both methods, and both work. Whatever you do, mix the batter very, very well. It should be a thinnish, somewhat translucent liquid.

Add sour cream to cottage cheese gradually, to insure that mix remains rather stiff. Cover; set aside.

You now prepare a large, clean surface and cover it with plain (not terry) cloth and very clean dish towels atop a bed of newspaper, or use a double layer of paper towels atop newspaper. You also can use washed unbleached muslin, or the backs of old cotton shirts (clean, and preferably broadcloth).

At this point let me explain what is involved in cooking blintzes. The batter is poured into a really hot pan, and encouraged to form as quickly as possible a thin—but solid—pancake. This process goes very quickly, and several things affect it: the heat of the pan, the kind of flour, the size of the eggs used, the thickness of the pan, the consistency of the liquid.

Two common methods are used:

A. The batter is poured into the pan and immediately poured back into the container. This leaves a just-right pancake in the bottom of the pan. The disadvantage of this method is that even the brief contact with a hot pan thickens the batter that goes back into the jug, and water must be added after a while to thin it down to proper consistency.

B. A measuring cup is filled with batter and just enough is poured into the pan to make a pancake of the right thickness. The cook then checks what the amount used was, and knows how much to pour in for each pancake. The disadvantage of this method is that an extra vessel needs washing, and the cakes tend to turn out thicker.

NOTE: *In cooking blintzes, one really must swirl the frying pan slightly to spread the dough. This is no doubt dangerous, and one cannot be too careful. Make sure you are wearing long, tight sleeves, no bracelets, that your hair is out of the way, that you have room to step back should the frying pan catch fire.*

Ready?

If you use method A, assemble butter, batter, a wooden-handled spatula, and a jug of lukewarm water within convenient reach. For B, you omit the water.

Heat the pan—your small one (8 or 9 inch)—till a drop of water sizzles away in it as soon as it hits the pan.

Place a little bit of butter in the pan, swirl it to cover the bottom. (The butter in the batter makes blintzes *almost* self-lubricating.)

In method A your 1-2-3 procedure is:

1. Grab the pan firmly, using a pot holder.

2. Pour about ½ cup of batter in the center of the pan, swirl to just reach the edges, pour the excess batter back into the jug.

3. Replace the pan on the flame, which should be medium, and cook the blintz till the edge is just brown. The inside will still have a wet, raw look.

It takes about a count of 15 to cook a blintz, so count to 15 and lift the edge of the blintz to see that the bottom is golden. Remove the pan from the fire, invert it over your spread-out cloth or paper toweling, and dump the blintz face side down onto the cloth.

Once you have the proper rhythm your pan will hardly cool, and you go on and on, blintz after blintz.

Using method B, you pour in just enough batter so when you twirl the pan, a thin pancake without any excess forms, reaching the edges of the pan. Then cook exactly as above.

When all the blintzes are cooked, you proceed to fill them with the cottage cheese mix. If your work area is not all that big, you may have to cook the blintzes in two batches. On the other hand, if you have a helper who fills and folds the blintzes as you fry, you can do all at one time.

Spoon your cottage cheese mix—which you can flavor with some lemon juice or vanilla if you like—into the center of the blintz. The cheese should be firm, not stiff, but certainly not liquid enough to spread sideways on its own. Into the center of each blintz you place a small mound of cheese. Then you fold the blintz north to south, south to north, east to west, and west to east. There should be enough fold-over of pancake to allow you to pick up the blintz without its opening, but the blintz should not look like an emaciated Indian wrapped in a double blanket either!

Place the folded-up blintzes, folded side *down*, on a plate if you will fry them, or in an ovenproof dish. *Do not stack them in layers.*

You can now store the blintzes till ready to use.

To cook: Heat 2 tablespoons of butter in a large frying pan and place the blintzes in, folded side down. Leave enough room to maneuver a spatula because, when the bottom is golden, you have to turn them over and cook the other side.

Or: Place the blintzes in a well-buttered overproof dish (pour some melted butter into the one you placed them in yesterday) and bake. I prefer this less classical method, since it is easier by far.

Variations

Austrians do not fold blintzes, but fry both sides, then roll them around the filling.

You also can fry the blintzes on both sides at the first sitting, then stack them with cheese between layers, and bake the "pie."

To make dessert crêpes, you fry on both sides at the first sitting, fill immediately with jam or preserve, and serve. You can also sprinkle with sugar and serve with flavored whipped cream.

As blintz making is quite complex (in the abstract—the work itself is fun), let's check out a few problems you may run into.

1. *The blintz is too thick.* This means it cannot be folded without breaking. Remedy: *roll* the blintz around the filling, or stack the blintzes and cheese into a layer-cake effect and bake. If you realize they are too thick as you are making them, a little extra water in the batter or less dough in the pan is in order.

2. *The blintz is too thin.* It has holes, or tears from the weight of the cheese. Use the blintzes double, or roll them, or try the layer-cake method of filling. If you realize they are too thin as you go along, and are using method B, change to method A till the batter thickens. Or, keeping the flame low, add a bit more batter, using method B. Or, for method A, let the batter sit in the pan a little longer before pouring the excess back.

3. *Cheese oozes out.* Cottage cheeses vary in solidness; some take more sour cream, others less. You may have added too much and gotten too liquid a mix. Or you may have overstuffed the blintz so it's "bursting at the seams." The layer-cake method in a really deep dish is the best remedy.

NOTE: Many people use about half the milk and flour per egg of this recipe. This makes an eggier, also more delicate and fragile, blintz. This recipe makes a hardier pancake, and is better for the first times out.

NOTE: Many recipes incorporate an egg yolk in the cheese mix. I do not, because the cheese does not get hot enough to guarantee against the survival of salmonella.

NOTE: Many people sweeten the cheese mix. The big disadvantage is that any cheese that oozes into the pan during the second frying will immediately caramelize and be almost impossible to scrape out. (Believe me, at a certain temperature cottage cheese and sugar make a glue tougher than epoxy!) There is no terrific advantage in sweetening the cheese. So *don't,* unless you like risk.

If you have leftover blintzes uncooked, they remain quite fine for two or three days in the refrigerator. If they have been cooked a second time, they can be eaten cold the next day. (After that they are likely to get soggy.)

If you have only pancakes left, you can roll them, slice them into something like noodles, and use as you would noodles—in a soup, or baked a few minutes to be eaten hot.

The leftover cheese mix can, of course, be used many ways. Just as is is fine. (Another reason not to add egg.)

Blintzes fried on both sides can be rolled around a hot meat or vegetable or fish filling and become crêpes. This involves a white sauce, to which we now proceed.

18 / Sauces: The Coward's Way to Heaven

Among the things one's mother should have told one is that a sauce is the simplest thing in the world to make, and one of the quickest, easiest ways to cook oneself out of a spot!

And of the sauces the cornerstone is the *white sauce*. Now the white sauce (which becomes a *brown sauce* if you allow the fat and flour to cook together till they turn dark tan) changes its name throughout *haute cuisine*—but it remains a mixture of fat and liquid thickened by starch over heat.

White Sauce

The best fat to use is butter. The starch should be all-purpose (or cake) flour, which does not, like cornstarch, get damaged by heat. You can use potato or rice flour, but as I said in the chapter on desserts, these are less standardized, so you have to experiment with quantities.

Basically a "normal" white sauce—which is the thickness

of melted ice cream—has 2 tablespoons (¼ stick) of butter and 2 tablespoons of flour to 2 cups milk. For a thinner sauce you use less flour and butter, and for a thicker sauce you increase flour and butter. As a matter of fact, for a thicker sauce you can quite easily *just* raise the amount of flour. It does not give as rich a flavor, but it works perfectly well.

To make the sauce, you melt the butter, remove the pot from the flame, stir in the flour, then cook, stirring constantly and vigorously till the mix foams. You then *carefully and slowly* add scalded milk or cream (light—or what rises to the top of unhomogenized milk) and cook stirring *constantly and strongly* until thick and smooth. Add salt and pepper and continue cooking over very low heat for about five minutes.

NOTE: This method is somewhat different from the one outlined under cream soups. The difficult part of a white sauce is the cooking of flour and fat without burning, and the addition of liquid without lumping. Since soup has to be cooked a while *anyway,* the method we suggested there of mixing fat and flour and adding the liquid right away is "safer." But you can follow this method just as well.

For appropriate dishes you can fry some very finely chopped onion in the butter before adding the flour, and cook the sauce a while longer, stirring very often over a tiny flame, or using a double boiler. (You need to cook it longer to get the flavor through and through.) You are not confined to milk for your liquid; either bouillon or the water in which a vegetable has been cooked is great. For a poached fish you use the liquid in which it was cooked, augmented with dry white wine, being sure to strain the poaching water before adding it to your sauce. You can use any of these liquids to dilute dry skim milk and make your sauce with that.

A white sauce need not end on a main course. Made with chocolate milk, or with cocoa added, it makes a hot chocolate sauce ideal for French toast or waffles. Made with the liquid from stewed fruit or from frozen raspberries or strawberries, it is lovely over ice cream, cottage cheese, custard, pudding.

One exciting variation—very close to the cream custard we had under desserts—is the following.

Mornay Sauce

Make a medium white sauce. Beat 2 egg yolks with a few spoons of milk, beat in the cooled but not cold white sauce. Return the mix to the stove, cook, stirring vigorously and constantly till it is just ready to boil. At this point one adds 2 to 4 tablespoons of grated cheese.

One need not add the grated cheese. The white sauce enriched with egg yolk is quite rich and elegant and is the white sauce used *de préférence* when the sauce is to be mixed with a food that will be baked. (Cauliflower or white onions or spinach, for instance, on occasions when you do not want cheese on them as well.)

NOTE: In the case of these sauces I not only say *stir constantly* but *stir vigorously*. Constantly means all the time, to keep the concoction from settling. This is enough for thinnish mixes, or when you are using a double boiler. But these starch mixes are quite thick and sluggish, and the *walls and bottom of a pot are considerably hotter than the center*. So you must work the mix energetically with a scraping of sides and bottom, and a near-beating motion.

NOTE: When you want to make a meat sauce—or thicken a pot roast gravy, or use red wine as your liquid—make a brown sauce. Simply allow the flour and butter to fry together till golden. Don't let them burn. Not only is the taste ghastly, but the thickening quality of the flour will be lost.

NOTE: That magic French invention *beurre manié*—which does not mean *maniac's butter*, but *manipulated butter*—is made by mashing an equal amount of butter and flour together, and adding it to the cooking juice of stews to thicken them. This is, I feel, a better method than flouring the meat, as it is done at the last moment when you *can* watch that nothing burns. For each cup of liquid, you want 2 tablespoons fat and 2 tablespoons flour. You drop the blend in bit by bit, and *allow to simmer, not boil.*

As you now understand, you make a brown sauce when you have a dry meat that needs a sauce. You use *beurre manié* to thicken existing sauces. Or you make a brown sauce out of stew "juice" and return to the stew at the last minute.

Yet another example of the endless possibilities available to you.

Uses of White Sauce

Close to endless. Add curry powder (first dissolved in cold water) or paprika, and use to turn leftover chicken or turkey into a ragout. (Add a fistful of seedless raisins to the curry sauce.) You can use to cook any otherwise dull vegetable—spinach, cauliflower. And of course for small white onions. You can mix with tuna and bake. With horseradish (added after the cooking, since horseradish, like capers, should not be boiled) a white sauce is the classic topping for boiled beef. But, most exciting, you can make crêpe fillings—which simply are a minced something, held together by white sauce.

The Mornay sauce is as versatile, and terribly good with baked cauliflower, or mixed with drained clams and baked.

Crêpes

Prepare blintzes, frying on both sides at one go—that is, do not flop them out onto a cloth, but turn in the frying pan to fry second side.

As a filling, leftover (cooked) chicken, ham, or any soft vegetable works fine. Chicken livers (already cooked) are lovely. Mushrooms are ideal.

Skin and debone the chicken and cut fine. Trim and mince

ham. Drain the vegetables you might be using (you can use the liquid in your white sauce).

Whatever you use as filling, mix the ingredient with a *thick* white sauce, roll the filling into a blintz, align the rolled blintzes in a greased baking form, cover with more filling, and bake till thoroughly hot.

Combinations can be used: chicken and ham; chicken and canned mushrooms; strips of mozzarella along with tomatoes or asparagus or ham; chopped hard-boiled eggs, some cheese, spinach; canned salmon, drained and boned and skinned.

Crêpes are *not* good reheated. But you can make your pancakes and your filling ahead of time, and roll and bake only at the last minute.

Clams Mornay

Can be extended by the addition of some cooked bland fish such as cod.

Buy 1 can (6 to 8 ounces) of chopped clams.

Have makings of a Mornay sauce.

Prepare half the amount of thick white sauce described above. Use 3 tablespoons butter, 3 tablespoons flour, but 1 cup liquid—which should be the liquid from the clam can* mixed with dry milk powder, or the liquid from the can mixed with 1 cup milk and boiled down to 1 cup. Use only 1 egg yolk. Mix the clams with the completed sauce, put in a buttered ovenproof dish, sprinkle with more cheese, and bake five minutes in a hot oven, then broil just long enough to get the top crusty.

Again, you can prepare the sauce ahead of time, but this dish cannot be reheated and should be cooked only till piping hot. If your baking dish is wide enough and the clams in it are shallow

---

*Although canned clams are far less sandy than the ones one shells oneself, it is still a good idea to strain the juice through a piece of filter paper or a doubled-over piece of muslin (or clean, old shirting or T-shirting).

(should not be more than an inch deep), five minutes is right. Do *not* overcook. With salad, supper for two. Appetizer for four.

19 / Salads: Pleasures and Pitfalls

Say "salad," and immediately visions of summer appear. In a series of books that regaled my childhood—the super-Victorian works of Madame de Ségur—there always were troops of sturdy French peasants (who knew their place under the broiling sun) feasting at noon on hard-boiled egg salad and cider. This seemed to me a repast worthier than any *we* ever got—and now that I can prepare it on my own, I still love it.

But say "salad," and just as quickly visions of newspaper headlines spring to mind: *Sunday school class poisoned on picnic; outing ends in death,* etc. That most harmless of foods, *salad,* that most delicious of summer delicacies, can easily, because it *is* blazing August, turn treacherous, and sometimes fatal.

So if you make salads that go beyond a simple mixing of greens and other vegetables, be very careful:

1. Keep all ingredients separate and refrigerated.

2. Whenever possible, sprinkle protein (that is, nonvegetable) ingredients with some acid, such as vinegar or lemon juice, before storing.

3. Use sour cream as a dressing instead of mayonnaise (if possible).

4. If you use mayonnaise, keep it iced till the last moment.

5. On real scorchers, use only oil and vinegar if you cannot keep the salad cool throughout the meal.

6. Mix too little rather than too much. Get rid of all leftovers.

7. *Do not,* in summer, make salads as sandwich filling.

8. If you buy a salad, be sure to go to a store that is busy enough, and reliable enough, to have absolutely fresh salads made daily, or preferably twice a day.

9. *Never* buy a salad that is not icy cold.

10. *Never* buy a salad you can't get back on ice within a very short while.

If you love egg salad and tuna salad and chicken salad as much as I do, you will forgive the negative notes, and understand I only wish you (and me) the longevity to feast on them through many another summer.

Mayonnaise

Know how to make your own, then don't! There are perfectly fine commercial mayonnaises (commercial salad dressings, even though they look like mayonnaise, are *not)* and good ones at the health food stores too. We buy the smallest jars in summer, larger ones in winter, and I make my own only on rare occasions. I am not fond of homemade mayonnaise, I do not prefer it to the brand I buy, and since homemade mayonnaise does not keep more than a day, I do not think it worth the effort.

There are a number of superstitions attendant to the making of mayonnaise, some of which cannot be repeated here. But *The Joy of Cooking* assures us that one really *cannot* make a mayonnaise during a thunderstorm or when one is lowering, and so scratch that as a myth and *believe* it. (Mrs. Rombauer is never wrong, I've found!)

To make a mayonnaise:

Take the yolk of one perfectly fresh egg, having checked the shell and washed it thoroughly before cracking the egg. The slightest defect in the shell makes it unwise to use it, because the yolk is to be eaten raw.

Beat the egg yolk thoroughly, and then drop by drop add your favorite oil. Literally add a single drop, beat the egg yolk, add a second drop, beat again, till each time the oil is totally incorporated. When you have added 1 tablespoon of oil this way, you can start adding the oil a bit more at a time. When the mix is really stiff, add lemon juice or vinegar, first drop by drop, then a little faster. I use a fork for the mixing. My mother uses a spoon.

For a single yolk you use ½ cup of oil. How much vinegar depends on you, and on how thin you want the mayonnaise. I use about ¼ cup. The oil thickens; the acid—lemon juice or vinegar—thins.

You can beat the white of the egg stiff as can be, then fold it into the finished mayonnaise. This gives a marvelously light, fluffy sauce for cold chicken or fish. (It also is better for those who must watch their fat intake.)

Some people add the acid first, then the oil. Some people alternate acid and oil. But *always* drop by drop. Some people beat, others stir. All the methods work, and all can fail, in which case the mayonnaise curdles. In my experience the fault generally lies with an unfresh egg or a too-hot room. The only remedy is to prepare a fresh egg yolk and make a fresh mayonnaise using the curdled one as your sole liquid addition.

Mayonnaise making is serious business, and I find it a bore. It leads to bitter family feuds, and all sorts of anxiety. In gourmet circles, however, it's *very* "in" to boast of always making one's own mayonnaise! So now you know.

Variations

Add as much raw, mashed garlic as you can tolerate, and you have *aïoli*.

Add chopped tarragon and chopped chives and chopped parsley. Nice with seafood or bland (chicken or turkey) fowl.

Add curry powder (first dissolved in a little water). Nice with hard-boiled eggs, or cold, boiled, bland fish.

Add mustard, or paprika, or capers and chopped pickles.

In all cases add salt and pepper after you have mixed the mayonnaise with the prepared food and/or other ingredients.

False Mayonnaise

Hard-boil 2 eggs. Cool. Discard whites. Mash the yolks well with oil, cut with vinegar. For a salad dressing this will just about replace mayonnaise. It gives the egg-yolk flavor, but of course none of the smooth richness.

Chef's Salad

From whenever the lettuces start coming out of the garden till they stop in early fall, this is our favorite fare, and although restaurants rarely use their imagination on it, it can be made in variations you never dreamt of.

Buy: ham; rolled turkey; one or two hard cheeses; tuna; fresh or canned shrimp; chicken breasts; etc.

Have: cold leftover meat; hard-boiled eggs; greens; oil, vinegar, or mayonnaise; salt; pepper.

Assemble a suitable quantity of several of the above ingredients. There should be one or two greens, and one or two nongreens. Possibly more. You can, for instance, use only tuna and hard-boiled eggs; hard-boiled eggs and Swiss cheese; ham and chicken. The one combination I do not like is tuna and shrimp *only*, because the tuna overpowers the shrimp. But tuna, shrimp, and hard-boiled eggs is very good.

Cook what needs cooking (chicken breasts or fresh shrimp). Drain what needs draining. Wash what needs washing, and dry on paper towels. If you use tuna canned in oil, rinse under very hot water to get the oil out, if the tuna is to be mixed with other things. Slice the meats and cheeses into thin slivers. *Very* thin is better. Quarter the eggs lengthwise.

Tear your greens or chop into suitable size. Greens, in this case, include tomatoes, peppers, avocados, celery, fennel, green onions, raw fresh peas, parsley.

Select your greens with your other ingredients in mind. Fennel or green pepper should be used in moderation in a big mix. But fennel can come on strong with just chicken and turkey.

If you like pickled beets, drain and use them. But just strew them on top at the last moment. Mixed in, they give a rather frightful color.

You can shred carrots into this salad. But I would avoid cabbage because of its too-strong flavor.

Mix the ingredients well and douse generously with salad dressing. A heavier-bodied dressing such as mayonnaise or sour cream is better here.

If you do your cutting and shredding ahead of time, keep the nonvegetable, that is, protein, ingredients in the refrigerator, doused with a little lemon juice or mild vinegar.

Other Salads

All to be mixed with mayonnaise.

Egg salad: Mashed hard-boiled eggs, with chopped green pepper and/or celery, and/or a tinge of onion. Mashed hard-boiled egg, some mustard. Mashed hard-boiled egg plus drained, chopped anchovies.

Tuna salad: Straight tuna. One 7-ounce can tuna and 1 or 2 hard-boiled eggs. Tuna and/or eggs with celery and/or green pepper and/or capers.

Chopped liver: Fried or broiled chicken or beef liver chopped fine with one-third to one-half the volume in hard-boiled egg; with or without some raw or fried onion. (This recipe, from our friend Ciceil, is more digestible and also better than the traditional chopped liver, made with chicken fat.)

Salmon salad: Drain, bone, and skin canned salmon. Use straight with mayonnaise or add some capers. Same can be done with cooked fish such as cod, flounder, haddock.

Chicken: Mince leftover chicken. Remove all skin and cartilage. Add celery, green pepper, and/or capers. Or you can add curry to your mayonnaise, then mix with chicken and celery.

Cold meat: Assuming you have well-done leftover steak or a rather dry pot roast. Dice meat small, sprinkle with some vinegar. Let sit in refrigerator a few hours. Add some pickled beets. Add mayonnaise or sour cream.

Herring salad: Chopped pickled herring. Do not get chopped herring! Buy pickled herring and chop it into ½-inch pieces. Add to 4 filets: 4 hard-boiled eggs, 1 medium-sized chopped apple, 2 or 3 chopped (cooked or pickled) red beets. Some people also add peas or a cold boiled potato. Mix well and allow to rest an hour or so before serving. You can use sour cream instead of mayonnaise. *This is a recipe for a perfectly delicious dish. But herring salad is and remains an acquired taste. Try the salad first at a German or Scandinavian restaurant, and do not spring it on unsuspecting friends!*

20 / Celebration: Special Dishes for Special Occasions

The time will come when you will want to celebrate something, or when you will suddenly have a guest of honor you don't quite know what to do with! I am assuming here that when you get together with friends and peers, you keep it informal, but that your celebration will include your parents, your hometown minister who drops in (!), your boss, a favorite teacher, or your lover's parents—something that brings out the conventional celebrant in all of us.

Food as celebration is as old as mankind and remains part of our religions and part of our social rite. So it should be taken seriously, and a successful dinner party requires planning. In fact, I'd say the key to a successful dinner party is three-fourths planning and one-fourth cooking. And if you are faced with the necessity of an instant party (John and Mary have not only eloped this afternoon but are leaving the country tomorrow!), keep it absolutely simple. (I'd suggest champagne and cheese for John and Mary.)

1. *Plan ahead.* The more hurried you are, the simpler your meal must be.

2. *Concentrate on one course, keep the rest minimal.* Decide which course to feature, build the meal around that. Do not, as I did in my youth, have a fancy appetizer, a fancy main course, a fancy dessert.

3. *Have a few people only.* Sounds unfriendly, but it's not. If you want a big group, have a party. (See next chapter.) But if you want your parents all to meet, restrict it to that. If you want Dad and Mom to meet the legendary Professor McGillicudy,

don't invite seven other students who also love the professor. Better to have the McGillicudys over twice.

4. If you live alone, give yourself time the day of the celebration. Arrange enough time between coming home and serving dinner so you do not have to rush. If you have a co-host (and you might find one just for the occasion), co-host can "play" with the guests and you can have a bit more time after they arrive.

5. A last word: *it's your home!* Even now that I've had a room of my own for more than half my life, I still am never as conscious of it as when I have guests. You do *not* need to say yes if someone asks if he may smoke. (A very good friend says firmly, kindly *no*. Smoke makes her sick.) You are *not* obliged to serve hard liquor if you yourself do not drink it. (You are also under no obligation to serve wine! Pity! If you are supergracious, you will have a few bottles of liquor for those who want it. Do not, however, propose to mix martinis or such if you do not know how. (The result may be undrinkable.) Do not feel that courtesy demands you permit anything that makes *you* uncomfortable. Courtesy demands that your guests bow to your preferences.

I mention this because I get sympathetic nervous twinges when I see young friends shoved into the background of their own dinner parties—generally by their mothers, who have a great way of taking over. *Everyone is your guest,* you are totally in charge, and while you certainly do not want to refuse well-intentioned help, you do not want your role usurped either.

While there are a number of recipes throughout this book that can easily be made in sufficient quantity for six or eight (all of the stews, the lemon chicken, meatballs, lasagne), here are a few recipes that, *a priori*, are party menus. Of necessity there is too much for two.

Pot-au Feu

Also called *petite marmite*, this is a simple boiled stew—equal parts of fowl and beef with vegetables—whose "secret" is that special care is taken with the slicing, dicing, and seasoning so everything looks very pretty and tastes perfect.

Buy: 2 pounds of chicken or chicken breasts and legs; 2 pounds chuck, flank, or other lean *pot-roast* cut; 2 pounds of soup bones; 4 or 5 leeks or a bunch of scallions; a bunch of soup greens or an old carrot, old celery, onion; carrots; 2 turnips (the size of oranges); fresh parsley.

Have: salt; pepper; nutmeg.

Cut the chicken into handy pieces, wash, place in your biggest pot.

Wash the meat, trim off all fat and skin, cut into small, bite-sized pieces. Place in pot.

Wash the soup bones, check for bone splinters. Add to pot.

Wash the soup greens, or the vegetables you will use as such, tie them up with a bit of twine. Include a few sprigs of parsley in the bunch. Peel, dice, add the turnips. (The onion will have to be separate.)

If you have leeks, pull them leaf from leaf and wash leaf by leaf. Leeks are inordinately sandy, and the sand remains in the bulb. Many people, who do not seem to mind sand, slice the leek across like an onion, but we cannot abide grit, so my method, not as pretty, is safer. Discard any faded or tired part of the leek tops, chop the whole thing, add to pot. If you use scallions, clean, wash, discard bad leaf tops, chop, add to pot. (Leek is more traditional, scallion cheaper.)

Cover the ingredients in the pot with water, bring to a quick boil without the lid. Skim, reduce flame to lowest possible, allow to cook, uncovered, till the chicken is done. (Cooking with the lid off keeps heat down, just as covering a pot increases heat. Also, boiling meat foams, easily cooks over. Keep skimming; feed foam to pet.)

When chicken is done, fish it out, cool as quickly as possible. (Meanwhile other ingredients go on simmering.) Skin and bone the chicken, slicing the meat as prettily as you can into bite-sized pieces.

Place the skin and bones in a second pot, over very low flame, giving them some of the broth as their cooking liquid. (You want to boil out all the goodness in that skin and bones without over-cooking the chicken meat.)

Go on cooking both pots slowly till the main pot has cooked two hours. Strain the chicken-bone stock into the main pot. *You can now interrupt the whole thing and let the pot and the chicken meat stay in the icebox overnight.*

A suitable time before serving:

Fish out the bunch of soup greens, give them a little squeeze to get the last drop of soup out, fish out your onion. Discard greens and onion. Remove fat that's formed at the top.*

Clean your carrots, slice prettily into circles or strips, add to the soup. Add the chicken meat.

Add salt, pepper, some nutmeg; taste and retaste till just right.

Serve with some fresh parsley sprinkled atop.

If you do not have chance to chill overnight allow to rest 20 minutes or so before heating to serve. Fat will rise to top and can be spooned off, or a piece of dry bread can be used as sponge to remove fat.

You can serve in individual bowls (soup and meats and carrots together) or have a main serving dish.

Prettiness and just-perfect seasoning are called for here, and are what turns a peasant dish into a feast.

A very light red wine can be served, though a white Burgundy seems safer. Spanish or French or California wines will do; German or Alsatian would, in most cases, be too fruity for this meal.

To start, serve an extremely well-made salad, with a touch of pungency, such as watercress or oranges. For dessert, fruit and a ripe, runny cheese.

Waterzooie

Although I spent my early childhood in Antwerp, don't ask me to pronounce the name of this queen of Belgian cuisine. The

*Save it in a lidded jar; use sometime soon in pâté.

W is a V sound, and the rest is like J. D. Salinger's hero. More or less.

Like pot-au-feu, Waterzooie can be made mostly the day before. *Unlike pot-au-feu, it cannot easily be reheated, and must be finished just before serving.*

So an Italian-style appetizer with a number of things—olives, celery, shrimp, cheese, salami—would be a good thought, which will keep your guests happily chatting and nibbling while you stalk off for the final touches.

Buy: 1 capon* or 7 pounds of chicken (buy the biggest you can get); 4 or 5 leeks or a bunch of scallions; 1 bunch soup greens or assortment of parsley, carrots, celery; 2 small onions; soup bones and 2 pounds soup meat, or 3 pounds chicken parts, or 2 cans beef or chicken broth; ⅓ cup heavy cream); 2 big lemons or 1 lemon plus lemon juice.

Have: thyme; bay leaf; nutmeg; (milk); eggs.

Make 3 or 4 cups of stock out of the chicken parts and/or bones. If you use soup meat, you have, of course, another meal. The stock will jell if kept in the icebox. Reheat and strain.

Cut the chicken or capon in a couple of big pieces, so it will fit tidily into your biggest pot. Rinse and dry, and broil skin thoroughly under broiler or fry really brown in pan with butter. Drain off excess fat.

Place browned fowl in your largest pot, and add cleaned soup greens, tying whatever you can into a bunch. Reserve some parsley for later. Add your vegetables. Add 1 bay leaf, ⅛ teaspoon thyme.

Add your strained stock, and enough water to cover fowl. Simmer slowly, uncovered, skimming any foam that comes up. When chicken is cooked, remove it from pot and chill it quickly. When it is cool enough to handle, cut into portion-sized pieces. Unlike pot-au-feu, Waterzooie is chicken with a sauce, not meat served in broth. You use knife and fork. Return skin and bones to the pot and simmer for a total cooking time of two hours.

---

*A capon is a castrated rooster, and in my judgment the best tasting of *all* fowl. Roast capon is my choice over roast turkey, or goose, or duck any day.

Strain the stock. If you do not have a fine sieve, line a coarse
one with cheesecloth folded triple, or a piece of muslin.

You can prepare the meal ahead of time up to this point.
When you are ready to serve:
Chop some parsley to sprinkle atop soup.

Wash and cut up one lemon so each diner has one or two
wedges.

Separte four eggs, and beat the yolks with ⅓ cup of milk
or cream.

Place the chicken meat in a small pot, with a few spoons
of broth, and cover. Heat.

Meanwhile slowly heat the rest of the broth, of which there
should be about 3 cups. Add salt, pepper, nutmeg, and the juice
of 1 lemon (or equivalent from bottled juice). Taste and retaste
till just right. There would be a faint taste of nutmeg, a stronger
one of lemon.

When the chicken and the stock both are good and hot, reduce
the flame under the stock so it no longer boils, and stir in the
yolk/milk mix. Stir thoroughly till the stock thickens, turn flame
off *immediately*, add the chicken and its liquid, stir again. Serve
out of the cookpot, sprinkling each portion with parsley and putting
some lemon on the side, or serve in a tureen. Serve with rice,
boiled potatoes, or noodles.

To keep this hot you need to keep it over boiling water.

An endive or watercress salad should follow this, and fruit
for dessert is fine. This is a fairly rich dish, and cheese might
be too much. A white wine, cider, or lager beer and lots of rye
bread and butter are the accompaniment for Waterzooie.

Noodles

•   Egg noodles have some extra merit over plain spaghetti or
rice. And they are a nice change from potatoes. Prepared with
lots of butter, and a bit of crushed garlic added at the very end,

buttered noodles are a delight, and very good served along with pot-au-feu or Waterzooie. (For the latter, omit garlic.)

Buttered Noodles

Buy: ½ pound egg noodles. Some like fine, some like wide. Pick what you prefer.

Have: ⅛ pound butter; (1 clove fresh garlic); salt; pepper; (herbs).

Bring 3 quarts of water to a full boil.

Add noodles. Count 2 minutes after the noodles are boiling for fine, and 3 minutes for wider. Fish out a noodle, taste. It should be cooked through (no hardness or starchiness in middle, but not soggy). Dump noodles in strainer, run cold water over them a second. Return to empty pot, and half a stick (⅛ pound) butter, toss till all butter is melted. Pot is warm enough to melt butter and keep noodles hot without flame. Add salt and pepper, serve.

If you plan to use garlic: crush, peel, chop clove ahead of time, sprinkle on the noodles at last toss.

This dish keeps warm quite well if covered with foil and placed in slow oven in a water bath.

Variation: Add lots of grated cheese, cottage cheese, or ricotta, and bake awhile in oven till brown at top. An excellent accompaniment to stews.

Add any herbs—oregano, fresh basil, fresh parsley, chives, premixed blends.

Pâtés: Liver and Otherwise

A pâté is nothing more than a steamed meat loaf. It is usually on the fat side, although most of the fat is squeezed out in cooling. It is usually made with lard, bacon drippings, goose or chicken fat rather than butter. *Pâté maison* (or like Maman used to make) frequently combines chopped-up *cooked* meat with finely ground *fresh* meat. Nothing is easier to make than a pâté, so here goes.

Lilly's Liver Pâté

Buy: 1 pound beef, chicken, or pork liver.

Have: ½ cup animal fat; nutmeg; allspice; bay leaf; salt; pepper; egg; ¼ cup bread crumbs.

Chicken liver is easier to work, pork is cheapest. Quite frankly, the next step sounds worse than it is. With a large, sharp knife peel and scrape the liver till it is pudding-like. Remove the veins carefully. Go on scraping and chopping till you have a smooth mass. (This takes no more than 3 minutes!)

Place liver in a bowl, add 1 egg per pound of liver, add salt, pepper, and a good pinch of allspice and nutmeg (about ⅛ teaspoon each per pound of meat at buying weight). Add ¼ cup crumbs on same basis.

Mix in ½ cup of fat. It will dissolve and permeate the mass, so don't work too hard at getting it blended in.

Place the mix in a fireproof dish and tie a double layer of aluminum foil over the top, tightly. Place the covered pot inside a larger pot with boiling water three-fourths of the way up the sides of the lesser pot. Cover the large pot and cook 45 minutes after water boils. If you use a pressure cooker, you will only need to cook 15 minutes, after pressure is reached.

Cool till you can handle with pot holders, cut the string but leave the foil, and place a heavy weight on top of the liver pot to press the fat out. This also gives it a sliceable texture. A #2 can is heavy enough, or use a saucer with a stone on it.

Chill well before serving. This is an appetizer for four or a main course for two. Unmold and slice.

You can make this with a bigger proportion of egg (2 per pound). This makes a fluffier pâté, and it should not be pressed, but left in the mold and served with a spoon rather than sliced.

Ham Pâté

Buy: 2 pounds veal, or veal and beef mixed, which you get the butcher to put through the grinder twice; 2 pounds boiled ham, sliced 1/8 inch thick.

Have: 1 small onion; some brandy; lard; bacon drippings or chicken fat; parsley; salt; pepper; 2 eggs.

Lay out the ham slices and cut them into slivers ⅛ inch by 1 or 1½ inches. Mix 1 or 2 ounces of brandy with the chopped meat. Add finely chopped onion and 3 tablespoons fresh parsley, chopped, or equivalent in dry parsley. *Taste your ham. If it is very salty, add no salt.* Otherwise add 1 teaspoon salt and generous sprinkle of pepper.

Work 2 eggs and ½ cup fat into the mass and mix in the ham. Cook exactly as the pâté above, for 1 hour in a regular pot, or 20 minutes in a pressure cooker with a 15-pound weight (time after the pressure is reached). In a water bath in the oven, this takes about 2 hours.

Since this recipe uses precooked pork, you do not need to worry about undercooking, but pâté should be well done for flavor.

Serve hot; or cool, press, chill, and slice like the pâté above. A fine summer dish for six to eight persons.

Pâté is best made a day or two ahead. It will keep three or four days in the refrigerator if well sealed. (It picks up flavors easily.) Cover with a double layer of foil or plastic, and be sure it is on tightly.

People will tell you pâté keeps for weeks. Actually if you seal it by covering with a layer of melted lard or chicken fat (as one seals jams with paraffin), it will keep a bit longer than three to four days. But it develops that gamy flavor called *faisandé* or *high.* It is an acquired taste, and I, for one, abhor it.

Raw pâté mix freezes very well. Cooked pâté loses all texture in the freezer. You need not be rigid about proportions, by the way. You can concoct quite a number of variations; all should work.

21 / Giving a Party: Cautionary Words, Mostly

Giving a party can easily turn into a disappointment. I have given parties for twenty to fifty people, and most of them I've not enjoyed. More recently we've kept ourselves down to fifteen or so—we have a very large house—and that is just about right.

Giving a party is really not a good way of enjoying *oneself*. It is a wonderful way of honoring a friend, celebrating someone else's occasion, but I think it wisest to own up to the probability that host and hostess will not have such a great time.

Then one can approach the subject calmly, as a labor of great love, and not face disillusionment.

1. *Don't crowd yourself.* If you have enough space for 6 for a sit-down dinner, and 8 or 10 buffet style, you can accommodate about 12 people at a party where no food is served, and about 20 quite likely if a program—such as a discussion or movie—will keep guests a homogeneous group, rather than little offshoots.

2. *Don't serve food.* Even sandwiches are a nuisance. Parties tend to develop a flow of their own, and anything that interrupts this flow may do so definitively. *Do have* bowls of fruit and nuts and maybe cookies about, and pitchers of something to drink.

3. *Do something about your pet.* My dogs hate noise, and I've been attacked at parties by animals who otherwise loved me. Animals dislike crowds. Shut your pet in a cozy room, if you can, or ask a neighbor or friend to keep the animal overnight, even if friend or neighbor comes to your party. Animals deserve courtesy too, and frankly, not everyone likes a bite or scratch!

4. *Warn your neighbors.* Not always possible, but thoughtful. One of the nicest gestures of this type I've encountered was an invitation from the girl next door (whom I did not know) to a jazz party. I could not come, but had I been home I would have gone. So wise, too, to circumvent my getting mad.

5. *Be realistic.* I lament the facts, but face them. Gatherings of young people, students, artists, etc. draw attention. *You* are

likelier to get a visit from the police than is a superannuated fraternal order, or a Sodality twice as old and three times as noisy as you.

6. *It's your party.* It's your house. You can say no to activities you disapprove of. You *must* say no, and be firm, about people who decide to move onto your landing to play the drums at 1:00 A.M.

7. *Prepare for emergencies.* If you are having a crowd, check the first aid kit. Try to arrange a place where someone under the weather might lie down. Air out the sleeping bag in case someone has to stay over. If you don't have a phone, know where the nearest all-night one is.

8. If you do serve food, observe all cautions about food poisoning.

9. *Put away all fragile objects.* I am not as negative as some folk who even remove valuables, and have told me of wrist watches and such disappearing at a party. But I have had rather fragile chairs crushed by "rockers," and good glasses smashed by people stepping on them, and even had bric-à-brac broken by alcohol-unsteady admirers. It is a pity, and can make for bitterness, so avoid it. Put your grandmother's lace mantilla away for the night. Do not use fragile china. If no one will be watching TV, put the set in the closet. (Put it in a neighbor's closet if necessary.) Clear the decks so everyone can relax and loaf, and move and enjoy, without anxiety.

If this sounds pessimistic, believe me, I have faced just about every problem envisaged here except someone calling the cops. I've had sudden illness, bad cuts, angry dogs, violent cats, too much booze, party crashers, fistfights. Take heed. These things happen.

If you live alone, and are having a crowd—a bunch of people who are not true intimates—ask a selfless friend who knows your house to co-host. When we gave those huge parties, we always asked one or two friends to keep a weather eye out for crises. This allowed us (my husband is doorman and wine steward, I cope with food and accidents) to chat and enjoy without that back-of-the-head anxiety that a fight is breaking out on the upper floor, or someone is desperate for aspirin.

APPENDIX

Some Statistics*

Butter:	1 stick = ¼ lb. = 8 T. = ½ c.
	4 sticks = 1 lb.
Sugar:	2¼ c. = 1 lb.
Cocoa:	1 T. regular = 1 oz. chocolate
	In otherwise fatless recipes, add 1 T. butter as well
Flour:	4 c. bread flour = 1 lb.
	4¾ c. cake flour = 1 lb.
	About 4 c. whole wheat flour = 1 lb.
Fruit:	1 lb. apples = 3 c. sliced pared
	1 lb. dry apricots = 3 c.
	1 lb. dates without pits = 2½ c.
	1 lb. dried figs, chopped or sliced = 2⅔ c.
	1 lb. raisins = about 3 c.
	1 lb. pitted prunes = 2¼ c.
Legumes:	Beans: 1 lb. kidney = 9 c. cooked
	Beans: 1 lb. lima = 6 c. cooked
	Beans: 1 lb. navy = 6 c. cooked
	Peas: 1 lb. = 5½ c. cooked
	Rice: 1 c. = 8 c. cooked

NOTE: British cookbooks are easy to use when they give weights, as 4 oz. translates into ½ c. But while the British use the same *terms* for volume, the measures are slightly different.

*Abbreviations
1 t. = 1 teaspoon
1 T. = 1 tablespoon
1 c. = 1 measuring cup
These are standard measures. 3 t. make 1 T. and 16 T. make one (8-oz. liquid) cup.

As I have said, this only matters in baking where complete accuracy is important. The reference section of a book such as *The Joy of Cooking* will give you all details.

KOSHER FOODS, Parve—Or Attention Vegetarians and Those Allergic to Milk and Pork

The Jewish dietary laws are clear and strict. No pork whatsoever. No meat (or derivative) is to be eaten or cooked with milk (or by-products). (Fish and eggs are *parve* or "neutral" in this split, though fish and meat are not mixed.) If you are allergic to pork, or milk, you can buy kosher sausages, as no pork or milk solids will be found in them.

You should also know that the word *parve* which appears on food packages (including many not made by Jewish firms) means the food can be eaten at meat or dairy meals; that is, no meat or milk is in it. So if you are allergic to milk, you can eat *parve* cookies. If you are allergic to pork, you can frequent an Orthodox bakery, sure there's no lard in the pie crust. You can always ask if a baked product is *parve*—except for the obvious cheesecake, most will be.

Bibliography

This bibliography is personal and pacific. It lists only books I cherish and use. That many splendid and popular cookbooks do not appear should not be taken as a condemnation on my part, but merely as a reflection of the equal limitations of a bibliography and a kitchen bookshelf.

Rombauer, Irma S., and Marion Rombauer Becker. *Joy of Cooking*. Bobbs Merrill Co.
> Admirably covers all details and possibilities of home cooking and the cuisine of most of the globe. *The* basic book to start with.

David, Elizabeth. *A Book of Mediterranean Food*
French Country Cooking
Italian Food
Summer Cooking
> All are in paperback (Penguin), all are charmingly written and entertaining, as well as inimitably informative.

Garvin, Fernande. *The Art of French Cooking*. Bantam.
> Simple, often inexpensive recipes, excellently explained, with Americans in mind.

Hazelton, Nika Standen. *The Best of Italian Cooking*. Signet.
> A remarkably good introduction, explained for Americans with American markets in mind.

Norman, Barbara. *The Spanish Cookbook*. Bantam.
> Spanish food is rarely found in restaurants. This very thorough book brings it home—and, particularly in summer, it provides lots of unusual, economical meals. (The chicken recipes are superb.)

The following Penguins require some skill to use. But they are a good thought for next year:

Hume, Rosemary, and Muriel Downes. *Penguin Cordon Bleu Cookery*.
> Requires time and money as well as skill to use, but is first-rate.

McDouall, Robin. *Cooking with Wine*.

A slim (and not costly) book, terribly handy when you have to perform miracles with leftovers. Shatters forever the notion that cooking with wine is some sort of magic.

To be borrowed from the library, for the copying of recipes:

Casella, Dolores. *A World of Baking*
A World of Breads
Both these David White books are fat and costly, but will provide those elusive recipes you've just *got* to have.

Johnson, Alice B. *The Complete Scandinavian Cookbook*. Macmillan.
Superb source book, very authentic, not difficult to use.

Watson, Betty. *Betty Watson's Greek Cookbook*. Macmillan.
Extremely good; relies heavily on lamb of necessity, which is costly. Excellent directions, and a shopping guide at the end tells where the Greek groceries are.

To be borrowed from the library for civilized joy:

Fisher, M. F. K. *The Art of Eating*. World.
No one writes about food, cooking, eating, with Mrs. Fisher's grace and verve.

Toklas, Alice B. *The Alice B. Toklas Cook Book*.
As much a journal as a book of recipes—what a circle of remarkable friends were served at the home of two very great ladies, despite a disintegrating and wicked world baying at the door.

NOTE: The U. S. Department of Agriculture and its Extension Services will deluge you with fantastic, mostly free, information at the drop of a postcard. What's not free is extremely low in price. Subjects range from clothing to roof repair, canning to building storage refrigerators.

NOTE: It has been our experience that manufacturers and their associations, will supply one with free, informative material, explaining products and their use. If the material is not free, the charge is minimal. I send away for, and keep on file, every booklet possible—whether it explains welding, the uses of manmade fibers, or offers canning recipes.

Index